Central Works of Philosophy

Central Works of Philosophy is a multi-volume set of essays on the core texts of the Western philosophical tradition. From Plato's *Republic* to the present day, the volumes range over 2,500 years of philosophical writing covering the best, most representative, and most influential work of some of our greatest philosophers. Each essay has been specially commissioned and provides an overview of the work and clear and authoritative exposition of its central ideas. Together these essays introduce the masterpieces of the Western philosophical canon and provide an unrivalled companion for reading and studying philosophy.

T0325298

Central Works of Philosophy
Edited by John Shand

Central Works of Philosophy Volume 1
Ancient and Medieval

Edited by John Shand

McGill-Queen's University Press
Montreal & Kingston • Ithaca

In memory of my parents, Alexander Hesketh Shand and Muriel Olive Shand

ISBN 0-7735-3015-0 (hardcover)
ISBN 0-7735-3016-9 (paperback)

Legal deposit third quarter 2005
Bibliothèque nationale du Québec

Published simultaneously outside North America
by Acumen Publishing Limited

McGill-Queen's University Press acknowledges the financial support of the Government of Canada through the Book Publishing Development Program (BPIDP) for its activities.

Library and Archives Canada Cataloguing in Publication

Central works of philosophy / edited by John Shand.

Includes bibliographical references and indexes.
Contents: v. 1. Ancient and medieval — v. 2. The seventeenth
    and eighteenth centuries.
ISBN 0-7735-3015-0 (v. 1 : bound).—ISBN 0-7735-3016-9 (v. 1 : pbk.).—
ISBN 0-7735-3017-7 (v. 2 : bound).—ISBN 0-7735-3018-5 (v. 2 : pbk.)

1. Philosophy—Introductions. I. Shand, John, 1956-

B21.C45 2005   100   C2005-902037-7

Designed and typeset by Kate Williams, Swansea.
Printed and bound by Biddles Ltd., King's Lynn.

Contents

CONTENTS

Contributors

Hugh H. Benson is Professor of Philosophy at the University of Oklahoma. He was educated at Oberlin College, Ohio and the University of Michigan, and has published articles on both Plato and Aristotle. He is author of *Socratic Wisdom* and editor of *Essays on the Philosophy of Socrates*.

Stephen R. L. Clark is Professor of Philosophy at the University of Liverpool. His books include *Aristotle's Man* and *From Athens to Jerusalem*. He is currently working on Plotinus's use of metaphors as spiritual exercises.

Richard Cross is Tutorial Fellow in Theology at Oriel College, Oxford. He has written extensively on medieval theology and metaphysics. Among his recent publications is *The Metaphysics of the Incarnation: Thomas Aquinas to Duns Scotus*.

Paula Gottlieb is Professor of Philosophy and Affiliate Professor of Classics at the University of Wisconsin-Madison. She recently completed an analysis of *Nicomachean Ethics* I and II for *Project Archelogos* and is completing a book, *The Virtue in Aristotle's Ethics*.

R. J. Hankinson is Professor of Philosophy and Classics at the University of Texas, Austin. He is the author of more than fifty articles on various aspects of ancient philosophy and science. His books include *The Sceptics* and *Cause and Explanation in Ancient Greek Thought*.

Peter King is Professor of Philosophy and of Medieval Studies at the University of Toronto. He has published translations of works of Augustine and

Buridan, and is the author of many specialized studies in medieval philosophy. He is best known for his work on medieval logic and metaphysics.

Christopher Kirwan is Emeritus Fellow and Lecturer in Philosophy at Exeter College, Oxford. His publications include *Aristotle: Metaphysics Gamma, Delta and Epsilon* and *Augustine*.

Harry Lesser is Senior Lecturer in Philosophy at the University of Manchester, where his teaching has regularly included courses in ancient philosophy. He is the author of a number of articles in ancient philosophy and ethics.

John Marenbon is a Fellow of Trinity College, Cambridge, where he teaches the history of philosophy. His recent publications include *Aristotelian Logic, Platonism, and the Context of Early Medieval Philosophy in the West* and *Boethius*.

Paul O'Grady is Lecturer in Philosophy and Fellow of Trinity College Dublin. He previously taught at St Catherine's College, Oxford. He has published papers in epistemology and philosophy of religion and is the author of *Relativism* (Acumen).

John Shand studied philosophy at the University of Manchester and King's College, Cambridge. He is an Associate Lecturer in Philosophy at the Open University and is the author of *Arguing Well* and *Philosophy and Philosophers: An Introduction to Western Philosophy* (Acumen).

Preface

The works in the *Central Works of Philosophy* volumes have been chosen because of their fundamental importance in the history of philosophy and for the development of human thought. Other works might have been chosen; however, the underlying idea is that if any works should be chosen, then these certainly should be. In the cases where the work is a philosopher's *magnum opus* the essay on it gives an excellent overview of the philosopher's thought.

Chapter 1 by Hugh Benson presents the central theme of Plato's *Republic*, that of the nature of justice. The *Republic* stands as arguably the most important work of Western philosophy. It is a pivotal work in Plato's thought, presenting a well worked out culmination of previous ideas, following which he subjected those ideas to considerable critical analysis, although he did not abandon them.

Chapter 2 by Paula Gottlieb discusses Aristotle's *Nichomachean Ethics*, central to understanding the key Greek idea in ethics of *eudaimonia*, usually translated "happiness". However, happiness here refers not to a subjective state of pleasure, but to *aretē* or virtue, whereby our actions should be guided by what truly contributes to our well-being or excellence as the kind of creatures that we are.

Chapter 3 by Harry Lesser gives an account of Lucretius's *On The Nature of the Universe*, which takes the form – not unusual for the time – of an extended philosophical verse. This work presents in poetic form a materialistic atomism, which not only attempts to present a coherent view of reality, but also aims to release men from superstition and fear of death simply by showing them that there is nothing of which to be afraid.

Chapter 4 by R. J. Hankinson explores in Sextus Empiricus's *Outlines of Pyrrhonism* the arguments for Pyrrhonian scepticism. This is deeply influential on those later philosophers for whom the function of scepticism is not as a test to establish knowledge on an unshakeable foundation, but rather to show that we should suspend judgement and cease the futile search for knowledge.

Chapter 5 by Stephen Clark looks at Plotinus's *The Enneads*, which extends Plato's view that thought is primary to philosophical understanding into a doctrine of the world as pure thought, in which one may escape the degradation of the material world by elevating the soul above it and become one with the true nature of reality, which is immaterial.

Chapter 6 by Christopher Kirwan brings out the philosophical substance from Augustine's masterpiece *City of God*, a work that partly seeks to demonstrate how Plato's philosophy is fundamentally in accord with a path to God, a path that for Augustine can only be travelled successfully with God's divine assistance. The influence of this work on Christian philosophical theology would be hard to overestimate.

Chapter 7 by John Marenbon looks at Anselm's *Proslogion*. Anselm is the father of the rational theology of medieval scholasticism. The logical proof for the existence of God found in this work is sometimes separated misleadingly from its function as a mystical meditation leading to a vision of God, a matter rectified in this essay.

Chapter 8 by Paul O'Grady gives an overview of Aquinas's huge *Summa Theologiae*, which literally attempts nothing less than a summation of theology. In it Aquinas strives to reconcile reason and faith as paths to understanding the world and our relation to God, drawing on the metaphysics of Aristotle.

Chapter 9 by Richard Cross examines Duns Scotus's *Ordinatio*. Scotus was dubbed the "Subtle Doctor", and his work is notable for its intricate logical reasoning. In it he undermines the metaphysics of Aquinas's Aristotelianism, and paves the way for the yet more radical ideas of Ockham. In this work he deals with fundamental issues concerning the nature of existence.

Chapter 10 by Peter King presents the prescient work of Ockham's *Summa Logicae*. On the logical side there are ideas about language, thought and meaning that have only relatively recently been fully matched in their depth of insight. The tension between reason and faith is yet more acute, as is the attack on the basic machinery of Aristotelianism that underpins medieval rational theology.

John Shand

Ancient and Medieval Philosophy
Introduction

John Shand

This book has two main strands of ideas that encompass not only the beginnings of philosophy, but also the foundation of Western civilization and much of what we take for granted in our mental outlook in the modern world. The two strands are: ancient – Plato, Aristotle, Lucretius, Sextus Empiricus and Plotinus; and medieval – Augustine, Anselm, Aquinas, Duns Scotus and Ockham. These comprise, roughly speaking, two thousand-year stretches from respectively 600 BCE to 300 CE, and 300 CE to 1600 CE. Without knowledge of these thinkers an understanding of the Western world would be a poor thing indeed. The ancient strand, which extends into the Roman period, is pre-Christian in its dominant ideas and contrasts with the medieval strand when Christian ideas prevailed. However, Christian European philosophy does not mark a break with ancient philosophy, but rather selectively incorporates it within the overarching Christian worldview. This is not a book of history that is concerned with the causes and influences of ideas whatever their merit, but a book of philosophy that is concerned with outstanding ideas and the quality of the arguments for them.

We begin with Plato (427–347 BCE) because philosophy proper begins with Plato. Plato's work marks perhaps the most important turning point in the development of mankind. For the first time in human history, when considering what is true, what we should believe, how we ought to live, the answers are advocated not on the basis of ideas found in supposedly holy books, or the word of great authorities, or the mere length of time an idea has been around. Rather, in a way that is a radical and systematic advance on what went before, we should

1

come to our conclusions about what is true, what we should believe, how we ought to live, solely on the basis of the strength of arguments; arguments moreover not restricted by a range of permitted starting places, but questioning-arguments that we follow wherever they lead with no holds barred, and that go as deep into what underpins all our beliefs as it is possible to go. That is philosophy. Philosophy is a growing-up of mankind, a coming of age. Plato is its father.

The battle to consider matters unrestrictedly purely on the strength of the arguments was not won by Plato and probably never will be; indeed, it took time to spread even to the educated. It is a way of going about things we still seem to find it hard to hang on to even to this day. In some places we seem to be going backwards. Philosophy characterized in this way has been a light that has brightened and dimmed according to the vagaries of human history. Some aspects of that history have been outside its influence while others have been caused by it. The craving for unshakeable certainty, which is antithetical to views arrived at by open argument – since there are always niggling doubts born of there being other possible arguments – can only be satisfied by mind-blinding dogma.

Of course it would be an exaggeration to say there was no philosophizing before Plato. But before him philosophy was hampered by restrictions in outlook that Plato is free of to a remarkable degree. Much of philosophical thought before Plato is bound by myth, the ulterior motive of establishing quasi-religious sects, and the desire to explain external reality in a way that points to the beginnings of natural science rather than to philosophy as such. Of course there was some philosophy, sometimes good philosophy, among this. Indeed, given the nature of human beings it is impossible for them not to philosophize in so far as they remain human and do not give themselves over to being automatons to habit and supine before the social pressure of the opinions of others. Free thought is almost impossible to extinguish entirely by threat or conditioning as it is part of the essence of what it is to be human. However, only with Plato do we find the first full sweep of issues that is characteristic of philosophy proper and the unremitting application of reasoned argument to them.

It may be said, even accepting the gist of the above, that philosophy began not with Plato but with Socrates (469–399 BCE). Socrates certainly stands as an iconic figure in philosophy: its earliest true proponent, the first to establish its methods and subject matter. Plato's works are written in the form of dialogues, where various characters represent different points of view and argue for and about them. We know next to nothing about Socrates as a man, and know him as a philosopher only through his appearance as the chief protagonist in the works of Plato, for Socrates may well have written nothing, and in any case no work by him has survived. He was the teacher of Plato, undoubtedly the greatest, but not the only, influence upon him. It is a measure of his importance for Plato that he used Socrates for what must be taken largely as Plato's own voice in the dialogues throughout his life. But apart from the suggestion that in the early dialogues Plato may have been reflecting quite closely the views of Socrates himself, before Plato gained much greater independence of mind, we can only weakly speculate as to what Socrates himself would have thought apart from what Plato suggests.

Talk of Socrates allows us to talk intelligibly of the Presocratic philosophers. We have no original extant works from the Presocratics, not even partial works, but only second-hand fragmentary quotes from their works in the works of other philosophers. The Presocratics should literally denote a group of philosophers who predate Socrates, but in fact some of them overlapped with his life. It is a crude label indeed for a group of philosophers whose doctrines often have little in common. What they do share, however, is the awakening of the philosophical ideal: the urge to speculate about the nature of the world in a way both imaginative and tempered by arguments open to inspection. Roughly speaking, their interests, compared to philosophy as it is recognized today, and indeed from Plato onwards, were narrow, focused as it were on the workings of nature. For this reason the Presocratics are often referred to as the first physicists. This is because they tended towards providing single natural unifying explanations for ranges of diverse phenomena and ones that moved away from special supernatural explanations for each phenomenon. This marks the step from explaining why a wall fell on someone, through suggesting that that person had in some way roused the displeasure of the gods, to an explanation of what physical objects such as walls do in general in certain circumstances regardless of who is underneath them. From this step was taken a further substantial one to philosophy. Philosophy broadens and deepens the questions that are raised. The deepening arises not only from attempts to explain the world itself, but also from considering problems arising from the conceptual tools involved in seeking such explanations. The broadening appears when we consider not merely what the world is like but how we should live in it, which is also, of course, closely connected to what it is like. Thus it is one thing to claim that we know the world is a certain way, and another to raise the question of what the claim to knowledge amounts to and whether in fact we ever truly have any knowledge. Further, we may think we have an accurate description of reality but we may also address the issue of how we ought to live our lives given the human condition in that world. Of course, our idea of the nature of the world cannot be completely severed from what counts as knowledge of it or how we should live in it, but philosophy makes knowledge as such and how we should live problematic matters that need to be addressed. This is the great advance made by Plato.

Plato was far from simply throwing off the Presocratics even if he did go far beyond them in philosophical sophistication. He absorbed the influences of many of them. In particular he carried with him the ideas of Heraclitus, Parmenides and Pythagoras. From Pythagoras he derives the notion that the key to explanation lies not in particularity and content but rather in generality and form. To explain the experience and nature of an octave rise in pitch one need not consider this or that octave, or one played on a particular instrument, but rather merely the general notion that halving the length of a string or tube doubles the pitch. The ideas of Heraclitus and Parmenides stand in opposition and run as a tension through Plato's philosophy. From Heraclitus he inherited the notion that the world we see around us is in constant change, and as such deeply unsuitable as an object of true knowledge. From Parmenides he inherits the influence of the argument that the world we see around us of change and plurality must in fact be an illusion, because when we think properly about it and treat it as real we find it full of impossible contradictions and so also not a subject of true knowledge. A choice between the world as a plurality in constant change, and the world of plurality and change as impossible, is not an enviable one. One answer would be to throw one's hands up and declare that knowledge is impossible, that people have different opinions, and there is no way of settling matters. This is not Plato's view. He is determined throughout his philosophy to give an account of knowledge and of how we can be said to know things. Knowledge needs to be given a place not only for its own sake, but also because without it knowledge of ethical standards – of good and bad, of how we should conduct our lives – collapses also, leaving us with a vast range of desperate arbitrary choices between which there is nothing to guide us. Knowledge proper is certain and eternal and must therefore be of suitable objects of knowledge, ones that can be known with certainty and are eternally unchanging. The truths of mathematics and geometry are a good step in the right direction. If the world as it appears around us is too changeable and imperfect to be an object of knowledge, or too riven with paradoxes to be fully real, then Plato's solution is to say there is yet a world that is a proper object of true knowledge, one we perceive not with the senses but with the intellect: the world of the Forms. The world of the Forms is fixed and perfect, and fully intelligible. It is the Forms that anchor knowledge and meaning to something fixed and eternal and that give the world of the senses that appears around us what order and intelligibility it has. In the world of the Forms, which we access by pure thought, we know that the sum of the internal angles of a triangle must always equal 180 degrees, even though no imperfect actual drawn triangle ever matches this exactly. Yet the Form of the triangle, the true and real triangle, enables us to explain the crude and imperfect triangles we come across in so far as we consider them to be triangles, without in any way being dependent on the existence of particular triangles. The order that Plato seeks, our knowledge, fixed eternal standards, is not to be found in the imperfect changing world around us, but in the fixed and eternal realm of the Forms. The Forms give the world as it appears whatever degree of order and reality it has and make it to that degree intelligible. Of the ethical concepts made intelligible objects of knowledge by the fixity of the Forms, none is more important, apart from the general notion of what is good, than the nature of justice. Any particular putative cases of justice will be flawed and ungeneralizable as accounts of justice itself. For a definitive and general account one must look to the Form of justice, justice as such, its essence, which makes all the particular cases of justice just in so far as they are just. This is not to say that Plato saw no difficulty in positing the realm of the Forms, and he indeed raises such difficulties in his later dialogues.

These beginnings, incomplete and later extended into matters and general approaches unenvisaged by Plato, basically set the agenda of the course of philosophy: to explore and give accounts of the meaning or nature of the tools with which we understand both the world and ourselves, as well as aspects of both the world and ourselves. It is not concerned with the mere meaning of words, as are the lexical concerns of a dictionary, but with the true nature of the concepts for which the words stand. Thus through philosophy has run concern for the nature of knowledge, truth, freedom, justice, good, God, meaning, reason, mind, substance, cause and reality. These concepts are, of course, open to all to use and think about. Philosophy is a particularly determined, systematic and open-minded attempt, through imagination guided by rigorous argument, to get to the bottom of what is involved in these concepts and the place they have in our view of the world, ourselves and our lives.

Aristotle (384–322 BCE) is the other intellectual giant of the ancient Greek world. He continues the philosophical tradition that Plato developed. The most significant aspect of this is not his doctrines as such, although they are significant too, but the breadth and depth of enquiry and the primacy of reasoned argument fundamentally unrestricted by matters being considered mysteriously off-limits. Plato was the teacher of Aristotle and his most profound influence. Aristotle both continued and opposed Plato's philosophy. He agreed with Plato that knowledge proper was certain and eternal, but found a way, disagreeing with Plato, of making possible knowledge of the natural world, rather than merely of a transcendent purely intellectual one. This was by contending that Platonic Forms did not exist separately from their instances in the world we see around us. The accidental features of things may vary, say between individual horses, and in the same horse over time, but what makes a horse the kind of thing it is remains the same. So the proper object of knowledge is the systematic study of things around us as natural kinds of things. The world chops itself up into various kinds of thing; it does not divide up the way it does by our subjective fiat. Real kinds interrelate in an orderly and fixed fashion, and how they do this is the proper object of knowledge. Aristotle's metaphysics is thus one of an ordered world, a world ordered by what makes things the kind of thing they are, their essences. The real division of the world into the natural kinds it appears to be divided into provide the proper individuated units of scientific explanation. One then studies their interrelations and their changes.

Aristotle's ethics connects immediately with his metaphysics, for his notion of the life we ought to lead is derived from the kind of creatures human beings are. The emphasis is the natural one of connecting the life we should live with what is best for our flourishing as the sorts of beings we are, just as one might connect watering and sunlight with the kind of things plants are. Thus ethics is not thought of as an abstract system of eternal rules binding for some perfect abstract ethical being, but as what is appropriate and good for the sort of beings human beings actually are. The significant intervening step is that our well-being consists not only in doing what is best for our flourishing as human beings, but that we develop ourselves in such a way that we would choose what is best for our flourishing. So it is not as if we take on ethical rules that run against the grain of our natures, but rather through living the right kind of life we are drawn towards the right kind of life and attain practical wisdom in a process of mutual reinforcement. The virtuous man would choose the virtuous life and the virtuous life is that which the virtuous man would choose. Although circular this is not the vicious circle one might suppose, for it is broken into by the facts about what human beings are actually like and what is good for them. There is, however, an underlying assumption that connects the ethical with what is best for human flourishing, and the obverse that somehow the unethical life will poison the well-being of the person who lives such a life. Aristotle's theory of virtue seeks to explain how this is so; how what is good for our well-being is what is virtuous. He does this by looking in detail at features of our life and connecting them through a consideration of our moral psychology to our well-being. It is not quite clear what the outcome of this is. Sometimes the self-sufficient contemplative life would seem to be the ideal, appealing as it does to the highest rational features of human character. Sometimes he seems to stress the importance of a connection with others through friendship and politics and the opportunity to be guided by virtues that involve others, such as courage and loyalty. What is clear is that Aristotle picks up the intuition that a bad life will lead to our downfall and our self-destruction. This is a strong thread in our ethical thought: that a life that is unethical – indulgent, excessive, lacking all control, say – is not only unethical but also harmful to ourselves. Aristotle makes the connection directly, rather than hopefully, by grounding the good life in what is good for the flourishing of human beings. From this one might be tempted to conclude that Aristotle is a safety-first avuncular finger-wagger, but this would be a gross distortion of his ethical outlook. What is good is not always what is moderate, but rather what is right and appropriate. For example, in the case of courage, great courage is sometimes appropriate regardless of whether it may lead even to our death; at other times we may consider such behaviour mere foolhardiness.

Before moving on to the medieval period, we should consider philosophy during Roman times, approximately the period 155 BCE to 500 CE. It should, however, be borne in mind that the delineation of anything that can be characterized as "Roman philosophy" is fraught with difficulty and vagueness. Apart from bare chronology, the term "Roman philosophy" points to philosophers writing in Latin during the period and those philosophers whose interests are distinguished by having a certain emphasis typical of the period. It would be tempting, but wrong, to make a tripartite division of ancient, Roman and medieval, in which "Roman" carried the same weight of difference as the other two terms. Although in Roman times the saturating hegemony of Christian ideas had yet to pervade philosophy in the way that marks out the medieval period, Roman philosophy is too derivative of Greek philosophy to be fully distinguishable from it. There are two reasons for the only partial separation of Roman philosophy from Greek: one is that much of Roman philosophy was devoted to commenting on and explicating the Greek heritage; the other is simply that not sufficient philosophy was written to stand as a distinctive body of work.

This should not lead us to regard the work done by Roman philosophers as negligible or insubstantial, nor to underestimate its influence. Its concerns were narrower than Greek philosophy; but just this concentration makes it a rich ground for philosophical study. The most obvious common guiding light of Roman philosophy is a concern for how best the individual should live his life, rather than theoretical speculation in epistemology and metaphysics for its own sake. Where there is theoretical thought about knowledge and the nature of reality, it is put at the service of, and motivated by, consideration of what one should conclude as being the good and ethical life. How the world is is connected directly to how we should live. The focus of interest moves away from scientific matters to ethics and religion. Here ethics should be understood in its broadest sense, not the narrow one of a system of moral prohibitions and obligations, but as a deep and also practical study of the human condition and the development of what one may call a philosophy of life that indicates what stance we should take to the world and how we should conduct ourselves both ethically and for the sake of our psychological well-being. In addition, the concern was for the practical: not just the way we should live, but how that way can be attained. The overriding aim of this philosophizing was to enable us to deal with life and what it can throw at us, so as to secure a dignified tranquillity, a sense of peace and equanimity, one that also encompasses the ultimate hurdle in the panoply of our fears, that of death.

The philosophers Lucretius, Sextus Empiricus and Plotinus share this aim, but are led down strikingly different routes. We find the same concerns in the Stoic Roman philosophers, such as Zeno of Citium, Lucius Annaeus Seneca, Epictetus and Marcus Aurelius, where again broad ethical virtues are extolled that emphasize self-mastery, restraint, reason, and our capacity to stand aloof from the chaos of the world around us, this based on our being part of a fatalistic bigger picture whereby the universe is governed by a divine intelligence.

Lucretius (99–55 BCE) is a chief proponent of Epicureanism. Here the practical aim of dignified tranquillity is brought about through knowledge, and the removal of the ignorance and superstition on which fear feeds. The foundation of this is an atomistic materialism, derived from the Greek Democritus. Although in some ways naive, in places the materialist doctrine is so strikingly modern that one could imagine going intellectually straight from it to the scientific materialism of Hobbes, Galileo and Newton, without troubling ourselves with the opposed Aristotelian metaphysics that dominated the medieval period. Our anxiety in life and our fear of death are to be lifted by arguing that human beings – including what we might call our "soul" – are purely physical, and that therefore there can be no survival after the dissolution of the body. Death is nothingness, and fear of it irrational. Death should not be feared as it would be when we suppose it might involve our persistence in a worryingly unknown supernatural world beyond the one we see around us; Lucretius opposes the damaging superstitions that engender fear by planting in our minds the worrying anxiety of survival. As opposed to valuing as an ultimate aim some world not yet reached, we are thrown back on valuing properly this world, which we should love for its beauty in the short time that we are in it.

Sextus Empiricus (c.200 CE) is our main source for a certain kind of scepticism, that of the Greek philosopher Pyrrho. The route that leads us to tranquillity is just the opposite, in one sense, to that of Lucretius; although it is still strongly epistemological in the way it gets there. Here we are saved from fear and anxiety not by knowledge but by the *denial* of knowledge; by a certain sort of scepticism. In this way we attain peace by denying universally the possibility of knowledge and thus we are freed from the desperate, worrying and futile striving for knowledge of the world, and can replace it with living quietly, always withholding the claim to know. Arguments are directed against our having more reason to accept one belief rather than its opposite. Pyrrhonian scepticism is not the same as Cartesian scepticism that is used as a tool to found knowledge securely, and which, should it fail in establishing such a foundation, results in a corrosive dark despairing nihilism as to our capacity to know anything. Rather, Sextus Empiricus embraces quietism with regard to our fever to know, bracketing and withholding all such claims. One gives up the futile pursuit of a putative knowledge of reality that should guide our life, but rather lives by appearances. This attains dignified tranquillity for we should not fear where we cannot know that there are things to fear.

Plotinus (204–70 CE) saw himself as a true heir and interpreter of Plato. He is characterized as a neo-Platonist. He would not have seen himself this way; he would have thought of himself not as setting up a new Platonism, but rather merely doing what Plato's philosophy truly and ultimately demanded. However, by most lights his interpretation of Plato is selective rather than definitive; it leads us into rarefied and personal philosophy that takes certain aspects of Plato's philosophy to and beyond the limits of comprehensibility. Lucretius led us to tranquillity through knowledge of the world and ourselves as material; Sextus Empiricus led us to tranquillity through a suspension of all knowledge claims, including any claims as to things we should be afraid of, or claims to know a reality of which we must take heed. Plotinus, by contrast, claims knowledge but leads us away from the material world, for it is in that world that we find the pain and anxiety of our existence if we take it as reality. This involves a denigration of the material world around us as a phantom in favour of a higher reality, ultimately the One (sometimes called the Good). The One is most truly thought of as ineffable, since applying predicates to it would render it many and no longer One. Such talk would call upon other Forms to express thought about the One; but the One stands as the highest of the Forms, so such talk would be at best misleading. Plato, too, talks of the inexpressibility of the Good, but thinks it may be grasped, as both he and Plotinus claimed sometimes to manage, by one intuitive revelation. It is from the One that anything has whatever degree of reality it can salvage. Thought, which the Forms encapsulate, is the foundation of reality and that from which all things are made. Lower but important realities, or "hypostases", are Soul and Intellect. Our souls, or true selves, are immaterial, and we can therefore stand aloof from the degradations of the world, for our true selves are untouched; our ultimate aim should be a wondrous union with the One, the path to which what we call death cannot touch as that is a mere dissolution of the body, which is not our true self.

We now move on to the long period of medieval philosophy, in which Christian ideas dominate. Aristotle's metaphysical vision of the natural world was the overwhelming conception of most of medieval Christian philosophy. It may seem surprising that Plato had so little influence on Western Christian thinkers in the medieval period. In fact, the reason was not owing to intellectual rejection, but rather to historical accident; Plato's full corpus of works, although held safely and studied in the East, did not re-emerge in western Europe until the end of the medieval period. Augustine was chiefly influenced by Plato, but then chronologically he predates the medieval period proper and lived at a time when Plato's works were still available, a time when East and West were not yet split.

Christianity had much to say of its own about ethics and so had little use or need for Aristotelian ethics. Christian religion essentially had little to say about the processes that determine the natural world. If, however, there was a good, all-powerful and all-knowing God, the world must surely have a systematically ordered structure, doubtless one of beauty and appropriate to the concerns of mankind. One can therefore understand that it was an easy and attractive step to adopt Aristotle's natural orderly view of the world, a world and its operations that are just as one would expect it to be headed by the Christian God. One has to remind oneself that the medieval outlook placed man at the centre of a meaningful universe, with no notion of a vast mechanistic inhuman universe that had no place for human beings or human values other than as an infinitesimal by-product of accidental causal events. The notion of a rich division into kinds within nature also fitted easily with the Christian conception of a hierarchy of Being ordered by value and perfection. The picture is one of God at the top, rocks and other inanimate objects at the bottom, and in between angels, man, animals and vegetables in that descending order. This was called The Great Chain of Being. The shattering of this conception in the seventeenth century, with the substitution of a notion such as matter in general as a single substance underlying and explaining the apparently vast array of kinds of things we see around us, was one of the most significant events in bringing to an end the medieval worldview. So there emerged a new view that opened up a gap between the world as it appears and as it really is. Crudely, on the Aristotelian outlook the world as it appears is pretty well how it really is. The ultimate constituents of the world are what they appear to be: horses, trees, people, water and so on. Explaining the systematic relation between these things and the process of change they undergo from one substance becoming another – say, wine turning into vinegar or Socrates becoming a corpse – or the same substance undergoing change – say, wine becoming sour or Socrates becoming old – is the job of the philosopher-metaphysician. This was all swept away when true substances were reduced to one or two. These underlying substances alone truly constituted reality, and the state of these substances and changes in them explained the apparent vast changing diversity of things that appear to us.

At the beginning of the medieval period all this lay hundreds of years ahead. Many of the questions taken up by medieval philosophers were not as easily resolved as the seventeenth- and eighteenth-century philosophers such as

Descartes and Hume supposed. For this reason there is much of value to study in their work.

The source of medieval theological doctrine was the Bible and the Church Fathers. While it would be foolish to suggest that medieval thinkers were the untrammelled picture of the philosophical free-thinker that we tend to associate with philosophers today, it would be wrong also to conclude that they were slavish apologists for theological orthodoxy. This is for three reasons. First, even within the strict bounds of Christian theology there were plenty of matters that could be explored philosophically and had general philosophical value outside their theological application: matters concerning free will, the limit of our cognitive powers, the nature of persons, for example. Secondly, much of the work of medieval philosophers in areas that were in most part theologically neutral – those of the philosophy of logic and semantics – has stood the test of time in continuing to be of profound philosophical interest. Thirdly, the thinkers involved were highly intelligent men and, in so far as integrity rightly guided them to follow arguments wherever they led, they were virtually bound through differences in judging the merits of those arguments to come into conflict both with each other and with prevailing orthodoxy. There may not have been any philosophers who were atheists or sceptics, but this did not stop the likes of Ockham – who to us would appear unexceptionally devout – being summoned by the Pope to have his teachings examined, it having been said that they were heretical. The examination lasted several years and in the end led to his excommunication. No one was safe from this kind of treatment.

The core of the difficulty for medieval thinkers was to reconcile the demands of philosophical reason and the demands of faith. This is the defining characteristic of what is called medieval scholasticism. It produced a tension in the intellectual framework that theoretically should not exist. One starts off with certain things one knows to be true. We know these truths because they are revealed to us by God either directly or through an intermediary we can trust. Now because these things are true there should be no problem in getting some if not all of the way to these truths by another route, that of reason. Reason properly applied takes us to the truth, so we should end up in the same place as truth revealed through faith. Theological orthodoxy may have constrained both the range of premises permitted in arguments and drawn the boundary of askable questions, but it should not be taken in the greatest thinkers to have led to the corruption of arguments and the debasement of the process of reasoning itself, a process whereby we try to pass validly from one step to the next. There may be questions as to how far natural unassisted human reason can take us, and whether with respect to some truths only divine intervention can help us take the final step, albeit divine intervention perhaps experienced by someone else; but this is a minor quibble. It is certainly so, compared to the worrying impression that reason seems to be taking us to other conclusions than those that are to be regarded as definitely true according to theological doctrine. What can one do then? Reject the truths? Try to reconcile the reasoning with the received truths by showing that the incompatibility is apparent not real? Give up on reason? Separate completely the deliverance of reason and faith as concerning different sets of truths? As the gap widened between the demands of reason and the demands of faith, so the medieval worldview began to crumble, although one must remind oneself that it had lasted for over a thousand years.

As one goes on, within theology, reason began to be undermined as a way of accessing religious truths so that reason and faith became increasingly separated. Further on still, there emerged areas of knowledge outside religion, where once nothing was outside religion's authority as part of its mission to give a complete account of the whole of reality. As reason faltered as a source of theological knowledge, so theology lost credibility elsewhere as a source of knowledge more generally, and of the natural world in particular. This had two main consequences. First, it laid the path to fideism, the doctrine that faith is the bedrock of religious belief and reason can neither support nor destroy it. Secondly, as the conclusions of reason became increasingly irreconcilable with the deliverances of divine insight, reason alone was seen as the way to understand the workings of the world, to the extent that ultimately no reference to theology was required at all. The first of these eventually gave rise to post-medieval Protestantism. The second, for those unconvinced by faith as a foundation for belief, gave rise later still to atheism and the total rejection of theology as a source of knowledge about the natural world, or indeed anything else.

The philosophers Augustine, Aquinas and Ockham neatly mark out the trajectory of medieval philosophy from certainty, through consolidation, to the beginning of dissolution. We can see this in their views on the relation of natural reason and faith founded in theological doctrine. For Augustine there is no fundamental distinction as divine help is required in order for reason to grasp eternal truths. For Aquinas there is a distinction based on that between the natural and the divine, but the two are complementary and overlap in part. For Ockham reason and faith are distinct and have no overlap, so conflicts are puzzlingly irreconcilable. Anselm and Duns Scotus fit both in chronology and in the development of ideas between Augustine and Aquinas, and Aquinas and Ockham, respectively. Anselm looks back to Augustine in seeing no problem in natural reason and the deliverances of divine insight running hand in hand; he looks forward to Aquinas in the emphasis on a rational theology of rigorous logical argument, in a way that makes Anselm the father of scholasticism. Duns Scotus employs rigorous logical argument in a natural theology, as does

Aquinas; like Ockham his position points to the limits of natural reason as a basis for theological belief and to a greater separation of reason and faith.

Augustine (355–430 CE) lived through the decline of the Roman Empire, and converted to Christianity following a licentious early life. He straddles the gap between Roman ideas and those of medieval Europe. Chronologically he is too early to count as medieval; but both because intellectually Christianity utterly dominates his thought and because of his huge influence on medieval thinkers themselves, he is often thought to be best considered as part of medieval philosophy and theology. One indication of his early chronology is that his chief non-Christian philosophical influence is Plato, and not Aristotle as it was later to be in medieval Europe. He was not concerned then with theoretical philosophizing as an end in itself, but with the way in which truth in philosophy would lead one down the path to the attainment of religious goodness and closeness to God. He spends some time refuting those sceptical of our being able to attain certain knowledge of eternal truths, the sort of truths held by Plato and the neo-Platonists. These intellectual truths are the proper objects of knowledge. Although he does not wholly dismiss the sensory-based judgements as illusory, as far as a source of knowledge is concerned, they are at best second-rate, for they lack both certainty and objectivity. Eternal truths require concomitant objects. But whereas Plato places the objects of eternal truths in the world of Forms, Augustine places them as immutable archetypal ideas in the mind of God. Such eternal truths extend not only to mathematics, but also to the moral and aesthetic. Unlike for Plato, such eternal truths would not be accessible to our limited temporal intellect or reason operating alone were it not for God assisting us with divine illumination. God enables our immaterial soul or mind to recognize the eternal truths that exist as latent copies in our mind or the originals in God's. This precludes making a distinction between natural reason and divine faith with respect to knowledge proper. It further emphasizes how all things depend on God. Indeed, the existence of such divine truths is proof of the existence of God, without whose immutable eternal nature in which to subsist they would be neither possible nor explicable. In the contemplation of eternal truth we satisfy a condition for moving nearer to God, but the conditions will not be complete unless we also go through a moral and spiritual purification.

Anselm (1033–1109) is seen as the father of scholasticism. By this is meant that he exhibits the conviction that rigorous natural reasoning can take us to the truths already delivered by divine illumination. Thus, he combines the mystical epiphany of Augustine and the great value placed on understanding through argument that is found later, at the highpoint of scholasticism in Aquinas. Argument and mysticism are guilelessly combined in Anselm's work; logic and prayer are natural companions. He is intent on leading us from blind faith through argument to rational understanding. To extract the logical arguments, as was done by later scholastics and indeed later philosophers, from their place as spiritual meditation leading to God, is to misunderstand both the content and flavour of Anselm's thought. His famous "ontological proof" of the existence of God is neither a logical exercise for its own sake, nor aimed at convincing an atheist. It is another way of arriving by rational means at a truth that Anselm already knows to be true. After all, it is not an implausible step to say that if something is true then there should be a convincing demonstrative proof for its being true. The central premise of the argument concerns "something than which nothing greater can be thought", and then a vision of God such that only He can so exist. The line of the argument is that the Fool, who denies that God exists, must admit that God characterized as "something than which nothing greater can be thought" can at least be thought. But such an entity cannot exist in thought alone, for if it did there could be something else existing in reality such that it would therefore be greater. If the entity existed only in thought something greater could be thought. To exist in reality is greater than to exist merely as a thought, so God as "something than which nothing greater can be thought" must exist. In addition, to exist as something that cannot be thought of as not existing is greater than to be thought of as something that may or may not exist. The Fool is only capable of entertaining the thought that God does not exist because his thought concerns the language in which the thought is expressed, and not the reality that the language signifies. In short, once properly thought of, God cannot be both so thought of and thought of as not existing.

Aquinas (1225–73) devises reconciliation between truths derived from our natural cognitive faculties of reason and the senses, and those derived from divine revelation embodied in theological doctrine. One could reject one or the other as worthless, or erase the distinction as Augustine does by holding that the two must operate together. Aquinas keeps the distinction, but looks upon them as two ways of looking at the same thing: understanding God "from below", naturally, or "from above", supernaturally through the faith of divine revelation. Faith, however, grants direct access to truths, whereas natural reason involves the addition of willed assenting judgement. While there is a certain class of truths we can come to know in two ways, there are some truths accessible only by divine revelation or illumination. Ideally a conflict should not arise, but since we err it will seem as though there is a contradiction; this appearance is dispelled as divine illumination trumps natural cognition, and in so doing shows us that we must have made a mistake in our reasoning. Aquinas's metaphysics follows that of Aristotle closely, although with some development and adaptation to the demands of Christian theology. All the main elements of Aristotle's metaphysics are there, including the distinction between the essence of things and their existence, wherein essences are universals subsisting in particulars. Essence, what it is that makes a particular the kind of thing it is, is contrasted with a thing's accidents, features that can change without affecting the kind of thing it is. Essences are discovered by giving the necessary and sufficient conditions for a thing to be the kind of thing it is. The distinction is a "real distinction" in that although only separable in thought, in that we do not find essence and existence separated in the world, the essence defining what a thing is is not a construct of our minds; the world chops itself up into kinds, it is not done through a certain way of thinking about the world. So, too, the distinction is made between the potential and the actual, whereby what a thing of a certain sort strives to fulfil is what it is according to its nature. An acorn grows into a tree, not a dog. But any essence can be actualized as something that exists if it is not logically contradictory. This primary actualization, from non-existence to existence, is God's work, who Himself is completely actualized and exists necessarily. Aquinas also distinguishes form and matter as Aristotle does; the form renders matter intelligible as, in taking on form, matter becomes a thing of a certain kind; as the same block of brass may be made into a vase or a helmet. Knowledge proper of things is knowledge of their essence, and we understand a thing through understanding the kind of thing it is and the ramifications of that. Universals are general defining concepts – such as "dogness" – that exist in objects, not separately as for Platonists. Thus, Aquinas is said to be a moderate realist about universals.

Duns Scotus (c.1266–1308) points to later medieval thought in two main ways. The first is his questioning of aspects of the Aristotelian orthodoxy. The second is the way in which theological arguments, although thought of as valuable, are often not viewed as totally convincing, and so do not form the ultimate basis for religious belief. He believes in both the immortality of the soul and, of course, the existence of God, but does not think any proof for the former is overwhelming, and finds Anselm's ontological proof for the latter only of "probable persuasion". His most distinctive doctrine is the univocity of being. By this is meant, in opposition to Aristotelianism, that there is only one sense in which things exist, not different senses according to their ontological status, which may be as substance, accident, potentiality or actuality. The term "being" means the same thing when applied to God's existence as to anything else. Only in this way can we, as limited intellects, move towards the understanding of the world that God has. Duns Scotus takes a significant step forwards in modal logic by separating possibility from time. A bare set of possible entities is antecedent to God's will, and the impossible is not thought of as that which does not exist in actuality at some time or other. God creates the world by conceiving of everything that is possible and then brings into existence a copossible collection of entities by His free choice. Thus, God creates out of freedom, not out of necessity. Another challenge to Aristotelian orthodoxy is in his understanding of individuation. Although he agrees with the moderate realist that universals (for example, humanity) really exist in particulars, he disagrees that individuals (for example, Plato, Socrates) are then distinguished by the parcels of matter making them up. Individuals are distinguished by a unique individual *haecceitas* or singularity: that which makes a thing different from everything else. He has trouble saying what *haecceitas* is in any individual case, and concludes that it is indeed incommunicable – although God can grasp it – unlike universal properties, which are communicable because they are common. What makes Socrates *Socrates*, as opposed to merely human, is something about him that can ultimately only be understood by God. The distinction between a thing's common nature and its individual nature, its *haecceitas*, is an "objective formal distinction", in that the two natures are inseparable in reality but distinguished by the one being communicable and the other not. This supposes a middle ground between a real and conceptual distinction.

There are in Ockham (*c.*1285–1349), albeit not with his conscious intent, insidious signs of the death of medieval scholasticism and the liberation of human thought, in particular philosophy, from theology. For in Ockham the tension between natural reason and religious faith is becoming acute. The two are separated: natural reason does not require divine illumination to come to truth (as in Augustine), nor is there a clear way of reconciling the two should they come into conflict (as in Aquinas). Ockham's arguments start to throw up too many conclusions incompatible with theological doctrine for it to be satisfactory simply to deal with them by saying that in that case the theology trumps the arguments and the arguments must be flawed. Of course, he does not remotely suggest that God does not exist; but the metaphysics of the theological apparatus filling out the detail of that belief starts to show why it cannot hold together. Ockham opposes even moderate realism about universals. This undermines our picture of the world as an orderly structure that is really "out there", rather than as something that is concocted and imposed by our minds. Ockham's explanation of what gets called universals is nominalism. This denies that universals even really exist in particulars, let alone exist in a separate realm of pure essences. The positing of real essences for Ockham is both unnecessary to account for how things fall into kinds, and an unacceptable restriction on God's freedom. God must be able to create unrestrained by essences defining what a certain thing has to be. Universality is a property primarily of thought and secondarily of language. Strictly speaking, the only thing that all things of the same kind have in common is that they fall under the same name. Nominalism contends that it is similarity and resemblance, not a literally common essence existing in particulars – identified by unique defining necessary and sufficient conditions – that lead us to classify a thing under a common name. We form universals out of our experience of particulars. "Ockham's razor", as it has become called, could be said to be exemplified by his nominalism. "Ockham's razor" holds that the entities of ontology should not be posited unnecessarily, if what they purport to explain can be explained without them; the simplest explanation should be chosen. Although the likeness should not be exaggerated, one can in his nominalism and his epistemology see a precursor of the empiricism of Locke and Hume. Probably unwittingly, Ockham is laying in his doctrines something of the groundwork for a time when philosophy would first partially, then utterly, cease to be dominated by theology. The natural course of events we see around us is as events disconnected from each other; there is nothing intrinsic in the events determining that they must unfold as they do. God is utterly free to change things within the bounds of the logically possible; although his goodness ensures that he will not do so, for without predictable order we should not survive. The world is radically contingent in all its aspects: existence, form and content. Strictly speaking, knowledge is only of necessary truths, but he extends science to include conclusions drawn from evident intuitive cognitions. The most radical claim is Ockham's denial that causal connections between things can be known by pure thought about the kind of things they are, as opposed to our experience of them.

It would be wrong to give the impression that theological doctrine and the scholasticism to which it gave rise was all conflict, with seminal philosophers trying to fight their way clear of religious oppression. The thinkers involved would not have seen it like that. They were sincerely and deeply religious men, with God at the centre of their lives. Indeed, it was only in the eighteenth century that such a picture of the relationship between philosophy, philosophers and religion appeared. No, these were devout men doing their best to give depth and understanding to matters they already believed as a matter of religious faith. The intention was to harmonize reason and faith. But one never knows what is going to happen when one starts thinking hard and truly open-mindedly about things.

1

Plato

Republic

Hugh H. Benson

Plato's *Republic* is many things to many people. To some it is among the first works in political theory in the Western tradition. To others it is a penetrating discussion of the relationship between the arts and the state, the nature of education or the sociological role of myth. To others still it may be the first examination of a fundamental ethical question, or the presentation of a fundamental metaphysical theory, or simply the *locus classicus* of classical Platonism. And as far as I can tell they may all be right. Nevertheless, I believe that the *Republic* contains a single thread of argument that one must come to terms with before the other issues in the *Republic* can be properly understood, and it is this thread of argument that will be the focus of this essay.

Before turning to the *Republic*, let me say a brief word about its author. To the best of our knowledge Plato was born to an aristocratic family in Athens in 427 BCE. His father, Ariston, who traced his lineage to the old kings of Athens, died in Plato's youth. His stepfather, Pyrilampes was a personal friend of Pericles, the great Golden Age Athenian statesman, and his mother, Perictione, was related to Solon, the famous Athenian legal reformer. Some time in his late teens or early twenties, Plato began to associate with Socrates (469–399 BCE), who was executed for impiety by the Athenians in 399 BCE. Around 387 BCE, Plato founded the Academy, which was named after the sacred olive grove in the outskirts of Athens in which it was located, and which boasted such members as Eudoxus and Aristotle. Plato died in 347 BCE. Plato flourished during the attempt by Athens to recover from its defeat at the hands of Sparta in the

Peloponnesian War (431–404 BCE), a war that ended the so-called Golden Age of Athens.

A quick outline of the *Republic*

The *Republic* falls into ten books. These divisions do not reflect Plato's choices, but rather the work of a later Greek scholar and the constraints of what will fit on a single papyrus roll. Nevertheless, it is traditional to trace the outline of the *Republic* by discussing what takes place in each of these books.

Book I resembles Plato's shorter so-called Socratic definitional and aporetic dialogues, dialogues like the *Euthyphro*, the *Laches*, the *Charmides*, the *Lysis*, and the *Hippias Major*. In these dialogues, Socrates examines with one or more interlocutors various answers to his "What is F-ness?" question, a question that aims to determine the nature of F-ness rather than various instances or examples of it. For example, in the *Euthyphro*, Socrates and Euthyphro consider a variety of answers to the question "What is piety?"; in the *Laches*, Socrates, Laches and Nicias consider a variety of answers to the question "What is courage?"; and in the *Charmides*, Socrates, Charmides and Critias consider a variety of answers to the question "What is temperance?" In none of these dialogues, however, does a satisfactory answer appear to be uncovered. The first book of the *Republic* has a similar structure.

In Book I, Socrates and his companion, Glaucon, while walking back to Athens after attending the feast of Bendis in the Piraeus, are invited to join a gathering at the house of Polemarchus. As is common in the Socratic dialogues, the discussion quickly turns to the nature of some moral concept. In this case, the question raised is "What is justice?" After dismissing the implied answer of Cephalus, Polemarchus's father, with a counter-example, Socrates turns first to Polemarchus's defence of his father's answer, that justice is to tell the truth and pay one's debts (331d), and then to Polemarchus's new answer, that justice is helping one's friends and harming one's enemies (332d). When Polemarchus proves unable to sustain either of these two answers, Thrasymachus angrily interrupts, complaining that Socrates will not provide an answer to the question himself and that instead Socrates ironically and disingenuously claims not to know what justice is. Socrates, however, professes to be genuinely ignorant, and persuades Thrasymachus to offer his own response that justice is the advantage of the stronger (338c). The remainder of Book I is devoted to an examination of this Thrasymachean conception of justice, culminating with the claim that injustice is never more profitable than justice contrary to the Thrasymachean conception. This leads Socrates to bring the first book of the *Republic* to a close as follows:

19

the result of the discussion, as far as I'm concerned, is that I know nothing, for when I don't know what justice is, I'll hardly know whether it is a kind of virtue or not, or whether a person who has it is happy or unhappy.   [*Republic* 354b9–c3][1]

Unlike many of the Socratic dialogues, the *Republic* does not end in this inconclusive or aporetic manner. Rather, Book II begins with Glaucon asking Socrates whether he wants to have appeared to persuade them that justice "is better in every way" than injustice, or to have genuinely persuaded them. When Socrates chooses the latter, Glaucon presents his threefold classification of goods. According to Glaucon there are three kinds of goods:

- Type 1: Goods "we welcome not because we desire what comes from [them], but because we welcome them for [their] own sake[s] – joy, for example, and all the harmless pleasures which have no results beyond the joy of having them" (357b5–8).
- Type 2: Goods "we like for [their] own sake[s] and also for the sake of what comes from [them] – knowing, for example, and seeing and being healthy" (357c1–3).
- Type 3: Goods "we wouldn't choose ... for their own sakes, but for the sake of the rewards and other things that come from them ... such as physical training, medical treatment when sick, medicine itself, and the other ways of making money" (357c5–d2).

Socrates and Glaucon agree that the Socratic conception of justice according to which justice "is better in every way" than injustice requires that justice is not simply a Type 1 good nor a Type 3 good, but a Type 2 good. The Thrasymachean conception rejected in Book I, on the other hand, only requires that justice is a Type 3 good. Glaucon challenges Socrates, then, to maintain that justice is a Type 2 good. After the challenge is clarified, developed and amplified, first by Glaucon (358c–362c) and then by his brother Adeimantus (362d–367e), Socrates accepts the challenge (368b–c), and proceeds to address it.

In typical fashion, Socrates suggests that in order to determine which kind of good justice is, they will first need to determine its nature; they will need, that is, to answer the question "What is justice?" To do this, Socrates maintains that since justice can be found in both the individual and in the city, and since the city is larger than the individual, it may be easier to uncover what justice in the city is than what justice in the individual is. Consequently, he proposes first to look for justice in the city and then to look for it in the individual (368c–369b), and so he sets out to describe the origins of the city, intending to find justice therein. Socrates begins by describing a simple city (369a–372d), but is quickly encouraged to describe a more complex or luxurious one (372d–427c). In the course of describing this complex city, Socrates is led to postulate three distinct types of citizens corresponding to the three fundamental needs of the complex city: the workers or craftsmen, who provide for the ordinary daily needs of food, clothing, and so on; the guardians or auxiliaries, who provide for the protection of the city from outside invasion; and the rulers, who provide decision-making for the overall advantage of the city. After describing the nature, selection procedure, accommodations and duties, especially of the guardians and rulers, Socrates concludes his description of this complex ideal city or Kallipolis about a third of the way through Book IV. Socrates now turns to the task that led him to begin his description of Kallipolis in the first place: the determination of the nature of justice. First, he provides an argument for the nature of justice in the city (427c–434c); then he provides an argument to the effect that the nature of the individual is sufficiently similar to the nature of Kallipolis that justice in the individual will be structurally the same as justice in the city (434d–441c); and he concludes that the nature of individual justice is each part of an individual's soul performing its own function (443c–444b).

Having determined the nature of justice, Socrates turns to meet Glaucon's challenge head on. Socrates begins a long discussion in which he lays out the five forms of government and the corresponding five forms of individual. The first form refers to Kallipolis and the corresponding virtuous individual; the next four forms refer to progressively degenerate forms of government and their corresponding degenerate forms of individual (445c–d, 545c–576b). Before Socrates gets very far with this discussion, however, Polemarchus and Adeimantus interrupt him at the beginning of Book V with a series of three objections – or three "waves" as Socrates calls them – to his description of Kallipolis completed earlier in Book IV. The first wave is the implausibility of the suggestion that women as well as men can and should serve as rulers of Kallipolis (451c–457b); the second wave is the implausibility of the suggestion that spouses, children and other possessions are to be held in common by guardians (457d–471c); and, finally, the third wave is the implausibility of the suggestion that Kallipolis could ever actually be brought into existence (471c–540c). Books V–VII consist of Socrates' attempts to address these three waves with most space devoted to addressing the third wave. Socrates attempts to turn back this wave by maintaining that Kallipolis is possible when and only when rulers become philosophers and philosophers become rulers. Beginning at the end of Book V, Socrates provides an elaborate account of the nature of the genuine philosopher (474c–502c) and his or her education (502c–540c).

21

Book VIII opens with Socrates returning to the main thread of argument. Recall that Socrates had just determined the nature of justice and was about to respond to Glaucon's challenge by discussing the five forms of government and individuals when Polemarchus and Adeimantus interrupted him. He had begun reviewing the nature of aristocracy and the aristocratic individual – the government of Kallipolis and the corresponding individual – and now he returns to where he left off. Socrates next discusses the nature and origin of the four progressively degenerate governments and their corresponding individuals: first timocracy and the timocratic individual (545c–550c); secondly, oligarchy and the oligarchic individual (550c–555b); thirdly, democracy and the democratic individual (555b–562a); and, finally, tyranny and the tyrannical individual (562a–576c). This leads to the first of three arguments for the profitability of justice in Book IX, according to which the tyrannical individual is worst, most unjust and most miserable, and the aristocratic or kingly individual is best, most just and most happy (576b–580c). Socrates follows this argument for the profitability of justice with a second argument according to which the just individual is best suited to judge the pleasure associated with the lives of reason, spirit and appetite, and he or she judges the life of reason, that is, the just life, to be the most pleasant (580c–583b). Finally, Socrates provides a third argument according to which the tyrant and tyrannical individual is farthest away from experiencing genuine or true pleasure and the king and kingly or aristocratic individual is nearest to experiencing genuine or true pleasure (583b–587b). Socrates draws these arguments to a conclusion with the image of an individual composed of a many-headed beast (corresponding to the appetitive part of the soul), a lion (corresponding to the spirited part of the soul) and a man (corresponding to the reason part of the soul) (587b–592b).

Book X begins rather awkwardly with a second defence of the banning of poetry, or at least the vast majority of contemporaneously available poetry, from Kallipolis (595a–608b). It then turns to an argument on behalf of the rewards of justice as it has come to be understood throughout the course of the *Republic*. Socrates begins this argument with an argument for the immortality of the soul (608d–612a). This is followed by a discussion of the rewards of justice in this life (612a–614a) and the even more impressive rewards of justice in the afterlife as described in the myth of Er (614a–621d).

While this outline of the *Republic* is hardly indisputable, it provides an arguably fair and unbiased summary of the text. As such, the main thread of argument in the *Republic* emerges. The goal of the *Republic* is the refutation of the Thrasymachean conception of justice first expressed in Book I. Book II explains that in order to accomplish this goal Plato must show that justice is welcomed both for its own sake and for its consequences ("what comes from

situations, and the cases themselves may differ a great deal. In Aristotle's terms, the actions performed in such circumstances would be mixed.

Finally, Aristotle tackles the problem of whether we are responsible for our characters. Aristotle sensibly is not interested in the question of whether we "could have done otherwise". Aristotle argues that we are responsible for the cumulative result of our actions, although he is not consistent about whether we must be aware of the result we are aiming at. Aristotle's view, in a nutshell, is that we are "in some way co-causes" of our characters. Presumably this means that however bad the circumstances of our upbringing, it is up to us to do or refrain from doing whatever bad actions others, and circumstances, may encourage us to do, on the way to developing our characters. But this raises a new problem. Suppose we are not responsible for whether things look good or bad to us in the first place? Aristotle assumes that such a questioner, like Socrates, thinks that virtue is voluntary, but vice is not, and points out that this would not be possible if how things look to us is never up to us. Modern philosophers are likely to object that perhaps *neither* virtue nor vice are up to us. Whether Aristotle has a response to their concern would require a full treatment of the medical analogies Aristotle uses to make his case.

Practical reasoning

We have now reached the heart of Aristotle's *Nicomachean Ethics*: his discussion of the type of thinking engaged in by the ethically virtuous human being. While wisdom (*sophia*) is the virtue of thought dealing with theoretical reasoning about necessary truths, practical wisdom (*phronēsis*) is the virtue of thought necessary for ethical virtue. Aristotle even includes the person with the virtue of practical wisdom in his definition of ethical virtue. Not only do the development of the ethical virtues and practical wisdom go hand in hand (Burnyeat 1980; Sherman 1989: 157–99), but neither is possible to the full extent without the other, and anyone who has practical wisdom will have all the ethical virtues. The reciprocal relationship of ethical virtue and practical wisdom shows that it is wrong to assimilate Aristotle's view to that of (the popular view of) Hume or Kant and to suppose that reason is either a slave of the passions or that reason rules the passions with an iron grasp. To make such claims, ethical virtue and practical wisdom in the good person need to be pried apart in a way that is against the spirit of Aristotle's account.

In order to explain what practical wisdom is, Aristotle has two tasks: to explain the practical nature of the reasoning it involves and how it differs from theoretical reasoning; and to explain how it is special to the person with ethical virtue. To accomplish the first task, Aristotle compares practical reasoning with the productive reasoning involved in skills like medicine (*EN* III cf. *Metaphysics* VII 7). To accomplish the second task, however, Aristotle has to show in what respect the practical reasoning associated with ethics differs from any merely productive or technical skill. As part of the explanation, he introduces what has been called "one of Aristotle's best discoveries", his practical syllogism (Anscombe 1957: 57–8).

Consider the following medical scenario. Dr Bloggs is at the theatre when someone asks if there is a doctor in the house. She immediately identifies herself and takes a look at the person who is ill. Seeing that the patient is shivering, she asks for some blankets or warm coats, and rubs the patient's hands. Recognizing the patient's symptoms, she first considers various possibilities, but finally ascertains that the patient has an idiosyncratic chronic condition and has forgotten to take his medication. Fortunately, the patient has some pills in his jacket pocket so the doctor can administer them now.

Here is how Aristotle would describe Dr Bloggs's deliberation. She does not deliberate about her end, curing, because she is a doctor and as such does not need to deliberate about whether to cure. To start deliberating she simply has to see that it is the right time to cure. If she sees *that* it is appropriate, deliberation about *whether* it is appropriate is redundant. Instead, then, she starts with a desire to restore the health of her patient, and then works out the best way to do this. In order to cure the patient, she first realizes that he needs warming up, and in order to warm him up, she realizes that she needs to find some blankets or other warm coats and so on.

Although we may be able to *explain* Dr Bloggs's actions by the linear piece of logic set out above, Aristotle himself realizes that there is more to medical reasoning than that. To cure her patient, the doctor needs to find out exactly what is ailing the patient, and consider the appropriate way to return the patient to health. The first requires perception and experience. The second, at the least, requires knowing what has cured, or at any rate helped, patients with similar conditions. This sort of general knowledge will not be simply book knowledge. Reading a Hippocratic treatise on the topics would not be sufficient for practical understanding; the doctor's grasp must involve experience. Furthermore, the general knowledge in question will only be what Aristotle calls "for the most part" because it will not necessarily be applicable to every single patient. (Recall that Dr Bloggs's patient had an idiosyncratic condition.) In this respect it differs from the knowledge of necessary truths that is the hallmark of theoretical reasoning, according to Aristotle. Finally, as modern scientists have discovered, while the process of seeing what information is relevant and pruning out unpromising alternatives seems easy for human beings, programming computers to simulate this aspect of human thought has proved notoriously difficult. Even medical deliberation, then, is far from mechanical.

Now consider the following scenario. Joe notices that his friend looks troubled. He asks in a sympathetic and gentle way what is the matter, and finds that his friend has just been diagnosed with a rare disease, and that the experimental drugs needed to cure the disease are not covered by his friend's health insurance. Being a generous person, Joe offers to help out, with money and support. He also discovers that there is a society funding research in the disease, and he makes a donation to that society, too, and finds out what he can do to support government initiatives in this area. As with the medical example, we can *explain* Joe's actions by a linear piece of deliberation, culminating with a good, Joe's own happiness: Joe helps out his friend, because helping his friend in such circumstances is what a generous person would do in those circumstances, and because being generous contributes to a happy life. No doubt Joe would assent to this line of thought, even if he did not consciously go through it at the time. However, it still leaves out some crucial parts of Joe's reasoning. In order for the view that generous people help out friends in need to have any purchase on Joe's action, he must *be* a generous person himself and he must see that his friend is in need. This part of Joe's reasoning can be represented by the following practical syllogism:

> Major premise: Generous people help out friends in need (at the right time, in the right way and so on).
> Minor premise: I'm a generous person and this is my friend in need (and this is the right time to help and so on).
> Conclusion: Help out!

It is the minor premise that makes the syllogism practical. The indexicals "I" and "this" are required for action, and in order to act Joe must have a certain kind of ethical character (he must *be* a certain kind of human being), or the major premise will be of no interest to him. The emotion of sympathy, according to Aristotle, involves seeing that someone is suffering undeservedly (*Rhetoric* II 8). Being virtuously disposed to have the right feelings on the right occasions, Joe has the sensitivity that gives him the information needed for the second part of the minor premise. But that information must be embedded in the whole syllogism, because a bad person could also see that someone was in need and yet use that information to harm, rather than to help. It is the way in which sensitivity and character are included in the practical syllogism that distinguishes the ethical practical syllogism from any purely technical reasoning. Aristotle's account is light years away from any utilitarian calculus.

How does Joe arrive at the major premise? Being well brought up he will be familiar from experience with the types of actions that ought to be performed in different situations. But any general thoughts he brings to bear on the situation will be only "for the most part", and so creativity, imagination and sensitivity will still be needed to see what is called for in a particular case. However, if Joe has full practical wisdom, he should be able to apply his priorities on a larger stage. In my example, he sees the importance of health care for his friend, and he also sees that health care should be a matter of general concern also. In discussing practical wisdom, then, it makes perfect sense for Aristotle to discuss varieties of practical wisdom that apply to legislative and political activities, too, and to discuss comprehension (*sunesis*) and judgement (*gnōmē*), related virtues of thought that can be used not just in one's daily life but also in jury service and in political gatherings (Gifford 1995: 58).

The reader may wonder how much Joe must know in order to be a virtuous person. Must he know everything that is discussed in the *Nicomachean Ethics*, or would too much knowledge undermine his own performance, like the fabled centipede, which is no longer able to walk when it starts to think about how it does it? Aristotle does not provide explicit answers to these questions, but the parallel with medicine suggests that, like the doctor, the good person can use the results of other disciplines in his deliberations, and will be aware of the different types of virtues and vices, just as the doctor is aware of the different conditions she may encounter from day to day. As for how much reflection is required, Aristotle would no doubt say that the answer depends on the particular circumstances.

Akrasia

Akrasia, roughly, is the phenomenon of knowing what would be good for you to do in a given situation, but irrationally and yet voluntarily doing something worse instead. Aristotle restricts *akrasia* to the sphere of temperance, where an appetite for food, drink or sex may clash with one's considered judgement about what to do. Given the tight connection between practical wisdom and ethical virtue, it is difficult to see how *akrasia* is possible for someone who has practical wisdom and, indeed, Aristotle says that it is not. *Akrasia* is only possible for those whose reasoning and appetites have gone awry.

Aristotle's discussion of *akrasia* is a case study in Aristotelian method. He discusses different opinions of the matter, raises various puzzles, and, in solving the puzzles, provides his own solution.

There are various reasons why *akrasia* still seems puzzling. First, for example, one needs to account for the knowledge the akratic has but acts against. If he has no reason to act against his knowledge, a second problem crops up: one needs to explain how the akratic act can be voluntary and therefore subject to blame. Thirdly, there is a logical problem. The akratic cannot have contradictory beliefs at the same time, on pain of violating Aristotle's principle of non-contradiction. Even though *akrasia* seems perfectly familiar from everyday life, then, difficulties in explaining it from a philosophical point of view can lead one to think, like Socrates, that it is not possible after all.

In order to combat the Socratic view that *akrasia* is impossible because knowledge cannot be dragged about like a slave (*EN* VII 2 1145b23–4), Aristotle begins his own discussion of the phenomenon by presenting examples where knowledge is had but not used, an apparent contradiction in Socratic terms. Aristotle draws distinctions between actual and potential knowledge, between knowledge of a universal premise versus knowledge of the particulars, and between the knowledge a person has when sober, and the way in which he fails to understand it, although he can still say the words expressing it, when drunk. Aristotle presents his full account in *EN* VII 3. The details are notoriously controversial, and there is even a dispute over whether Aristotle agrees with Socrates in the final analysis or not (cf. Charles 1984: 109–96). Some think that there are two syllogisms in play here, but that would contradict Aristotle's claim that while appetite clashes with belief, belief does not clash with belief. There is also a debate about what premise (or premises) the akratic lacks, according to Aristotle. My interpretation is as follows:

> The akratic's behaviour can be explained by considering which parts of the following correct syllogism the agent has or lacks.
>
> Major premise: Temperate human beings ought not to eat (too many) sweets.
> Minor premise: (a) I'm a temperate human being. (b) This is (a) sweet (too many).
> Conclusion: Don't eat this!

The akratic human being has the major premise. He believes that temperate human beings ought not to eat too many sweets, and he sees that this is a sweet too many. But directly he sees that this is sweet, his appetite jumps in (cf. *EN* VII 6 1149a35), seeing that any sweet is pleasant, and literally makes off with part (b) of the minor premise so that the akratic eats the sweet, contrary to his original better judgement. The akratic also fails to be the right sort of person to have part (a) of the minor premise. The akratic, then, has all the information to form the correct syllogism, but his appetite prevents him from putting the information together in the right way (cf. the way in which one may have all the information for a theoretical syllogism, but fail to put two and two together; *Posterior Analytics* I 21). Aristotle concludes that the akratic lacks the minor premise.

To respond to our original puzzles, on Aristotle's account, the knowledge, or information, the akratic has that he acts against is that expressed in the major premise. Aristotle concludes that this is what Socrates was looking for, because it is only perceptual knowledge, expressed in the minor premise, that is dragged about like a slave. However, this is disingenuous, since Socrates would hardly agree with the sea change in his view of knowledge. According to Socrates, if the akratic fails to apply his general knowledge, it would make no sense to attribute it to him in the first place.

As for the problem about voluntary action, the appetite that makes the agent do his akratic act is in the agent, and so the act is voluntary. If there is any ignorance involved, it is appetite that is the cause of the ignorance and so the agent is responsible for his act, in accordance with Aristotle's earlier discussion of voluntary action. Unlike Oedipus, who would not have killled his father had he known who he was, the akratic would still have acted in the same way had he been aware that this was sweet, which he was.

Modern commentators debate whether the akratic's mistake is intellectual or a flaw in character. If my interpretation is right, and the practical syllogism represents one's character and reasoning at the same time, the answer is both.

Pleasure

According to Aristotle, pleasure is important for several reasons: virtue and vice involve pleasure and pain; moral education should lead people to take pleasure and pain in the right things; and pleasure is also related to the happy life. Aristotle's analysis of pleasure is one of the most sophisticated to be found in the philosophical canon, even if it raises more problems than it solves. Modern philosophers, following Bentham, usually assume that pleasure is a subjective feeling, although they have generally abandoned Bentham's idea that pleasure can be quantified, as if it were a heap of homogeneous stuff. Aristotle thinks that there are objectively good and bad pleasures, and that there is no one homogeneous feeling associated with all pleasant activities.

Aristotle's account is directed against his predecessors, who, from the time of the doctor Alcmaeon of Croton, thought that pleasure was a felt process that brings someone back into his natural state. For example, they thought that the pleasure of eating is a felt process that brings someone back from the unnatural state of hunger to the natural state of equilibrium, being replete. In Plato's *Gorgias* (493–4), Plato uses an analogy of a leaky jar to illustrate the theory. While the jar is being filled up we feel pleasure, and when it is being emptied we feel pain. Once it is filled, there is neither pleasure nor pain. Aristotle himself gives the traditional definition of pleasure in his *Rhetoric*: "Let it be assumed by us that pleasure is a certain process (*kinēsis*) of the psyche, an intense and perceptible settling down into its natural state and pain the opposite" (*Rhetoric* I 11 1369b33–5).

The traditional picture of pleasure can be used to support different accounts of the happy life. For example, in Plato's dialogue, Callicles concludes that it is the process of satisfying our appetites and having appetites as large as possible that makes for a pleasant and hence happy life, since once our appetites are satisfied there is no pleasure any more. It is no surprise that he thinks that the tyrant's life is best, since a tyrant would be able to keep increasing his appetites and have access to the resources to satisfy them. Of course, one might conclude the opposite, that neither pleasure nor pain are good, because pleasure is a process that aims at a better end than itself, the state of equilibrium, and *that* must be what we are really after for a happy life.

Aristotle's arguments against the traditional view are relatively uncontroversial. Not all processes that restore us to our natural state, for example, recovering from an illness, are intrinsically pleasant. It may be the healthy part of our nature that is enjoying the recovery. There are also pleasures that are not preceded by pain and do not fill any lack, for example the pleasures of studying and seeing. Finally, the traditional model focuses too much on physical pleasures such as eating, making the body the subject of pleasure. While it may seem reasonable to refer to the pleasure of eating as a process of "refilling", it is less plausible to describe, say, the pleasure of studying mathematics in the same way. In short, there are pleasures we enjoy when we are in our natural state, not just returning to it, and the traditional model leaves these out. Pleasure is not a process. We are not pleased quickly or slowly. If the traditional model is wrong, the views of happiness it engenders also come into question.

Aristotle's positive account of pleasure is more controversial. The discussion of pleasure comes in two books, Book VII, a book common to the *Eudemian Ethics*, and Book X. Although Aristotle clearly rejects the idea that pleasure is a process (*kinēsis*) in both books, it is less clear what precisely he thinks pleasure is. In Book VII he says that pleasure is an unimpeded activity (*energeia*) of the natural state (*EN* VII 12 1153a14–15), but in Book X he says that pleasure *completes* the activity as a sort of supervenient end (*EN* X 1174b30–33). There are two difficulties here: to explain the difference between an activity and a process; and to see if Aristotle's accounts of pleasure are consistent (Penner 1970; Gosling & Taylor 1982).

While it is clear that those things that take place when one is in one's natural state, for example, seeing, thinking and so on, differ from those that bring one back into one's natural state, for example, recovering from illness, eating and so on, it is less clear that the distinction between activity and process neatly captures this distinction, or shows how we can enjoy the latter as well as the former. According to Aristotle, an activity is complete at any moment, whereas a process is not complete until it has reached its goal (cf. *Metaphysics* IX 6 1048b18–35). For example, seeing is complete at any moment – it has an intrinsic goal, seeing – whereas eating is not complete until I have finished the last morsel in my mouth. The problem is that a sophisticated process theorist might argue that, for example, when we see, we are carrying out the process of scanning the room, and that, for example, when we are thinking, we are carrying out the process of following out a train of thought.

The second difficulty relates to Aristotle's two definitions of pleasure. Perhaps the second definition is a clarification of the first. The relationship between activity and pleasure is not one of identity. Instead, if a person is fully engrossed in an activity and doing it well, then it will be enjoyable. From a phenomenological point of view, this is a plausible account, especially for the pleasures of thinking and sense-perception that Aristotle has in mind. Rawls even incorporates Aristotle's insight into his "Aristotelian Principle": "Other things being equal, human beings enjoy the exercise of their realized capacities (their innate or trained abilities), and this enjoyment increases the more the capacity is realized, or the greater its complexity" (Rawls 1971: 426).

Aristotle's analysis of pleasure also completes his account of happiness and virtue in a brilliant way. According to Aristotle, virtuous actions have an intrinsic goal. At the beginning of the *Nicomachean Ethics*, Aristotle argued that happiness depends on the human function (*ergon*) and that it is exercising of our function (*en-erg-eia*) well, that is, in accordance with virtue. It now turns out that exercising our function well is itself pleasant. According to Aristotle, then, the happy life is pleasant, but not identical with pleasure. He therefore keeps the intuitive connection between happiness and pleasure, without being saddled with the paradox of hedonism, that the best way to achieve one's goal of pleasure is to have any goal but pleasure.

Friendship

Aristotle says that a friend is the greatest external good, and he accordingly devotes two whole books of his *Nicomachean Ethics* (Books VIII and IX), as well as another whole book of his *Eudemian Ethics* (Book VII), to the topic of friendship. Aristotle's discussion ranges from friendship between individuals to family ties and the bonds between fellow citizens. According to Aristotle, a human being can only be self-sufficient if he has friends, because it is friends and family who enable him to be independent in the first place. Friends, including family, are necessary not only for living a happy life, but also to help one develop the good character to be able to enjoy a happy life in the first place. We learn about ourselves by interacting with our friends, and we also enjoy activities far more when they are shared (Cooper 1980: 320–30; Sherman 1997: 187–216). A friend is "another self", someone one can identify with and whom one notices reciprocating one's own good wishes. It is not surprising, then, that Aristotle thinks that the best, the most reliable and the most pleasant friend a person can have is someone of good character. There are two other types of friendship based on utility and pleasure respectively, but these are not as good, and are more easily dissolved.

According to Aristotle, only good people can be friends with each other "because of the friend himself", but what this means is unclear. Vlastos (1973) and Whiting (1991) take Aristotle to mean that if X and Y are friends of good character, (a) X cares for Y simply because Y has a good character (where good character is a repeatable general property), and they chide and praise Aristotle for this suggestion respectively. Is one good friend just as good as another, and is it only pragmatic reasons that make one remain friends with X rather than become friends with Y? Is one friend replaceable by another? Would you want a friend who cared primarily about your good qualities and only incidentally that they were good *for you*?

Aristotle's discussion is more complicated. He seems to conflate (a) with two other possibilities: (b) X cares for Y because of Y himself; and (c) X cares for Y because Y is (or has) the very good character that she has (a non-repeatable character). The conflation is understandable if Aristotle believes that only a good person has the integrity that would allow a friend to relate to him himself. If that is the case, then one can only relate properly to a friend *as a particular individual* if that friend has a good character, and the questions above become moot.

Other questions remain. Is it best to have friends who all have the same character, rather than different ones? The question assumes that friends of good character will all have exactly the same interests and backgrounds and personalities, but there is no reason to suppose that this is the case. Why is civic friendship based on utility, rather than virtue? It takes a long time to establish a friendship with a virtuous person, since one cannot just look at a slice of behaviour but must ascertain the person's general motives and character. Therefore, one cannot have many good friends, according to Aristotle. Certainly, if one needs to ask directions on the street, one has to trust that the bystander is virtuous enough to tell the truth, but it would be out of place to call her later to find out how she is. Is Aristotelian friendship too parochial? Perhaps, but the nameless virtue of friendliness deals with the correct attitude to have towards those near and far.

Happiness revisited

At the beginning of his *Nicomachean Ethics*, Aristotle presented his function argument to show that happiness is reasoning in accordance with virtue. Since there are two main virtues of thinking, practical wisdom and wisdom, and the former requires and is required by the ethical virtues, the question remains whether the happy life (a) involves the exercise of all the virtues, (b) involves the exercise of wisdom alone, or (c) involves the exercise of practical wisdom and the ethical virtues alone. In the final book of the *Nicomachean Ethics*, Aristotle appears to be trying to rank these alternatives. On the face of it, he ranks (b) in first place, with the proviso that it would be impossible for a human being, as opposed to a god, to live such a life without exercising practical wisdom and the ethical virtues, and (c) in second place, but the discussion goes back and forth, allowing puzzled commentators to attribute every possible combination to Aristotle as his first choice, and to give different answers to the question of whether Book X is consistent with Book I.

While Aristotle's discussion is controversial for many reasons, there is a prior problem to be addressed: that the whole project of ranking happy lives appears to go against the grain of the doctrine of the mean. If happiness is doing well, and what counts as doing well depends on one's particular circumstances and what is called for at the time, then it makes no sense to give a ranking of happy lives in the abstract. What counts as a happy life depends on the particular human being who is living it, her particular abilities and the very particular circumstances encountered in her life. While a philosophical life might suit one person, it might be inappropriate for another, and so on.

To understand the point of Aristotle's ranking, we must turn to Book VII of Aristotle's *Politics*. There Aristotle takes it as agreed that what happiness is for the city is the same as what it is for the individual. Someone who thinks that the happiness of an individual consists in wealth will think that the city as a whole is happy when it is wealthy. Similarly, those who rank the life of the tyrant as happy will rank the city with the largest empire as happy also (*Politics* VII 2 1324a5–13). Thus to rank types of happiness is not to rank the quality of individual lives as much as it is to rank the priorities that should govern the society in which individuals live. Those who rank the tyrant and empire-building life best will be making war their first priority. Aristotle is especially scathing about the Spartan way of life. While the Spartan system was geared for war, it failed to prepare its citizenry for peace. Aristotle concludes that the point of war is peace and the point of work is leisure (time for study), so these should be the priorities for the legislator to implement via education. While practical reasoning is necessary at all times, theoretical reasoning requires leisure, according to Aristotle.

On this account, then, there is no clash with the doctrine of the mean. What counts as a happy life for a particular individual still depends on her particular circumstances and abilities, but Aristotle's ranking is first and foremost for the legislator who is arranging the city and its education so that the citizens can take full advantage of the abilities they have (*Politics* VII 15 1333b27 cf. *EN* X 9). The ranking has a further consequence. If peace takes priority over war, the peacetime virtues should also take priority in the happy society. While bravery may be "more familiar to us", it is Aristotle's "nameless" virtues that we need more.

Aristotle is often criticized by modern philosophers for failing to address the immoralist and for being insufficiently critical of the customs of his times. However, his account of moral psychology shows what is defective about the Thrasymachean ideal, and his prejudices are often best combated by adopting a general Aristotelian approach (e.g. Nussbaum 2000). Aristotle claims that his account of the happy life is only a sketch. If the sketch is correct, he says, anyone can fill in the details, and here time can also help (*EN* I 7 1098a20–24). A good deal of time has passed since the fourth century BCE, and a good many famous philosophers have been inspired to elaborate Aristotle's ideas, but there are still plenty of details left for future philosophers to provide.[3]

Notes

1. When it comes to good translations, the student of Aristotle is spoilt for choice. See the beginning of the Bibliography for a selection of the best, most readily available translations. For a discussion of the difficulties in translating Aristotle's *Nicomachean Ethics* and different ways of addressing them, see Gottlieb (2001a). I have transliterated key Greek words for ease of reference in the authors' glossaries.
2. In the biblical book of Jonah, Jonah is sent by God to tell the people of Nineveh to mend their sinful ways. Nineveh is also immortalized as "a city of sin" in Michael Hurd's musical version, *Jonah-man Jazz*.
3. Thanks to Claudia Card and Henry Newell for helpful comments on an earlier draft. Thanks also to John Shand for many helpful suggestions.

Bibliography

Translations

Broadie, S. & C. Rowe (eds) 2001. *Aristotle's Nicomachean Ethics*, translation and commentary. New York: Oxford University Press.
Crisp, R. (ed.) 2000. *Aristotle's Nicomachean Ethics*, translation and introduction. Cambridge: Cambridge University Press.
Irwin, T. H. 1985. *Aristotle's Nicomachean Ethics*, reprinted 1999 with revised introduction,

expanded notes and glossary. Indianapolis, IN: Hackett.

Ross, W. D. 1923. *Aristotle's Nicomachean Ethics*, translation revised by J. L. Ackrill & J. O. Urmson. Oxford: Oxford University Press. Ross's original translation can be found on the web at www.epistemelinks.com

Sachs, J. (ed.) 2001. *Aristotle's Nicomachean Ethics*, translation, glossary and introductory essay. Newbury Port, MA: Focus Publishing. The introduction is also in the *Internet Encyclopedia of Philosophy* at www.utm.edu/research/iep

Thomson, J. A. K. 1976. *Aristotle's Nicomachean Ethics*, translation with appendices by Hugh Tredennick and introduction and bibliography by Jonathan Barnes. Harmondsworth: Penguin.

Secondary literature

Ackrill, J. L. 1978. "Aristotle on Action". See Rorty (1980), 93–101.

Ackrill, J. L. 1981. *Aristotle the Philosopher*. Oxford: Clarendon Press.

Annas, J. 1993. *The Morality of Happiness*. Oxford: Oxford University Press.

Anscombe, G. E. M. 1957. *Intention*. Cambridge, MA: Harvard University Press.

Anton, J. P. & A. Preus (eds) 1983. *Essays in Ancient Greek Philosophy*, 6 vols, vols 2 & 4. Albany, NY: SUNY Press.

Austin, J. L. 1956/7. "A Plea for Excuses", reprinted in his *Philosophical Papers* (1961). Oxford: Clarendon Press.

Barnes, J., M. Schofield & R. Sorabji (eds) 1977. *Articles on Aristotle, vol. 2: Ethics and Politics*. London: Duckworth.

Bostock, D. 2000. *Aristotle's Ethics*. Oxford: Oxford University Press.

Broadie, S. 1991. *Ethics with Aristotle*. Oxford: Oxford University Press.

Brown, L. 1997. "What is 'the mean relative to us' in Aristotle's Ethics?", *Phronesis* **42**(1), 77–93.

Burnyeat, M. F. 1980. "Aristotle on Learning to be Good". See Rorty (1980), 69–92.

Card, C. 1999. "Groping Through Gray Zones". In *On Feminist Ethics and Politics*, C. Card (ed.), 3–26. Lawrence, KS: University Press of Kansas.

Charles, D. O. M. 1984. *Aristotle's Philosophy of Action*. Ithaca, NY: Cornell University Press.

Cooper, J. M. 1975. *Reason and Human Good in Aristotle*. Indianapolis, IN: Hackett.

Cooper, J. M. 1980. "Aristotle on Friendship". See Rorty (1980), 301–40.

Dahl, N. 1984. *Practical Reason, Aristotle and Weakness of Will*. Minneapolis, MI: University of Minnesota Press.

Driver, J. 2001. *Uneasy Virtue*. Cambridge: Cambridge University Press.

Foot, P. 2001. *Natural Goodness*. Oxford: Oxford University Press.

Gifford, M. 1995. "Nobility of Mind: The Political Dimension of Aristotle's Theory of Intellectual Virtue". In *Aristotelian Political Philosophy*, vol. 1, K. J. Boudouris (ed.), 51–60. Athens: International Association for Greek Philosophy.

Gosling, J. C. B. & C. C. W. Taylor 1982. *The Greeks on Pleasure*. Oxford: Clarendon Press.

Gottlieb, P. 2001a. "Translating Aristotle's Ethics", *Apeiron* **34**(1), 91–9.

Gottlieb, P. 2001b. "Aristotle: *Nicomachean Ethics* I–II" and long bibliography for *Project Archelogos* at www.archelogos.com

Hursthouse, R. 1999. *On Virtue Ethics*. Oxford: Oxford University Press.

Irwin, T. H. 1980. "The Metaphysical and Psychological Basis of Aristotle's Ethics". See Rorty (1980), 35–53.

Irwin, T. H. 1988. *Aristotle's First Principles*. Oxford: Clarendon Press (esp. Part 3).

Kenny, A. 1978. *The Aristotelian Ethics: A Study of the Relationship between the Eudemian and the Nicomachean Ethics of Aristotle*. Oxford: Clarendon Press.

Kosman, L. A. 1980. "Being Properly Affected: Virtues and Feelings in Aristotle's Ethics". See Rorty (1980), 103–16.

Kraut, R. 1989. *Aristotle on the Human Good*. Princeton, NJ: Princeton University Press.

Leighton, S. 1992. "Relativizing Moral Excellence in Aristotle", *Apeiron* 25, 49–66.

Lloyd. G. E. R. 1968. "The Role of Medical and Biological Analogies in Aristotle's Ethics", *Phronesis* 13, 68–83.

McDowell, J. 1980. "The Role of *Eudaimonia* in Aristotle's Ethics". See Rorty (1980), 359–76.

McDowell, J. 1995. "Two Sorts of Naturalism". In *Virtues and Reasons: Philippa Foot and Moral Theory*, R. Hursthouse, G. Lawrence & W. Quinn (eds), 149–79. Oxford: Clarendon Press.

Meyer, S. S. 1993. *Aristotle on Moral Responsiblity: Character and Cause*. Oxford: Blackwell.

Nussbaum, M. C. 1986. *The Fragility of Goodness: Luck and Ethics in Greek Tragedy and Philosophy*. Cambridge: Cambridge University Press.

Nussbaum, M. C. 2000. *Women and Human Development: The Capabilities Approach*. Cambridge: Cambridge University Press.

Pears, D. 1980. "Courage as a Mean". See Rorty (1980), 171–87.

Penner, T. M. I. 1970. "Verbs and the Identity of Actions: A Philosophical Exercise in the Interpretation of Aristotle". In *Ryle: A Collection of Critical Essays*, O. P. Wood & G. W. Pitcher (eds), 393–460. New York: Doubleday.

Price, A. W. 1988. *Love and Friendship in Plato and Aristotle*. Oxford: Clarendon Press.

Rand, A. 1964. *The Virtue of Selfishness: A New Concept of Egoism*. New York: Signet Books.

Rawls, J. 1971. *A Theory of Justice*. Cambridge, MA: Harvard University Press.

Reeve, C. D. C. 1992. *Practices of Reason*. Oxford: Oxford University Press.

Rorty, A. O. (ed.) 1980. *Essays on Aristotle's Ethics*. Berkeley, CA: University of California Press.

Santas, G. 2001. *Goodness and Justice: Plato, Aristotle, and the Moderns*. Oxford: Blackwell.

Sherman, N. 1989. *The Fabric of Character: Aristotle's Theory of Virtue*. Oxford: Clarendon Press.

Sherman, N. 1997. *Making a Necessity of Virtue: Aristotle and Kant on Virtue*. Cambridge: Cambridge University Press.

Sim, M. 2004. "Harmony and the Mean in the *Nicomachean Ethics* and the *Zhongyong*", *Dao: A Journal of Comparative Philosophy* 3(2), 253–80.

Smart, J. C. C. & B. A. O. Williams 1973. *Utilitarianism: For and Against*. Cambridge: Cambridge University Press.

Sorabji, R. 1973–4. "Aristotle on the Role of Intellect in Virtue". See Rorty (1980), 201–19.

Stocker, M. 1990. *Plural and Conflicting Values*. Oxford: Clarendon Press.

Urmson, J. O. 1973. "Aristotle's Doctrine of the Mean". See Rorty (1980), 157–70.

Vlastos, G. 1973. "The Individual as Object of Love in Plato". In *Platonic Studies*, G. Vlastos (ed.), 3–42. Princeton, NJ: Princeton University Press.

Whiting, J. E. 1988. "Aristotle's Function Argument: A Defense", *Ancient Philosophy* 8(1), 33–48.

Whiting, J. E. 1991. "Impersonal Friends", *Monist* 74(1), 3–29.

Wiggins, D. 1975–76. "Deliberation and Practical Reasoning". See Rorty (1980), 221–40.

Williams, B. A. O. 1985. *Ethics and the Limits of Philosophy*. Cambridge, MA: Harvard University Press.

Woods, M. J. 1992. *Aristotle's Eudemian Ethics Books I, II and VIII*, 2nd edn. Oxford: Clarendon Press.

3

Lucretius

On the Nature of the Universe

Harry Lesser

Introduction: Lucretius's method

Titus Lucretius Carus, to give him his full name, lived probably from 99 to 55 BCE. Virtually nothing is known of his life, or why he died young; there is no reason to believe the story that he was driven mad by a love potion and committed suicide. He was probably of aristocratic birth, married, and a fairly prosperous farmer, prosperous enough not to have to work on the farm with his own hands, but not so prosperous that he could employ a bailiff. There are references in his poem to the management of the farm keeping him very busy, so that he could find time for writing only at night. His work consists of one long philosophical poem, *De rerum natura*, literally, "On the Nature of Things", but often translated, more philosophically, as "On the Nature of the Universe", unfinished at his death but already in six books and over 7000 lines. This poem is the most complete account we have of the philosophy of Epicurus (341–271 BCE), because all that survives of the works of Epicurus himself are three letters, two collections of aphorisms and an account of his "Principal Doctrines", plus fragments and later reports of what he wrote.

These writings provide evidence that Lucretius largely stayed very close to Epicurus, and often simply put his doctrines and arguments into poetry. He does appear to claim originality for the doctrine of perception in Book 4, although the passage may simply mean that he is the first to put it into poetry; and it is reasonable to think that he adds examples and arguments of his own in many places; at least once, in Book 2, he says that what he will now say was "sought out by my own sweet labour" (l. 730). He certainly adds a deep feeling for the beauty and fecundity of nature. The poem opens with an invocation to Venus, not as the goddess of love as such, but as the goddess of procreation. He may also have had a deeper scientific interest than Epicurus. Epicurus's main concern was ethical, and he probably dealt with the philosophy of nature mainly to back up his ethical views, whereas, apart from Lucretius's obvious enthusiasm for his subject, there is the fact that, even if one allows for the unfinished state of the poem, there is far more space given to natural philosophy than to ethics. But in any case, our concern is with philosophy, rather than the history of ideas, with the study of Lucretius's thought as we find it, rather than with the reconstruction of Epicureanism. We should also remember, even while reading a prose translation, that Lucretius was a great poet as well as a philosopher. Indeed, it may have been awareness of his gifts that led him to choose the medium of poetry to express his philosophical ideas, which was rare, although not unprecedented: there were Parmenides and Empedocles before him. The reason he himself gives is that the "honey" of poetry will make the bitter medicine of philosophy more acceptable, and beguile people into swallowing it (1, 935ff.).

Nevertheless, it may well be asked why the ideas of Lucretius, however magnificently expressed, are of more than historical and literary interest. The answer is that one possible and plausible general theory of what the world is like is the theory of materialism: the theory that everything that exists is either physical, whether solid, liquid or gaseous, or, like consciousness, an attribute of something physical. Materialism may or may not be true, but anyone who wants to try to understand the world around them, including the human world, needs to consider whether it might be true. Now Lucretius's poem still supplies both some of the main arguments for materialism and a systematic working out of what it entails. Much of what is said is known now to be scientifically incorrect, and this applies, as we shall see, to the general theory itself as well as to points of detail. But much also remains, and we still need to ask how much the arguments of the poem establish.

To understand Lucretius's philosophy, one must first understand its purpose and its methods. The purpose, and the purpose of all Epicureanism, is to destroy the basis and power of superstition by providing a proper scientific account of the workings of nature. The aim of life, according to Epicurus and his followers, is happiness, and the function of philosophy is to remove obstacles to happiness. One of the main obstacles is fear, and especially fear engendered by superstition, such as the fear of divine vengeance, which both causes psychological misery and motivates acts of injustice and cruelty, such as the sacrifice of Iphigenia by her father, described in Book 1 (80–101). The cure for this is knowledge, and this is what philosophy and science will provide. It should be noted that, as always with ancient philosophy, no distinction could yet be made between science and philosophy. This was not because the ancients despised empirical observation – this was not true even of Plato and Aristotle (claims to the contrary are based on misunderstanding), and is even less true of Lucretius – but because the equipment for controlled experiments and really accurate measurement was lacking, and therefore the ability to test a theory was severely limited.

Nevertheless, Lucretius's method of enquiry, which is to be found in the surviving writings of Epicurus in a less fully developed form, has much in common with modern scientific method. The starting-point is the evidence provided by the senses: sight, touch, hearing, smell and taste. The argument for this – which first appears, almost incidentally, in Book 1 (699–700) as part of the criticism of Heraclitus – is that there is nothing more trustworthy that one could use to correct the senses: either one accepts them as a guide to what is true and false or one has no guide at all. This is elaborated in Book 4 (469ff.). The first point made here is that radical scepticism, apart from being impossible in practical life (see 507ff.), cannot be stated coherently: if anyone claims that he knows nothing, he cannot also claim that he knows that he knows nothing. So either he simply does not distinguish true and false, or he accepts the guidance of the senses. Reason is not an alternative because it "has risen entirely from the senses" (484), by which Lucretius presumably means that we can use reason to find out about the world only if we base our reasoning on premises derived from sense-perception, for example, by arguing from effects to likely causes. Moreover (499), no reasoning or further perceptions can alter the fact that we really do experience what we seem to experience. Where we go wrong is in the conclusions about the world that we draw from our experience. One of Lucretius's examples (436ff.) is refraction. People ignorant of the sea think that the oars in the water are broken. They really do see bent or broken oars; the mistake they make is to think that this is because the oars really are broken.

So to find out about the world we have to ask what will explain the things that we observe through the senses. But to do this we have to posit what is unobservable (1, 270). Lucretius points out that innumerable things happen that are only explicable if we suppose that they are the result of many events too slight to be visible: growth, the drying of wet clothes and the erosion of cliffs are among his examples. So what we need is a theory that refers to unobservables in order to explain what we do observe. How, though, is such a theory to be tested, if our only guide is the senses?

Lucretius gives no explicit answer, but he demonstrates repeatedly what his answer is. In order to test a theory, he derives from it the consequence that, if the theory were true, a particular type of event would occur and be observed to occur. For example, if matter could be created, or could arise, from nothing, we would see this happening. If this type of event is not in fact observed, he concludes that the theory is false. Now the logic of this – If p, q; not q; therefore not p – is valid. And the form of the enquiry corresponds to what is now known as the hypothetico-deductive method: the method of dealing with a hypothesis that cannot be directly tested by deducing something from it that is directly testable and testing that. The difference is that Lucretius could not use laboratory experiments, and therefore had to rely on everyday observation of natural processes in order to test any theory.

But, as is well known, the limitation of the hypothetico-deductive method is that it can falsify a theory, but it cannot prove any theory to be true. A million observations of white swans may render it more and more probable that all swans are white, but do not prove it; the observation of a single black swan in Australia (or in Fog Lane Park, in Manchester) shows that the theory is incorrect. For the same reason, the method cannot prove a theory to be false on the grounds that something has never been observed; given the total absence over millennia of any sighting of a unicorn, it is highly unlikely that there are any, to put it mildly, but their existence has not actually been disproved. This is a problem for Lucretius, but he is able to use the method to get positive results that, if not 100 per cent certain, are at least highly probable. He achieves this, first, because the theories he uses the method to destroy are sometimes so general that the mere assertions that they are false are theories in their own right. If, for example, we can show that the theory that matter can be created from nothing is false, we have thereby established the very interesting proposition that matter cannot be created from nothing. Secondly, although the fact that we have not observed x so far does not mean that we never shall, if x is something sufficiently general, something that we could not avoid observing if it happened, or cannot avoid observing that it has not happened, such as the destruction of all matter, then, although the method does not yield certainty, as Lucretius thought, it does yield a very high probability. But to see this one must turn to the work itself.

The plan of the work is very clear, although our exposition will not always follow Lucretius's own order. The basic principles of materialism and of the atomic theory are explained in Book 1. Book 2 explains the details of the theory; Book 3 applies it to the human mind or soul; and Book 4 applies it to mental life, especially perception and emotion. Book 5 gives an account of the origins of the world-system we inhabit and of the origins of human society, and Book 6 uses the theory to explain a range of natural phenomena, especially those such as thunder and earthquakes that are particularly apt to cause superstitious fears if their causes are not understood. In this exposition I shall give an account in turn of the most important ideas in Books 1–3, followed in each case by comment. Passages from Book 4 will be used, as they have been used above, to explain Lucretius's theory of knowledge and perception. Book 5 will be discussed, in part, together with Book 2, since both deal with how atoms come together to produce everything else. Book 6 will occasionally be referred to in order to illustrate a particular point. In the main, it is of more interest for the history of science than for philosophy, but even here there are points made that are of importance for the general theory.

Lucretius's basic ideas

We should begin by considering Lucretius's (and Epicurus's) two most basic propositions (1, 146–264): that matter can neither be created out of nothing nor be utterly destroyed. The use of the method described above is immediately apparent. Thus, the argument for the first proposition is that if generation from nothing were possible we would see it sometimes happen. But not only do things never come into being from nothing, but they require, whether they are animal or vegetable, seed of a specific sort and conditions of a specific sort for their generation to be possible. Similarly, not only do things never disappear into nothing, but, given that an infinite amount of time has elapsed already (Lucretius does not say how we know that time is infinite, but presumably would argue that if we posit any start of time we can always intelligibly ask "What happened before that?"), then, if it were possible for things to be annihilated, by this time everything would have disappeared. So matter must be indestructible and uncreated, and have always existed.

Now if this is the nature of matter, an atomic theory follows as an inevitable consequence. For all observable material objects, however large or small, are clearly perishable eventually. So if matter as such is imperishable, the only possible explanation is that everything physical is composed of tiny particles, much too small to be visible, that are totally solid and indestructible, so that what we call "destruction" is simply the resolution of something into its constituent parts and ultimately its constituent atoms. Moreover, atoms must be unsplittable – it is one of the ironies of history that the word, from the Greek root "tom" ("cut") and the negative prefix "a", originally meant "unsplittable" rather than "very small" – since otherwise by this time everything would have crumbled away into particles too small to recombine.

But as well as atoms there must be void, or empty space. If there were no empty space motion would be impossible, since everything would be jammed together and there would be nowhere for anything to move (1, 329ff.). But we observe that there is such a thing as motion; therefore there is empty space. This empty space must be infinite in extent (1, 958ff.). For suppose that it has a boundary. Then imagine that someone stands on the boundary and throws a dart. Either the dart moves or its path is blocked; there are no other possibilities. But if the dart moves there must be more empty space beyond the boundary, and if it is blocked there must be something solid beyond the boundary, and in neither case is there a boundary. And if space is infinite, so must matter be (1, 1008ff.). Otherwise, if there were a finite number of atoms, however large, in infinite space, they would by this time have been separated from each other and become unable to combine to form anything else.

So matter, in the form of atoms and things composed of atoms, exists, and void (i.e. empty) space exists, and both are infinite in extent. Everything else that exists, such as events or consciousness, exists only as an attribute of one or the other of these (1, 418ff.). Two arguments for this are given. First, everything that exists must be either tangible or intangible. If it is tangible, no matter how slightly, it must be material, and if it is intangible it must be space. Secondly, everything that exists must either be capable of acting and being acted upon or provide a place in which action takes place, that is, be part of space. But action is impossible without body; therefore everything that is not space must have a body. Consciousness does indeed exist, but as an attribute of physical bodies: not, of course, of individual atoms (2, 865ff.), but of those combinations of atoms that form living animals. So the universe is eternal and infinite: it has already existed for an infinite length of time, and will exist for an infinite time more; it is infinite in extent; and it contains an infinite number of beings, animate and inanimate. It did not come into being from nothing, it has no purpose (1, 1021ff.), and it contains no beings that are not totally physical.

Comment on the basic ideas

This basic position of Lucretius, set out mainly in Book 1, can be expressed in two key propositions: first, that matter consists of minute particles that cannot be created or destroyed, and, secondly, that nothing except empty space exists that is not physical.

The argument for the first of these propositions is that this is the only theory that does not have consequences incompatible with the observed facts. The argument for the second is that it is logically impossible for anything else to exist, because it would have to be neither tangible nor intangible. This, however, is question-begging; it simply asserts the impossibility of anything non-physical except empty space, and provides no further argument. The important question here is whether consciousness, as mind or soul, can exist independently of anything physical. This will be considered at greater length when we discuss

Book 3. Meanwhile, we should note that Lucretius has put forward a view that is coherent and plausible but has not proved it. It is true that it is hard to imagine a pure non-physical consciousness, but it is not a logical impossibility. Also, the alternative, that matter can be conscious, leaves us with an equivalent problem of how it is possible for this to come about. Nevertheless, it is worth noting that even if non-physical consciousness exists and has physical effects, the point that everything must be tangible or intangible can already serve to deliver us from much superstition, since the ghosts, witches, vampires and so on of folklore could only do the things they are credited with if they were simultaneously physical and non-physical, which is impossible. So the serious student of Lucretius can already sleep a bit more easily!

The first proposition is more complex. There are two issues: whether Lucretius is right about the nature of matter, and whether he is right that it is uncreated and indestructible. On the first point, modern science would appear to have confirmed the atomic theory, but to have shown that the atom is something very different from the totally solid particle conceived, reasonably enough at the time, by Lucretius. It is very small, but it is not simple, solid or unsplittable. In fact, the appropriate conclusion seems to be that Lucretius, and the atomists before him, were right to say that the real nature of matter is something very different from what we observe on the macro-level, but neither they nor we, even though we know more than they did, really understand what matter is. Possibly, if and when we do, the problem of how matter and consciousness are related will look altogether different. What is certain is that if anything is uncreated and indestructible, it is not simply matter but matter/energy.

But has Lucretius proved that matter or matter/energy cannot be created or destroyed? He has shown at least that within the system of nature this is highly unlikely. Indeed, he has perhaps given enough evidence to show that it is almost certainly impossible in our particular part of the universe, and that, while it might happen elsewhere, there is no reason to think that it does. For the matter with which we deal contains no capacity to generate itself from nothing, or we should see this happen sometimes, and no liability to perish, or it would by now have perished. Admittedly, we cannot take it for granted, as Lucretius does, that matter is the same throughout the universe, but this is a reasonable hypothesis as long as there is no evidence to the contrary.

However, what he has not proved is that the system of nature as such is uncreated or uncaused. He has shown that this is a coherent possibility, that matter in its basic form, as opposed to the things composed from it, may be eternal and require nothing to bring it into being or keep it in being. But he has not shown that this is in fact so. For one cannot argue from what is true of each thing within the system to what is true of the system as a whole, without committing the fallacy of composition: for example, some things that are true of individual people, that they have a heart and a brain, say, are not true of humanity as a whole. So, while it may well be true that absolute creation and destruction do not occur in nature, this does not show that the whole system was not created, or is not kept from destruction, by a cause outside itself rather than within itself. It is true that some, although not all, arguments for God as the first cause of the universe, whether as creating, preserving or both, commit this same fallacy. But this shows only that the question is so far unsettled. In short, Lucretius has shown that we should study nature with the assumptions that spontaneous generation and destruction are impossible and that to understand matter we must understand what it is on the micro-level. He has also shown that it is a coherent possibility, to be taken seriously, that everything in the universe is material. But he has neither shown this to be true nor investigated the metaphysical question of whether it is likely to be true: it is assumed, not demonstrated.

The nature of atoms, and of what is composed of atoms

With this conclusion in mind, accepting much of the atomic theory, but recognizing that it needs modifying in the light of modern science and that the conclusions Lucretius draws from it are possibilities, not proven certainties, we may proceed to the account of the properties of atoms in Book 2, together with the account of the formation of our world-system in Book 5 and the account of perception in Book 4. We will not follow Lucretius's own order, but deal first with Book 2, 333–729. Lucretius argues that atoms, although all absolutely solid, and microscopic, differ in size and particularly shape, and this is why there are many different things in the world. The things in the world differ both because they are composed of different types of atom (for example, some atoms are rough and jagged and some are smooth) and because, although there is some void or empty space in everything except individual atoms, there are variations in how closely the atoms cling to each other and are packed together. This explains, for example, the difference between solids, liquids and gases (444ff.). But there is a finite, although large, number of types of atom (480ff.). This must be so for two reasons. First, a limit in size imposes a limit on the number of possible shapes. Secondly, the number of different kinds of things in the world, although large, is finite, which shows both that there are a finite number of elements and also (700ff.) that there are a finite number of possible combinations: not every potential combination of atoms will hold together. However, Lucretius also holds that nothing is made out of only one sort of atom. Interestingly, modern science, with its table of elements differing in the properties of their atoms, is on this point more in line with the supposedly less empirically concerned Plato of the *Timaeus*, who posited five elements – earth, air, water, fire and the substance of the heavens – which differed in the shape of their atoms, than with Lucretius.

Lucretius's reason for maintaining this has to do with his theory of perception. As we have seen, he is committed to the theory that only matter can have any causal effect. He also believes that causal effects are possible only if there is physical contact, and he is emphatic that all perception is really touch (434ff.). Hence, sight, hearing, smell and taste are all brought about by the effect of atoms on our sense-organs. This is explained in detail in Book 4. Since all objects have multiple effects on our senses, they all must be composed of many sorts of atoms. The reason they act on our senses from a distance as well as when in contact is that they are constantly giving off atoms that strike our senses, these being constantly replaced as long as the object exists. Thus our experiences of sound, smell and taste are all the result of atoms given off by physical objects entering the pores of the appropriate sense-organ – ear, nose or tongue – and making contact. Rough atoms, which tear the pores, produce harsh and unpleasant sensations; smooth atoms produce pleasant ones; atoms that slip through without making contact will produce no sensation. Since different people, and different animals, as species and as individuals, have pores of different shapes and sizes, and since the state of the pores can be changed by sickness (e.g. by becoming clogged), both what is experienced and what is found pleasant change from individual to individual, and species to species, and for the same person if the state of their body changes. Also, atoms are lost as the stream passes through the air, so that sounds become indistinct and softer, and smells fainter. (On all this, see Book 4, 522–705).

Sight (4, 1–468) is more complex. As well as emitting streams of atoms, all objects are constantly peeling off very thin films from their surfaces; these fly through the air and produce sight as they strike the eye. The variations in what we see, whether accurately representing the objects themselves or distorted in some way, are explained by what happens to the films as they pass through the air, or by the state of the eye itself. Thus the sense of distance is produced by the amount of air that is driven into the eye by the film (244–68); mirror images are reversed because the film rebounds from the mirror "straight back in reverse" (292–323); distant objects look blurred because the films lose atoms as they travel, through collisions (353–63); and sufferers from jaundice see everything yellow because particles from their own bodies are clogging their eyes (332–6). The existence of these films also explains imagination and dreaming (722–822; 962–1036). For there are innumerable films of every sort flying around, some being films of actual objects and some being composites that are the result of collisions, such as the image of a centaur, produced by a collision of images of man and horse (741). If we are concentrating on what is around us we do not see these images, but if we are not attending to this, as in sleep, images will strike the eye at random. But in particular, if we think of anything, an image of it will nearly always be to hand, and this is what we then see. Similarly, even in dreams we tend to see those things we are most involved with when waking; even dogs act in sleep as if they were dreaming of hunting (991ff.).

So our perception and our mental life are the result of the direct action of atoms on our bodies. But in Book 2 (730ff.), Lucretius explains that atoms themselves lack colour, temperature, sound, taste and smell, and have therefore only size, shape and solidity. For our perceptions of all these are constantly changing, but atoms cannot change their properties. We must therefore conclude that our experiences of all these are the result of the effect on us of large combinations of atoms, but could not be produced by individual atoms, even if we could perceive them. Similarly (865ff.), sentience and consciousness are said to be not qualities of individual atoms, which would be absurd, but of the appropriate atoms appropriately combined. We shall return to this later. Meanwhile, it is worth noting that we have here, although for different reasons, an early appearance of the distinction later worked out by John Locke between primary and secondary qualities, primary qualities being those that are possessed by objects themselves, such as size and shape, and secondary qualities, such as colour, which do not exist unperceived, and so are really powers to affect sense-organs. Whether this distinction really should be made, and why or why not, has been a much discussed philosophical question. It is interesting and important to note its appearance here.

But the formation and nature of things is to be explained not only by the nature of atoms but also by their movements (2, 62–332). Uncombined atoms move downwards constantly, since they have weight, and, since the universe has no bottom, this will continue for ever. If this were the only movement, they would forever move parallel to each other and never combine to form anything. But at random times and places atoms swerve, and therefore collide. The results of these collisions are determined by the speed and direction of the impact and the shapes of the atoms involved. Sometimes they cling together and combine, sometimes they rebound, and the rebounds produce further collisions, and more and more combinations, involving larger and larger numbers of atoms, so that there are more and more recognizable physical substances.

Above all, although this is not fully described until Book 5 (416ff.), world-systems are formed by this process: systems like our solar system, except that Lucretius, like most people before Copernicus, assumes that our system has the earth at the centre and includes the stars. What happens is that as a result of the various collisions and combinations a huge number of atoms become relatively isolated, and combine more and more. Since only certain combinations are possible, there will be more and more of certain substances, especially earth, water, air and ether (air in its lighter and fierier form). The heavier material falls towards the centre and coalesces, the place where it caves in being filled by water, and the light, fiery bodies are pushed outwards but have sufficient weight to remain in the system, being left with freedom to move but only by revolving round the earth at the centre. The first living beings, plants and later animals, of all species, including human beings, came into being from the earth (783ff.), as a result of the action of sun and rain on it. Those species that could survive and reproduce then did so, but the earth then lost its power to produce anything of any size by itself. Incidentally, the belief that flies and worms were spontaneously generated in this way continued at least until the early modern period and was in no way peculiar to Lucretius.

Since the universe is infinite, all this has happened not once but an infinite number of times, and there are an infinite number of world-systems. They all have, so to speak, a birth, of the kind described very briefly above, and will all eventually disintegrate and perish (see the final section of Book 2, and Book 5, 91–145), since only atoms are eternal, and everything made out of them eventually breaks up. They are all produced as a result of the operations of the laws of nature – which determine what is inevitable, given the conditions, and what is impossible – and not as the result of any purpose or design. The atoms did not come together purposively (1, 1021ff) and the organs of our bodies were not designed for our use, but simply used once they happened to develop (4, 823ff).

In particular, our world was not created by any divine being. Surprisingly, Lucretius, although he denies that the earth or the heavenly bodies have any divine nature or any consciousness, since only certain kinds of being can be conscious (see 2, 652ff and 5, 110–45), follows Epicurus in recognizing the existence of gods. But they are physical beings, although relatively ethereal, living a carefree existence in a remote and isolated part of the universe (5, 146–55), and able to remain in existence indefinitely because they can avoid colliding with other bodies. Lucretius gives three reasons why we should not suppose that they either created or in any way preserve or control the physical universe. First, even divine beings, given that they must still be physical, lack the necessary power; in particular, they would have to be in several places at once, which is impossible (2, 1090ff.). They also lack the necessary total knowledge of the nature of the atoms out of which they would have had to create the world (5, 181ff.). (We have already established, for Lucretius, that creation from nothing is impossible, and are considering creation from atoms.) Secondly, beings already living a happy existence could have no possible motive for creating a world: they have no reason to be dissatisfied with things as they are, they gain nothing from the existence of the rest of universe and of humanity, and they would do us no harm or injustice by leaving us uncreated (5, 156–80). Thirdly, the imperfect nature of the world shows that it could not be the product of divine creation, least of all by divine beings seeking to benefit human beings, who are in their natural state less well equipped to survive than most animals (5, 195–234; also 2, 167–82).

Comment

In considering Lucretius's account of the order of nature, we need to do much more than admire the poetry, and the intellectual power and ingenuity, both of the man himself and of his avowed master Epicurus. We should certainly admire; but we then have to try to determine, as always, where he was wrong, where he was right, and where things are still undecided. We should not despise him for not knowing what science would discover in the two thousand years after his death; but we do need to read him in the light of later discoveries, and also we need to be philosophically critical.

If we do this, we find several mistakes. First, atoms in empty space would not have weight or fall downwards. "Downwards" has meaning only in relation to movement towards the earth or towards the centre of the earth, or similarly towards any other planet or star; and there is no "down" in space. Atoms in empty space might all move parallel, but there is no reason why they should. This could also mean that there is no need to posit a swerve in order to explain why atoms collide, although it is worth noting that, admittedly coincidentally, modern physics does also speak of indeterminacy at the micro-level. Lucretius's other reason for positing the swerve – that it is needed in order to explain human free will (2, 251ff.) – is also unconvincing, for two reasons. First, to establish free will one needs to show that we have some control and choice over our actions, not that we are random and unpredictable, which is what the argument from indeterminacy suggests; the attempt to derive free will from the indeterminacy at the micro-level posited by modern physics runs into the same problem. Secondly, as we saw above, Lucretius argues at length in the final part of Book 2 that many characteristics of the objects composed of atoms are not possessed by the atoms themselves. If sentient beings are composed of insentient atoms, why cannot beings with free will be composed of atoms that are subject to determining laws? (There is no need to suppose that, if the position of each atom is determined, the position of the animal itself is determined, because the decision of the animal to move in a certain direction may itself be one of the determining factors.)

So we are unlikely to accept Lucretius's account of the movement of atoms. His astronomy, his rejection of the notion of elements, his account of the origin of life, his belief in the absolute solidity of atoms and his theory of perception (briefly touched on above) all similarly belong to outmoded science. The fundamental difference between Lucretius and modern science is that he assumes that the physical world consists of bodies that can act on each other only by physical contact: no notion exists of forces of attraction or repulsion, or of fields of energy. Thus the explanation of magnetism (6, 1002ff.) is that the Magnesian stone emits a stream of particles that clear away the air between it and the iron. This causes some of the atoms in the iron object to fall into the vacuum; and because the atoms of iron are exceptionally tightly packed and entangled they pull the rest of the object along with them. This point is fundamental, because it relates not just to particular theories but to what we now call philosophy of science. Lucretius supposed – reasonably enough, at the time – that a scientific explanation, or, as he himself might have put it, a non-superstitious explanation, of any phenomenon must be in terms of physical bodies acting directly on each other by touch. And this has turned out to be incorrect.

However, Lucretius did identify, or take over from Epicurus, much about the features of a proper investigation of the natural world that has proved correct. First, he has seen that, if one is to offer x as an explanation of y, one must be able to show how x and y are connected. Indeed, he went wrong only in supposing that there could be no such connection unless x and y were in actual physical contact. This may seem obvious, but there are still superstitions surviving, such as belief in actions that bring good or bad luck, or belief in signs and omens of various sorts, and also systems of thought, such as astrology, or most of it, that ignore this; and there were probably even more in Lucretius's day.

Secondly, he takes it that the natural world operates according to regular laws, so that the same causes always produce the same effects. It is true that this assumption cannot be proved, as Hume and others have pointed out. Nevertheless, it has to be assumed for any serious scientific investigation to take place. (Hume, for instance, clearly wished to retain it, and was merely concerned to point out that it can't be proved, even though our psychological make-up, very fortunately, means that we cannot help believing it.) It has also served us very well, both in theoretical and practical matters. Admittedly, Lucretius is sometimes too quick to establish a general principle on the basis of observations that may relate only to a special case, as when he assumes that the other world-systems, infinite in number, must all be broadly similar to our own, or, in the later part of Book 5, that human nature is more or less uniform. But this was, at the time, a weakness in the right direction; he was by no means the first to see that we must assume the uniformity of nature, but he probably operated the principle more thoroughly than anyone before him, including Epicurus. He also uses the principle in support of particular theories, by arguing that a proposed explanation is at least a possible one, since it is in line with what happens elsewhere in nature. This is not proof, and Lucretius did not think it was, but it is rational supporting evidence.

Thirdly, he takes it that the natural world must be explained in its own terms, without reference to the activity of supernatural beings or causes. As we shall see shortly, this does not of itself settle the issue of the truth of religious claims. But it does do away with superstitious fears and practices, and direct attention towards discovering how things actually do work and what their causes really are, and then if necessary using this information practically as well as theoretically. Again, this principle cannot be proved but must be assumed if nature is to be seriously investigated.

Finally, there is the point, discussed earlier, of the importance of observation. A theory that does not fit the observations cannot be a correct theory. The appeal to the observable facts is constant throughout the poem, and rightly so. Sometimes the facts prove less than Lucretius thinks, either because he is drawing conclusions from too few observations, or because he has for the moment overlooked the fact that more than one theory may fit the observations. He was, though, well aware of this possibility; and in Book 6 (703ff.) he points out that sometimes one may be able to say only that one of a number of possible causes must be active, and not know which one it is. He then demonstrates this by offering four alternative explanations of the flooding of the Nile in summer. But any theory offered must at least be consistent with the observations.

This, then, seems to indicate where Lucretius is wrong and where he is right. Where matters are uncertain is, as indicated earlier, with regard to religion. Once again, as when discussing Book 1, we need to distinguish what is true of the things that happen in the physical universe with what is true of the universe as a whole. Lucretius's arguments show the extreme unlikelihood – to put it no more strongly – that any being within this universe could have the power, the knowledge or the motivation to create even one world-system. But there is still the question whether the universe itself has a Creator and Sustainer. Such a being, unlike any physical being, could have the necessary power and knowledge, and also the motivation: not a motivation from need, but a motivation to create something beautiful, and Lucretius was as sensitive as any man to the beauty of nature. Whether this is the case is something about which philosophers, like other people, differ. There are those who argue that the universe must have a cause beyond itself, and those who deny the cogency of this argument. There are those who fully accept Lucretius's third argument, that the universe is too imperfect to be the work of a divine Creator, and those who think it is evidence against the existence of a Creator, but for various reasons not conclusive. Philosophically, the question is not settled. But both materialists and believers in transcendent religion should be grateful to Lucretius for delivering us from superstition.

The nature of consciousness

Deliverance from superstition is indeed Lucretius's aim, and in the prologues to the books of the poem he repeatedly praises Epicurus as the man who first saved us from irrational fears and terrors (1, 62ff.; 3, 1–30; 5, 1–54; 6, 1–42). This is partly achieved by knowledge of what the world is really like and what are the real causes of natural phenomena (6, 43–95). But this leaves one great fear: the fear of death. This not only poisons people's lives, but also creates discord between people and motivates them to crime. For the fear of death produces fear of poverty, which brings one close to death, and this leads to exaggerated greed for money; and it also leads to envy and hatred of the successful, who are seen as a threat (3, 31–93).

Now Lucretius, like Hamlet in "To be or not to be", thinks that the fear of death is really the fear of "something after death": of divine punishment in the next world. The cure for this is to understand the true nature of consciousness and of the mind and vital spirits. Once one grasps that the mind is as physical as anything else in the universe, and as much composed of atoms, one will realize that at death it simply disintegrates and consciousness ends for good. Death, being nothing, is nothing to be afraid of; matters after one's death will be as they were before one was born. Lucretius suggests that when people are sad because of what will happen to their bodies after death they are unconsciously but quite wrongly imagining that they will still be around to experience this, rather than, as is actually the case, being in the equivalent of an eternal dreamless sleep. As for those who are reluctant to leave a happy life, they should remember that the world owes them nothing – this is a very free, but I think faithful paraphrase – and be prepared to make way for the new generation. (On all this, see 3, 830–977.)

One interesting question is whether Lucretius, who died young, wrote this with an awareness that he was terminally ill, and whether he was tackling his own fear of death as well as other people's. Similarly, there is a question about the last 200 lines of the poem, in which, after beginning an account of the causes of epidemics, he goes into a long "purple passage" that is based on Thucydides' history and describes the Athenian plague of 430 BCE. Was he ill himself, and did he find a grim satisfaction in facing the facts of illness and death? The answer is unknown, and makes no difference to the philosophy; but it is worth reminding ourselves that Lucretius was a man, and not a set of ideas.

Our real business, however, is to consider Lucretius's account of consciousness and the arguments he brings for it. The account is in Book 3 (94–416). It is, as was said above, a physicalist account, but different from modern physicalism. Modern physicalism regards consciousness – thinking, feeling, and so on – as an attribute or activity of the brain, and therefore as something material and physical. Lucretius regards it as having its own organ, distinct from the rest of the body, but still composed of atoms, so that there is an identifiable "soul", not to be identified with the heart or brain or blood, but still physical. This has two distinct parts, although they are interconnected and "form one nature" (137). The mind, which is the seat of intelligence and emotion, is located in the breast, near the heart; Lucretius argues that it cannot be scattered through the body because it is not necessarily affected by what happens to the body (94–116). One might have expected it to be located in the brain, even if Lucretius thought it was not part of it, but many of the ancients, including Aristotle, although not Plato, located thought in the heart. Jung once suggested that this attribution of thought to the heart was a feature of cultures where people think only about things important to them, so that all their thought is accompanied by emotion.

In contrast, the source of sentience, for which the best English term is probably "vital spirit", as used by Latham in his translation (see Bibliography), is diffused through the body, as indicated by the fact that we can feel pleasure and pain in nearly every part of the body. Nevertheless, Lucretius maintains (3, 323–69), it is not the spirit that has sentience, but the combination of body and spirit, or even the combination of body, spirit and mind. Indeed, the spirit seems to perform the functions that we now ascribe to the nervous system; Lucretius does not say that it conveys information to the mind, but he does say (136–60) that the mind is the controlling agent, and works on the body through the vital spirits. In Book 4 (877ff.) he explains how this happens. The mind conceives a desire, for example to move in a certain direction, and strikes the vital spirits to move them appropriately. In their turn they strike on the body and send it in that direction. As he observes, there is nothing unusual in a light body causing movement in a heavy one. Nevertheless, just as we would say that it is the person who perceives and feels pleasure and pain, and decides, for example, to move, rather than saying it is the brain or nervous system, similarly Lucretius wants to say it is the person, rather than the mind or spirit. But the mind is the ruling organ; as long as there is mind there is life, and when mind goes, life goes (3, 396–416).

The crucial point, for Lucretius, is that mind and spirit are composed of matter (161–322). Four kinds of atoms make up mind and spirit. To paraphrase, since a living body, as opposed to a dead one, has breath, warmth and energy, what leaves the dying is "a rarefied wind mixed with warmth, while the warmth carries with it also air" (232f, Latham (trans.)). But since these three, wind, air and warmth, even combined, still cannot produce sentience, we must suppose there is a fourth component that, in combination with the other three, yields sentience and consciousness. Although all four of these are very fine matter, they are still matter. So, since the soul is material, it is perishable. Even in sleep, enough atoms from the mind and spirit leave the body to produce a loss of consciousness, although not of life; and at death they all leave and scatter, and that particular consciousness ends for good. One will be recycled, and the same atoms will go to help form many other sentient beings; but one's individual consciousness will not return. "The minds of living beings and the light fabric of their spirit are neither birthless nor deathless" (417f, Latham (trans.)).

Discussion of Lucretius's arguments for the mortality of consciousness

To show that the mind is mortal Lucretius first has to show that it is physical. He has two arguments for this: the argument in Book 1 that nothing non-physical can exist, except empty space; and the argument in Book 3 (161–76) that since the mind and body clearly interact with and affect each other, and since one thing can act on another only by touch, the mind must be physical. I have argued above that the first argument is question-begging. The second argument will not do as it stands, since it rests on the false premise that all causation must be by touch. But it raises a question that is still with us: if mind and body interact, as all the evidence suggests they do, is it then more likely that they are both physical than that the body is physical and the mind a non-physical pure consciousness?

It must be noted that although Lucretius's account of the mind is physicalist, it is not, to use the modern term, "reductionist". A reductionist theory is one that claims that in principle everything we do could be explained in terms of the activity of the brain (the modern equivalent of Lucretius's soul-atoms), without reference to such things as motives, emotions, perceptions and so on. Lucretius's theory, however, obviously requires us to consider mind as being conscious, perceiving, feeling, taking decisions and so on. We see a friend; we feel pleased; we decide to walk towards them; the mind strikes the vital spirits accordingly; and they push the limbs forward. Although all these five stages are physical, and in Lucretius's view could not happen if they were not, we can make sense of what happened only if we consider the first three in their mental aspect: as a perception, an emotion and a decision. Indeed, on Lucretius's theory we can explain why some of the films hitting our eyes have an effect on us and others do not only by saying that we gave mental attention to the first group of images and therefore noticed them, and failed to notice the others. This in its turn would be the result of our tastes and feelings, and what we found interesting or important. So although, for Lucretius, there is just the one entity, mind plus vital spirits, which is both physical and conscious, he has to make as much reference to its conscious activity as to its physical activity in order to explain human or animal life (See Books 3 and 4, *passim*).

Does this mean that Lucretius is a "double aspect" theorist, to use the jargon, rather than a physicalist, that is, that he believes that the mental and physical are identical, but both sets of properties, those of our experiences and mental life, and those of the atoms, are equally fundamental? It seems not. Consciousness is still based ultimately on the coming together and maintenance of certain types of atom in certain numbers. The state of the atoms does not control everything we perceive or do once we are conscious, but it does control whether we are conscious, or alive, or not. Since every combination of atoms eventually breaks up, our consciousness is therefore bound to be temporary.

This is Lucretius's position, but is he right? The two arguments considered so far certainly show that physicalism is possible; but they do not prove it, either in Lucretius's version or the modern one. So we need to turn to the battery of arguments deployed to establish the mortal nature of the mind, to see if they establish anything more certain. There are anything up to thirty of these arguments, depending on how one distinguishes them, but they reduce to four.

The first argument is that since the soul is composed of very fine atoms held very loosely together, when it leaves the body at death it must dissipate and disintegrate, like a gas, resulting in a permanent loss of that particular consciousness (3, 425–44; cf. 806–19). This argument depends on Lucretius's version of physicalism, which no one would now hold. It also has problems for Lucretius himself, because he holds, as we saw above, that, although the gods did not create the world and take no interest in human affairs, they do exist and are ethereal beings of this sort (5, 146–55). Perhaps the conclusion that the gods cannot exist would not really bother Lucretius, but he would have to alter his account of how belief in them has arisen.

A second argument is somewhat similar. It is that the process of dying is often gradual and not instantaneous: there is a gradual loss of sensation (3, 526–46), of consciousness (607–14) and of physical movement, even when a body is cut into pieces (634–69) and no longer conscious. Lucretius would say this is because of the composite nature of the soul; a modern physicalist would say that the organs of the body do not all die at the same time. So this argument, unlike the preceding one, can be translated into modern terms. It is certainly evidence for the physical nature of consciousness, but it is not clear that it is conclusive. There might be a moment when consciousness withdraws permanently from the body, even though this is preceded by a gradual loss of sensation and followed for a time by physical activity, even including some types of brain activity.

The third argument, or group of arguments, is much stronger. It is, in effect, that mind does not just interact with body, but is subject to the effects of: heredity (741–54); growth and decay (445–58; cf. 760–68); stimulants such as wine (476–86), which has bad effects, and medicine (510–25), which has good ones; and above all disease and injury, both mental (459–62) and physical (463–73; 487–509; 592–606; 819–29). The placing of this last passage at the conclusion of the arguments suggests that Lucretius regarded the argument from susceptibility to disease as the strongest of them all. Was he himself terminally ill when he wrote it? One might see all these arguments as summed up in lines 800–805, which assert that it is simply impossible for mortal and immortal to be yoked together in this way. The argument is that if the mind is subject, like the body, to all the effects of inherited characteristics, growth and decay, and health and disease, and moreover undergoes these along with the body, then it must perish with the body also.

How strong are these points? The weakest is perhaps the argument from the effects of alcohol and medicine. All this shows is that if mind and body are different, they nevertheless constantly interact. Next weakest is the argument from mental illness. (Lucretius here and elsewhere is, as a good Epicurean, treating unhappiness and misery as illness, although he does also recognize the existence of insanity in the ordinary sense.) Mental illness, either in Lucretius's sense or in ours, can distort the working of the mind, but does not enfeeble or weaken it, in the way that illness weakens the body; life would be easier for the mentally disturbed if it did. A similar point was made by Plato in the *Phaedrus*: what is evil for the soul (Plato meant by this moral evil, but one can apply it to whatever distorts the working of the mind) is unlike physical evil in that it does not act as a weakening or destroying agent.

Similarly, although perhaps less obviously, physical illness does not weaken the mind. It can make people disinclined for mental exertion, and it can distort or limit mental activity, sometimes very drastically, either by creating inappropriate emotions, distorting or preventing perception and/or memory, or producing visual or auditory hallucinations. But it does not prevent mental activity as such; and whether it distorts or limits the activity depends not on the severity of the illness but on its nature. We may use a Lucretian-type argument against Lucretius: it is observable that many people on the verge of death are capable of acting with total rationality, which would not be possible if the mind and body died together. The same point can be made with regard to ageing. Children do not have weaker minds than adults, in the way that they have weaker bodies; their capacity to learn is at its peak, and needs to be, and what they lack is experience and the ability to control their emotions, and also the willingness to concentrate even on what is dull. As regards the problems of the elderly, which are by no means universal even when they have physical difficulties, a view still plausible is that of Aristotle in the *De Anima*: this is due to gaps and distortions in memory and perception, so that the mind is provided with false or no information, rather than to a failure in the working of the mind itself.

We can thus resist Lucretius's conclusion. But we have to concede that there is a physical basis to perception and memory, and also, with regard to heredity, that there are mental capacities and characteristics which we get, at least potentially, from our genetic make-up. This brings us to the fourth and last set of arguments: that the notion of a disembodied consciousness, or of a consciousness that passes from body to body in reincarnation, is impossible. Consciousness exists only when there is a union of body and mind (558–79). A disembodied consciousness could not, for example, see or hear; we imagine such a consciousness as still having the five senses, but this is impossible without the physical organs (624–33). If, on the other hand, the soul goes from body to body, why have we no memory of an earlier existence (670–78), and why is our nature so determined by the species to which we now belong, that is by heredity (741–53)?

Once again, this shows that much of our consciousness, particularly perception and memory, is either physically based or the result of physical interaction with the mental. But it does not show that it all is, and it does not show that a disembodied consciousness is an impossibility, or that we may not have been or may not become either disembodied or differently embodied. What is still true is that this is outside our present experience, which is an argument against it, although not a conclusive one.

Conclusion

So, if I am right, Lucretius has not proved the case for materialism. He has not proved that the universe has no Creator, or that a non-physical consciousness is impossible, or that we do not survive death in any way. What he has shown is that materialism is a coherent possibility for which there is evidence, and which ought to be taken seriously. He has also shown something about the alternatives, although he himself would not have been aware of this. With regard to religion, I think he has shown that the alternatives are atheism or belief in a transcendental Creator who is outside the universe as well as manifest in it; superstitious beliefs in beings or forces that are part of the universe but have supernatural powers are, apart from their bad moral effects, incoherent. (The modern equivalent is the attribution of causal powers to abstractions, such as nature, history or race.) With regard to mind and body, he has shown that whether we adopt a form of physicalism or of dualism, it must be one that squares with the facts.

This is the other big thing established by Lucretius, and it may well go beyond what was said in the Epicurean tradition before him. It is that whichever metaphysical line we take, we need a scientific approach to nature. Even though we know now that a true scientific picture will look very different from the one Lucretius provides, especially because he was wrong in supposing that all action is by touch, it remains true that we need to assume that the laws of nature are constant; that we have to posit unobservables; that within the system of nature, matter/energy is not created or destroyed; that theories must be tested against observations. Much in Lucretius has been proved wrong, and some crucial things are unsettled, but some very important things survive. And apart from his philosophical doctrines there is the excellent example he sets us of being both poet and scientist. He may or may not be right in supposing that the world has no purpose other than those we give it, and that nothing follows death. But he was certainly right in showing us that our response to nature, whether it has purposes or not, should be simultaneously to try to understand it and to enjoy, value and appreciate it.

Bibliography

Clay, D. 1983. *Lucretius and Epicurus*. Ithaca, NY: Cornell University Press.

Fowler, D. P. 2002. *Lucretius on Atomic Motion*. Oxford: Oxford University Press.

Long, A. A. 1986. *Stoics, Epicureans, Sceptics*. Berkeley, CA: University of California Press.

Long, A. A. & D. N. Sedley 1987. *The Hellenistic Philosophers*. Cambridge: Cambridge University Press.

Rist, J. M. 1977. *Epicurus: An Introduction*. Cambridge: Cambridge University Press.

Sedley, D. N. 1998. *Lucretius and the Transformation of Greek Wisdom*. Cambridge: Cambridge University Press.

Segal, C. 1990. *Lucretius on Death and Anxiety*. Princeton, NJ: Princeton University Press.

Further reading

By far the most accessible translation of Lucretius, and the one that has the most help for someone trying to understand the philosophy, is the Penguin Classic, Lucretius, *On the Nature of the Universe*, R. E. Latham (trans.), J. Godwin (rev.) (Harmondsworth: Penguin, 1994). For a Latin text with English translation, again with much help in seeing the philosophical points, there is the Loeb edition, Lucretius, *De Rerum Natura*, W. H. D. Rouse (trans.), M. F. Smith (rev.) (Cambridge, MA: Harvard University Press, 1975; 2nd edn 1982). For a detailed commentary in English on the Latin text, preceded by an excellent general study of Lucretius's art and thought, which can be read on its own, see C. Bailey, *Titi Lucretii Cari:De Rerum Natura* (Oxford: Oxford University Press, 1947). For the writings of Epicurus, see *The Epicurus Reader*, B. Inwood & L. P. Gerson (trans.) (Indianapolis, IN: Hackett, 1994).

4

Sextus Empiricus
Outlines of Pyrrhonism

R. J. Hankinson

Until recently, Sextus Empiricus's *Outlines of Pyrrhonism* had been little read in modern times, and less understood. But in the last quarter-century, a revival of interest in later Greek philosophy in general, and scepticism in particular, has seen it largely restored to its rightful place as one of the most influential texts in the entire history of Western philosophy. In this chapter, I shall concentrate upon producing my own outline of its contents; but I shall also seek to put it in its proper place in the Greek sceptical tradition, as well as within the longer tradition of Western epistemology, upon which, principally through the mediation of Descartes, it has exercised an incalculable, if often largely obscured, influence.

Sextus the empiricist

The sobriquet *empeirikos* indicates in all probability that Sextus was a member of the empirical school of medicine, which flourished from the middle of the third century BCE at least until the third century CE.[1] We cannot date his career with any certainty; but it must have unfolded in the late second or early third centuries CE. He is mentioned in Diogenes Läertius's *Lives of the Philosophers*, in the list of prominent Pyrrhonian philosophers (DL 9.116); but we do not know precisely when Diogenes wrote (although, again, the third century seems likely), and nor can we date those philosophers said by Diogenes to be his teacher and his pupil (Herodotus of Tarsus and Saturninus). He was still famous – infamous – in the fourth century, when St Gregory of Nazianzus held him (among others) responsible for "the vile and malignant disease" of arguing, in good sceptical fashion, on both sides of the same issue, a pestilence infecting the church of the time.

Empiricism was an anti-theoretical school of medicine, whose adherents held that there was no point in trying to understand the inner workings of the body in order to treat disease. In the first place, those inner workings were by definition hidden, and no amount of investigation could serve to show them unequivocally as they really are; but in any case such knowledge was therapeutically useless. All the good doctor can – and needs to – do is to tabulate the results of past experience, both personal and reported, and determine on that basis how a particular condition is likely (epistemically) to progress, and what sorts of treatments might seem to be indicated for it. This refusal to speculate about hidden matters is what links empiricist physicians with the various strands of Greek philosophical scepticism; and they called their opponents, doctors who believed in the importance and the attainability of such theoretical knowledge, dogmatists, just as the sceptics labelled their philosophical enemies.

But curiously, in spite of his moniker, Sextus himself says that a third school, the methodists, is in fact more congenial to the Pyrrhonian spirit (*PH* 1.236–41),[2] since, on Sextus's account at any rate, empiricists tend "to maintain that what is non-evident is inapprehensible", which is, in Sextus's sceptical book, a form of dogmatism (sometimes nowadays called "negative dogmatism"),[3] whereas the methodists make no pronouncements about the non-evident one way or another, as the good sceptic should (cf. *PH* 1.13–17; and "Differences from other schools", below).[4] Why this matters should become apparent in what follows.

In addition to *Outlines of Pyrrhonism*, Sextus wrote several medical works, none of which are extant, and two other texts on scepticism, of which we possess one in its entirety, and the other partially. He wrote a longer treatment of scepticism in general, the bulk of which survives as *Against the Professors* Books 7–11,[5] and a set of six self-contained essays against the practitioners of various arts known as *Against the Professors* 1–6 (*M* 1–6). The relations between these various works, and whether they all embody precisely the same type of scepticism, are disputed issues, but we may leave them to the scholars. However *Outlines of Pyrrhonism* is his distillation of the sceptical spirit; and whether or not it is at all original in content (and here again scholars disagree) it is at the very least an intelligent and intelligently organized authoritative summary of Pyrrhonian scepticism, and evidently swiftly became accepted as such, as St Gregory's fulminations bear eloquent witness.

The origins of Pyrrhonism

Sextus came at – or at any rate near – the end of a long dubitative line. As he himself says, "the sceptical persuasion is called ... 'Pyrrhonian' too, on the grounds that Pyrrho seems to us to have applied himself to scepticism more thoroughly and conspicuously than any of his predecessors" (*PH* 1.7). Pyrrho of Elis lived in the fourth century BCE, and is the subject of a typically fanciful "Life" in Diogenes. Such was his detachment from the ordinary concerns of the world, that he is said to have washed pigs with equanimity, and relied upon his friends to keep him from falling off precipices (DL 9.63–6). Such stories are clearly apocryphal, being the calumnies of his philosophical detractors, but they are still philosophically pointed, indicating as they do what were taken to be the shortcomings, indeed absurdities, of the position.

Pyrrho, like Socrates, wrote nothing, but an immediate disciple, Timon, memorialized him in both prose and mock-epic verse. Timon's works survive only in fragments, and often brief ones at that, but a paragraph of a prose work describing Pyrrho's philosophy has come down to us, at two further removes of quotation. Its import is still controversial: some[6] see it as describing a genuine scepticism about the way things are, while others[7] prefer to interpret it as committing Pyrrho to a Heraclitean metaphysics of constant flux, which in turn he holds responsible for epistemological uncertainty. At all events, Sextus himself mentions Pyrrho only a handful of times, and then usually in the general terms of *PH* 1.7, while other ancient testimony (such as that of Cicero) suggests that he was primarily concerned with ethical (in the broad ancient sense) questions.

From the third century BCE on, a different type of scepticism arose in what had been Plato's Academy, under the initial impetus of Arcesilaus (head of the Academy 272–243 BCE). Arcesilaus sought to return Platonism to its Socratic refutational and aporetic roots, and he made a practice of destructive argument, a practice aimed particularly (although not exclusively) against the ethics and epistemology of the Stoics.[8] Whether he also adopted (limited) positions of his own (for example, in order to show how action, and hence life, is still possible even if one rejects beliefs: *M* 7.158), or whether rather his entire procedure began and ended with refutation, is again controverted.[9] But however that may be, Academic scepticism was developed in dialectical conflict with the Stoics, a conflict that persisted through the second century with Carneades, the greatest refuter of them all. Carneades (*c.*219–*c.*129 BCE) argued (as had Arcesilaus) that the Stoics's ideal of indubitable knowledge founded upon secure impressions was unattainable; but he also argued (again it is unclear whether in his own voice or simply for the sake of argument) that we could be satisfied with impressions that were plausible and tested as practical guides to life.

In the course of this epistemological debate each side softened their positions,[10] and by the first century, the scepticism of the Academy under Philo of Larissa had become seriously diluted.[11] Antiochus of Ascalon broke with Philo some time in the 90s BCE over questions having to do with epistemological justification, and effectively returned to "dogmatic" philosophy. The details of this rift are obscure,[12] but they appear to have also caused Aenesidemus to react in the opposite direction; denouncing the Academics as "Stoics quarrelling with Stoics", he apparently sought to recover a more unsullied scepticism by returning to the Pyrrhonian tradition.[13] In particular, he collected a sequence of "Modes", or families of argument, which were designed to induce scepticism in the receptive listener ("The Modes of scepticism", below). Whether Aenesidemus's scepticism precisely anticipates that of Sextus a couple of centuries later is also controversial (and the figure of Aenesidemus himself in Sextus is a puzzling one), but whether or not he adhered to an earlier (and less completely sceptical) form of scepticism,[14] it is clear both that he is of pivotal importance in the generation of the neo-Pyrrhonist position of Sextus, and that later figures, pre-eminently (if obscurely) Agrippa (of whom more below, "The Modes of Agrippa"), added further crucial elements to the brew.

I have sketched that history partly because it is of importance to see how Sextus's scepticism is the culmination of a long tradition, but also because Sextus himself is our best source for most of it, and for much else besides; indeed, he is our single most important source for Hellenistic philosophy (Cicero runs him a close second). *Outlines of Pyrrhonism*, and to an even greater extent Sextus's other works, are important not just for the position they themselves exemplify, but for the wealth of detail with which they furnish us regarding the nature and the vivacity of philosophy in the centuries after Aristotle.

The sceptical life

That *Outlines of Pyrrhonism* furnishes us with such a wealth of detail is no accident, for Pyrrhonian scepticism, in its mature Sextan form as presented in *Outlines of Pyrrhonism*, is, like its Academic predecessor, fundamentally a matter of refutation, and in order to refute a view, you need to present it (how fairly, of course, is another matter). Thus, a typical section of Sextan argument will consist (for example) of the presentation of a number of different (and incompatible) views on the nature of motion (*PH* 3.63–81), with the upshot that it is impossible to say anything for certain about the subject one way or the other. But this is more than merely an argumentative practice: it is, according to Sextus, a way of life. Indeed the first thirty sections of *Outlines of Pyrrhonism* are devoted to describing (and defending the possibility of) such a way of life against opponents who were quick to charge that scepticism made life itself impossible.

All philosophy, Sextus writes (*PH* 1.1–4), consists of seeking answers, and there are three possible outcomes of the search. You may think you've found them, as do the dogmatists (Sextus mentions "Aristotle and Epicurus, for example, and their followers, and the Stoics, as well as others": *PH* 1.3); you may think that they are by nature undiscoverable (the position Sextus ascribes to the Academics: *PH* 1.3; cf. "The origins of Pyrrhonism", above, n. 11; "The sceptical slogans" and "Differences from other schools" below); "but the sceptics keep on searching".

Scepticism is, as Sextus puts it:

> a capacity for finding oppositions, between appearances and judgements, in any way whatever, as a result of which we arrive firstly at suspension of judgement (*epochê*), and then afterwards at tranquillity (*ataraxia*), on account of the equal strength (*isostheneia*) of the opposing objects and arguments. (*PH* 1.8)

That sentence includes three key technical terms. *Epochê* ("thought coming to a halt, as a result of which we neither deny nor affirm anything") is the supposed preliminary result of the *isostheneia* of considerations on every question; but this in turn leads to *ataraxia* ("undisturbedness and serenity of the soul"), which was the goal of most of the later Greek philosophies (explicitly of Epicureanism: see e.g. *Letter to Menoeceus* 127 (Long & Sedley 1987: 21B1); implicitly of the Stoics: Seneca, *Letters* 92.3 (Long & Sedley 1987: 63F1)).

Ataraxia is portrayed as a causal consequence of *epochê*, albeit an unexpected one; and this is true even though "the causal origin of scepticism … was the hope of tranquillity" (*PH* 1.12). This is because sceptics started out, like everyone else, as dogmatists:[15]

> having begun philosophizing in order to decide about the appearances and to grasp which of them were true and which false in order to attain *ataraxia*, they fell into disputes of equal strength [i.e. on each side], and being unable decide about them and so suspended judgement; but along with *epochê* there came along also, fortuitously, *ataraxia* in matters of opinion. (*PH* 1.26)

In a vivid metaphor, Sextus cites the case of Apelles the painter, who, despairing of being able to represent realistically the foam on a horse's mouth, threw his cleaning sponge at the picture "which produced an image of the horse's foam as it struck it" (*PH* 1.28).

The preamble to *Outlines of Pyrrhonism* is also notable for the extreme philosophical sensitivity Sextus exhibits in regard to the questions of the consistency and livability of his scepticism. In a sense, the sceptic has no real concern for consistency as such, since it is a dogmatist's virtue (although central to his sceptical method is an aggressive questioning of the dogmatists' own claims to consistency: cf. especially "Signs and proof"). But sceptics of all varieties were open to the charge that their professed attitudes (or lack of them) to such things as belief render even the basic sorts of action required for the continuation of human life an impossibility. The charge, familiar in a modern context from Hume,[16] was taken seriously by Sextus, and he answers it by making subtle philosophical distinctions in the language of belief and motivation. The sceptic, he says, follows the *phainomena*, the appearances (*PH* 1.17, 19–20, 21–4): "he states what appears to him and announces his own experience undogmatically, affirming nothing concerning the external objects underlying them" (*PH* 1.15). "Undogmatically" means without commitment to a *dogma*, or firmly held belief:[17] "he does not dogmatize ... in the sense of 'assent to one of the non-evident objects of scientific inquiry'" (*PH* 1.13). In this sense (*PH* 1.16), he has no methodological commitment (*hairesis*) either; however if you define *hairesis* as "method which, in accordance with appearance, follows that argument which shows how one may live rightly (in a broad sense of 'rightly'), and tending towards the capacity for suspension of judgement", then he may allow that in that sense he has one. Indeed, he also allows that he has a criterion (see further "The criterion") "of action, by attending to which in the course of our life we do some things and not others" (*PH* 1.21). This too is a matter of attending to the appearances, which Sextus is at pains to emphasize the sceptics do not do away with: "for we do not overturn those things which lead us involuntarily to assent in accordance with an affective impression: and these are the appearances" (*PH* 1.19). When presented with the appearance of an object, the sceptic "accepts that it does appear, and inquires not about the appearance as such but about what is said regarding the thing which appears" (*PH* 1.19), that is, about what non-sceptics assert to be the real natures of things that (supposedly) underlie the appearances: "that honey appears sweet, we allow, since we are perceptually sweetened; but whether it really is sweet as regards its own definition we doubt, since this is not the appearance but something said about the appearance" (*PH* 1.20). By "attending to the appearances we live undogmatically in accordance with the ordinary observances of life, since we cannot remain wholly inactive", he says (*PH* 1.23); and these "ordinary observances" consist in "the guidance of nature, the compulsion of the passions, the tradition of laws and customs, and the instruction of the arts (*technai*)" (*PH* 1.23). Thus a sceptic will not only be moved by his various drives; he will also adhere to conventional values, and may even legitimately learn a trade – but of course "we say all these things undogmatically".

Ironically, Sextus's scepticism in fact turns out to be rather like Hume's mitigated or Academic scepticism, and not at all like the caricature he offers of Pyrrhonism itself. The sceptic is not, it turns out "wholly untroubled; rather we say that he is troubled by things which are forced upon him; for we grant that he is sometimes cold and suffers thirst and other things of this sort" (*PH* 1.29); in the case of the unavoidable pains, the sceptic's goal is not an unattainable *ataraxia*, but "moderation in affection (*metriopatheia*)" (*PH* 1.25, 30). But even so, on Sextus's account, the sceptic is better off than others, who are oppressed not just by the pains themselves, but also by the "additional belief" that they are really bad (*PH* 1.30).

The Modes of scepticism

At *PH* 1.5, Sextus distinguishes between a "general" and a "special" type of sceptical argument. The general type involves the deployment of general argument forms ("Modes"), as well as a discussion of the "sceptical slogans" and the differences between scepticism and other philosophies; and it occupies the rest of Book 1. (Books 2 and 3 treat the various "special" arguments, directed topically.) There are three sets of Modes, or general argument-types, discussed by Sextus. The best known and most influential, the so-called "Ten Modes of Aenesidemus",[18] occupy *PH* 1.31–163. Versions of the Modes (all or some of them) are also found in Philo of Alexandria (*On Drunkenness* 169–202) and Diogenes Laërtius (DL 9.78–88). The arguments all have the same structure. In some domain, it is said, there is disagreement as to whether or not *p*; there is no non-question-begging way in which the dispute (*diaphônia*: another key technical term) can be decided; so we suspend judgement as to *p*. In Sextus's presentation of them, the Modes largely involve the collection and setting up in opposition of allegedly contradictory facts and beliefs ("we oppose appearances to appearances, conceptions to conceptions, or *vice versa*": *PH* 1.31). The First Mode is that "derived from the differences between animals" (*PH* 1.40; cf. 1.36); these differences are elaborated at great length (*PH* 1.40–78), and they include differences of physical structure (particularly of the sense-organs) but also of modes of reproduction, which (allegedly) allow us to infer that different animals see things differently.

Two obvious difficulties arise here: (i) on what grounds can a *sceptic* argue from such differences to what must be non-evident claims about the facts of animal perception; and (ii) what in any case does reproduction have to do with it? As regards (i), it seems best to treat the arguments as dialectical: that is, they are supposed to take off from premises conceded by the dogmatists themselves. Thus it is not the sceptics who ought to be convinced by the arguments, but their opponents (this facet of sceptical argument will be important later: "Signs and proof"). As for (ii), I suppose that what Sextus is driving at (and examples of this are to be found later in the Mode) is that different creatures differ in their appetitive behaviour, hence it is reasonable to suppose that things present themselves differently to them (pigs prefer foul water to fresh: *PH* 1.56; for the general principle, see *PH* 1.87); and so animals that reproduce sexually will differ from one another in the direction of their desires, and from animals that reproduce asexually in having the desires (and hence the appearances associated with them) in the first place.[19]

The Second Mode (*PH* 1.79–91) concerns differences between different human beings, either as individuals ("Demophon, Alexander's batman, used to shiver in direct sunlight or in the bath, but to feel warm in the shade": *PH* 1.82) or as ethnic groups ("a Scythian's body differs in morphology from that of an Indian; and what causes the difference, so they say, is a difference in the predominant humours": *PH* 1.80); the "so they [the dogmatists] say" is obviously significant. The conclusion is similar to that of the First Mode: "necessarily then we are led to suspension owing to the difference among men" (*PH* 1.89). The causal language ("we are led") is significant, here and elsewhere in the presentation of the Modes. Whereas the dogmatists are portrayed as being rationally committed (by their own lights) to abandon their dogmas, the sceptics are simply moved. And this is obviously in line with Sextus's careful programmatic remarks about the nature of the sceptical way ("The sceptical life" above).

"The Third Mode [*PH* 1.91–9] is based on the differences between the senses" (*PH* 1.91). Different things appear differently (in regard to their apparent desirability) to different senses; the Fourth Mode (*PH* 1.100–17) narrows the field even further by recording discrepancies between the information conveyed (at different times or to different individuals) by the same sense: "so objects affect us differently according to whether the mental state is natural or unnatural" (*PH* 1.101). Once again, the sceptic does not endorse the implications of the descriptions "natural" and "unnatural": "just as the healthy are in a state natural for the healthy but unnatural for the sick, so the sick are in a state unnatural for the healthy but natural for the sick" (*PH* 1.103); while dream objects exist for the dreamer but waking objects do not (*PH* 1.104). Moreover, emotional states affect judgement: "many men with ugly lovers think them most attractive" (*PH* 1.108). But there is no non-question-begging way of settling these disputes; everyone is a party to the case, and there are no independent criteria upon which to rely (*PH* 1.114–17). This latter is a fundamental sceptical contention, and we will examine it further in "The criterion" below.

The Fifth Mode, that "derived from positions, distances and location" (*PH* 1.118–23), makes the familiar point that how things look depends upon where and how you view them; but this (and some of the examples used to illustrate it: the tower which seems round from a distance but square close to and the oar that seems straight in the air and bent in water: *PH* 1.118–19) is familiar only because of the influence of the sceptical tradition, and pre-eminently of Sextus. The Sixth Mode (*PH* 1.124–8), "based on mixtures", argues that "since none of the underlying objects affects us solely in itself, but always along with something, we may perhaps be able to say how the mixture of the external thing and what it is seen mixed along with is, but we will never be able to say how the external thing really is" (*PH* 1.124). Some of the "mixtures" are external (different atmospheric conditions affect the way we see and hear things: *PH* 1.125); others are internal: "our eyes contain within themselves membranes and liquids; so since visible things are not perceived without these, they will not be apprehended with accuracy ... jaundice-sufferers see everything as yellow, those with bloodshot eyes as red" (*PH* 1.126). Again the examples (cf. *PH* 1.44, 101) became epistemological commonplaces quite independently of their truth (cf. e.g. Descartes, *Replies* II.4); and again they did so by way of Sextus.

The Seventh Mode (*PH* 1.129–34) deals with "the quantity and constitution of the underlying objects"; things present different appearances (and have different effects) according to how they are arranged and how much of them there is, and requires no further comment.

The Eighth Mode (*PH* 1.135–40), the Mode from relativity, is a different beast. In his preamble to the Modes, Sextus remarks that in a way relativity underlies all of the Modes: it is a sort of super-Mode of which the others are sub-species (*PH* 1.39). And yet it also figures among the ten, and so is a sub-set of itself. This awkward (not to say incoherent) arrangement is to be explained in terms of the development of Pyrrhonism itself. In the original modes (and presumably in Aenesidemus's version of them), considerations of relationality were taken to supply a separate set of arguments for the undecidable indeterminacy in things. But following the work of Agrippa ("The Modes of Agrippa", below), Sceptics came to see that relativity underlay the strategies of the Modes in a more general sense. It is worth quoting Sextus at some length:

> the Eighth Mode is that ... by which we infer that since everything is relative we shall suspend judgement as to what things are absolutely and in their own nature. It is essential to note that here, just as in other cases [cf. "The sceptical slogans"], we employ the expression "it is" in place of "it appears"; so that in effect we are saying "it appears that all things are relative". This has two meanings: first (a) relative to the

judger (since the external underlying object appears and is judged relative to the judger), but in another way (b) relative to things seen along with it (*ta suntheôroumena*), as left is to right.   (*PH* 1.135)

Sextus's distinction between (a) and (b) suggests the conflation of the two types of appeal to relativity (although it does not precisely reproduce them), with (b) answering to the earlier, non-architectonic invocation of relativity; and in Diogenes' presentation of the Mode, "which rests on the placing alongside one thing of another, such as light by heavy, strong by weak, bigger by smaller, up by down" (DL 9.87), in spite of the fact that Diogenes probably wrote later than Sextus, we seem to have the residue of the earlier presentation of the Modes.[20] Sextus's report, by contrast, concentrates on the general features of relationality itself, attempting to establish the strong conclusion that everything is (or at least appears) to be relative, and hence nothing properly speaking appears to be in its own right. We shall return to this in a moment.

The Ninth Mode (*PH* 1.141–4) derives from the fact that things seem remarkable (or otherwise) in virtue of the rarity or frequency; hence "being remarkable" is not a genuine property of things in themselves. Once more the scope of the Mode is modest, and the conclusion (relatively speaking) unexceptionable (although one might balk at some of Sextus's examples: are earthquakes really less terrifying the more you experience them (*PH* 1.142)?); it is a further question whether or not they have any genuinely sceptical force.

The Tenth Mode (*PH* 1.145–63) deals with "practices, customs, laws, mythological beliefs, and dogmatic suppositions" (*PH* 1.145), all of which are shown to generate conflicts, both within and among themselves (*PH* 1.148); thus "we oppose custom to custom: some Africans tattoo their children, but we do not … And while the Indians have sex in public, while most others think this shameful" (*PH* 1.148; cf. 3.200). Similarly, law is opposed to law: "among the Crimeans, it was the law that strangers should be sacrificed to Artemis, but with us human sacrifice is illegal" (*PH* 1.149); and similarly with the other categories (*PH* 1.150–51). The oppositions between the categories evince a similar salacious interest in the curiosities of comparative ethnology: homosexuality is customary in Persia, illegal in Rome; adultery is a crime among the Greeks but "an indifferent custom" for the Massagetae; while various forms of incest are not only condoned but encouraged in Persia and Egypt (*PH* 1.152). The conclusion drawn, however, is not one of moral or cultural relativism, but rather that "we will not be able to state what the underlying things are in their real nature, but only how it appears relative to this or that practice, etc." (*PH* 1.163).

The Modes of Agrippa

Immediately after his presentation of the Ten Modes, Sextus proceeds to discuss five other Modes (*PH* 1.164–77), ascribing them to "more recent sceptics" (*PH* 1.164). Diogenes, in his shorter notice (DL 9.88), attributes them to one Agrippa, about whom nothing else is known. The Five Modes are completely different in scope and structure from the Ten; instead of dealing with different types of opposition, they purport rather to offer, conjointly, a total sceptical strategy.[21] The First Mode in general notes the apparently chronic undecidability of philosophical questions, while the Third Mode recapitulates the general claim that everything is apprehended in relation to something and so its real nature, if any, cannot be discerned; the remaining Modes deal rather with the formal limitations on probative argumentation: argument will proceed either *ad infinitum* (the Second Mode); or terminate in an unargued (and hence insecure) hypothesis (the Fourth Mode); or move in a circle (the Fifth Mode). The three formal Modes recapitulate Aristotle's strictures on epistemically worthwhile argument (*Posterior Analytics* 1.3); but whereas Aristotle's realism explicitly demands that there be first principles that are self-evident (or at least are certain and rest on no prior premises), this possibility is precisely what the Agrippan sceptic disallows. And if there are no such principles (arguments against there being any such come under the general heading of the criterion ("The criterion", below), but they also derive from the material considerations of relativity and dispute of the First and Third Modes), then there can be no soundly based propositions at all. Thus the Agrippan procedure is global in scope. If successful, it undermines all claims to rationally based belief (and *a fortiori* to knowledge). It is also noteworthy that these Modes, unlike the original Ten, are designed to be deployed in combination:

> Will they say that the dispute is decidable or undecidable? If undecidable, we hold that we should suspend judgement [Mode 1] ... But if they say that it is decidable, we must ascertain how it can be decided ... If by something perceptible (since we are inquiring about perceptibles), then that too will require another to confirm it; and if that is perceptible, it too will require another to confirm it, ... and so on ad infinitum [Mode 2]. But if the perceptible object is to be decided by an intelligible object, then since intelligibles too are disputed, this intelligible will require judgement and confirmation. But whence will it derive its confirmation? If from something intelligible, then it will fall foul of the regress argument in the same way. But if from something perceptible, then since an intelligible was

adduced to support a perceptible and a perceptible to support an intelligible, the Mode from circularity [Mode 5] will be introduced. But if our adversary should seek refuge from this in claiming to introduce as agreed an undemonstrated assumption in order to demonstrate what follows from it, the hypothetical Mode [4] will be introduced. (*PH* 1.170–73)

There are some curiosities about Sextus's presentation of the Agrippan modes (in particular he presents the Mode from circularity as though it involves cycling between perceptibles and intelligibles, while the Mode from regress deals with an infinite sequence of intelligibles), but they need not concern us here, since the general outlines of a clear, serious and generalized attack on the very possibility of epistemic (or doxastic) justification are clear enough. And in a sense they have set the agenda for all subsequent discussion of such issues; whether they acknowledge the fact or not, all later epistemologists are in Agrippa's debt.

The sceptical medicine is further boiled down by Sextus into two Modes, "since everything is thought to be apprehended either by means of itself or by means of something else" (*PH* 1.178); this introduces (and rejects) the further possibility, not explicitly covered by the Modes of Agrippa, of a proposition's being self-supporting. We shall deal with this issue a little further below ("The criterion").[22]

One further set of Modes deserves brief consideration. At *PH* 1.180–85, Sextus offers a brief account of "Eight Modes against the Aetiologists", attributed (firmly this time: see Photius, *Bibliotheca* 212 (Long & Sedley 1987: 72L4)) to Aenesidemus.[23] "Aetiology" is the sort of causal explanation practised by natural philosophers and rationalist doctors: the attempt to account for the workings of the world in terms of hypotheses regarding its deep structures. Such structures are, in the nature of things, non-phenomenal, and it is this fact that supplies the sceptics with their obvious starting-point: "the first is the Mode according to which aetiology in general, being concerned with non-apparent things, has no consistent confirmation from the appearances" (*PH* 1.181). This claim is buttressed by "the second Mode [which] shows that often, when there is an abundance of ways of assigning an explanation to what is under investigation, some of them account for it in one way only" (*PH* 1.181). In a modern jargon, theory is underdetermined by data. The Third Mode "is that according to which they assign to orderly occurrences explanations which exhibit no order" (*PH* 1.182); piecemeal explanations of evidently related sets of phenomena are no good. The Fourth Mode castigates investigators for "supposing that they grasp how the non-apparent things are because they have seen how the apparent occur" (*PH* 1.182); here Aenesidemus presciently questions the ancient (and early modern) tendency (notoriously eschewed by modern physics) to suppose that the micro-world must resemble, in its basic array of properties, the ordinary world of experience that it purports to explain. The Fifth, Sixth and Seventh Modes develop the theme of the Second Mode; researchers are prone to treat as the explanation the one that accords with their prejudices, and are inclined to overlook awkward anomalous evidence that apparently contradicts them, while "they often give explanations which conflict not only with the appearances but also with their own theories" (*PH* 1.183–4). Finally the Eighth Mode notes that "they frequently ... seek to explain doubtful things on the basis of things equally doubtful" (*PH* 1.184). Evidently the aetiological Modes are not all of equal scope and power; some are avowedly (although in no derogatory sense) *ad hominem*. But equally evidently, taken both severally and in tandem, they constitute a powerful challenge to the practice of explanation in general, and not merely to that of its ancient practitioners.

The sceptical slogans

As we noted above ("The sceptical life"), Sextus is extremely careful to avoid presenting his scepticism as in any way dogmatic. The next few paragraphs (*PH* 1.187–208) elaborate on this in so far as it concerns the "sceptical slogans" (*PH* 1.187), in order "that every sophism ranged against them may be destroyed" (*PH* 1.208). These "slogans" are: "no more [i.e. this way than that] (*ouden mallon*)" (*PH* 1.188–91); "non-assertion (*aphasia*)" (*PH* 1.192–3); "perhaps, maybe and possibly (*tacha, exesti, endechetai*)" (*PH* 1.194–5); "I suspend judgement (*epechô*)" (*PH* 1.196); "I determine nothing (*ouden horizo*)" (*PH* 1.197); "everything is undetermined (*aorista*)" (*PH* 1.198–9); "everything is inapprehensible (*akatalêpta*)" (*PH* 1.200); "I have no apprehension", "I do not apprehend (*akatalêptô, ou katalambanô*)" (*PH* 1.201); "to every account (*logos*) there is opposed an equal account" (*PH* 1.202–5). Sextus's general strategy is straightforward enough. For example, "*ouden mallon*" might be taken quasi-dogmatically to express the actual indeterminacy of things: they really *are* no more this way than that. And the phrase was indeed so used, to relativistic and negative dogmatist ends, by various philosophers (see "Differences from other schools", below). But such an implication is non-sceptical. Here, as elsewhere, the sceptic only reports the appearances, and makes no claim, explicit or otherwise, about what state of affairs (if any) underlies them:

> thus, although the expression "no more" has the form of an assent or denial [i.e. in a dogmatic sense] ... we use it non-committally and

loosely …, to mean "I do not know which of these things I should assent to and which not" … Observe that in using the phrase "no more", we do not affirm of it [i.e. the slogan itself] that it is true or securely established: here too we say only how things seem to us.

(*PH* 1.191)

The same goes for *aphasia*, non-determination, non-apprehension, and the rest: they "manifest a certain sceptical attitude and feeling" (*PH* 1.187). But there is a further interesting twist; Sextus at any rate conceives of the Academics as *affirming* that "everything is inapprehensible" (*PH* 1.226; "Differences from other schools", below). Such a position is profoundly un-Pyrrhonian; indeed, it may be self-refuting.[24] But this is not Sextus's view. Rather, "the sceptical slogans … destroy themselves, being cancelled along with what they apply to, like purgative drugs" (see "Sceptical medicine", below). When you "affirm nothing", you do not thereby (and potentially inconsistently) affirm that you affirm nothing. Your attitude to the slogan is the same as it is to everything else; it seems that way to you, but you do not assert that it is.

Differences from other schools

In line with these strictures, Sextus is at pains in what remains of Book 1 to differentiate his own attitude (better not say "doctrine") from that of other, superficially similar schools. We have already seen why he rejects the view (common enough in later antiquity) that there is no real difference between Academic and Pyrrhonian scepticism. He expands upon this stance at *PH* 1.226–35 (after rightly rejecting the image – popular in some circles in antiquity, not least that of Arcesilaus – of a sceptical Plato: *PH* 1.221–5), drawing attention to additional differences (as he sees them) in regard to their attitudes towards good and bad (on which see further "Ethics"): the Academics think "that it is plausible (*pithanon*) that what they call good really is good (and the same goes for bad)" (*PH* 1.226), while the Pyrrhonian simply "follows ordinary life" (cf. "The sceptical life"). Moreover, the Academics (in particular Carneades) make elaborate distinctions in regard to plausibility: impressions can be merely plausible, or they can be "plausible and tested" or "plausible, tested, and unreversed" (*PH* 1.227–8; cf. *M* 7.150–75); "testing" consists in seeking further perceptual data to confirm (or disconfirm) the original impression; an impression is "unreversed" if its content does not conflict with any of the cognizer's other commitments. Thus, in a stock example, when Admetus is faced with Alcestis brought back from the dead, his impression is both plausible and tested, but not unreversed, since he does not believe in the possibility of resurrection. But for the Pyrrhonist, no impression is any more convincing or plausible than any other. Sextus draws a general moral: while both Academics and Pyrrhonists say that they "go along with" certain things, the crucial term is used in a different sense in each of their cases, for while the Academics follow things "with a strong inclination", Pyrrhonists do so only in the sense of "yielding without adherence" (*PH* 1.230). Sextus proceeds to distinguish Pyrrhonism from the epistemology of medical Empiricism in a similar manner; empiricists positively affirm, on his account, the inapprehensibility of hidden conditions. And in a famously puzzling comparison, he goes on to conclude that, in fact, Pyrrhonism has most in common with the medical approach known as "methodism", since just as sceptics follow the "ordinary observances of life" (*PH* 1.237; cf. 1.23, "The sceptical life", above), methodist doctors "are led by their passions to what answers to them: by constriction to dilatation, and by flux to stopping-up" (*PH* 1.238); indeed, "everything that the Methodists say in this regard may be ranged under the compulsion of the passions" (*PH* 1.239); the methodists, like the Pyrrhonists, apparently hold no beliefs; they are moved to action directly and unreflectively, just as the sceptic is by hunger and thirst (*PH* 1.240).[25]

Earlier, and in a similar fashion, Sextus has distinguished his Pyrrhonism from Heracliteanism, which makes "dogmatic assertions about non-evident matters" (*PH* 1.210); Heracliteans hold that nothing is really as it seems and that everything is in a state of flux, with contraries holding at the same time of the same things. For the Pyrrhonian, things only seem that way (they are part of the *diaphôniai* which drive *epochê*). The same goes for Democritus, in spite of some of his sceptical-leaning pronouncements in epistemology,[26] and his agreement with the Pyrrhonists that honey appears sweet; for he holds positively that it is *not* sweet in reality – he is an eliminativist about perceptual properties – and he also holds that what really exist are atoms and the void. And, as Sextus rightly emphasizes, such a position is not sceptical (*PH* 1.213–14). The minor Socratic school of the Cyrenaics seems sceptical in that it allows access only to feelings, but again it is unsceptical in positively asserting that the nature of things is inapprehensible, as well as endorsing a positive (hedonistic) doctrine of the good life (*PH* 1.215). Finally, Sextus differentiates Pyrrhonism from relativism of the sort espoused by Protagoras (and perhaps also by earlier Pyrrhonists: "The origins of Pyrrhonism", n. 14 above).[27] He famously held that "man is the measure of all things", and, at least as interpreted by Plato (*Theaetetus* 151e–171b), that amounts to the claim that as things appear to each person, so they are for that person. And Sextus endorses this reading: everybody is his own criterion (*PH* 1.216). Hence "he posits only what is apparent to each individual, and thus introduces relativity" (*PH* 1.216), and so "he is thought to have something in common with Pyrrhonists" (*PH* 1.217). Sextus rejects this assimilation on the grounds that Protagoras (according to him at least, and here, too, Plato is on his side) espoused a positive metaphysics of flux (*PH* 1.217–19), incompatibly with scepticism. But he might also have said that, in so far as relativism is a positive epistemology, it is also un-Pyrrhonian; for a genuine sceptic will allow that it is possible, for all he knows, that things really are, non-relatively, a certain way, and no dogmatic relativist will allow that (see further "Ethics").

The criterion

So Sextus concludes his "general account" of scepticism (*PH* 1.241), turning in Books 2 and 3 to deal with specific areas of enquiry. Although this occupies the bulk of *Outlines of Pyrrhonism*, our own assessment of it will be much more restricted and cursory than what has gone before, since (in my view at least) it is the general lineaments of scepticism and its strategies that are of more intrinsic interest (and probably of greater historical significance as well). But before turning to his case-by-case treatment, Sextus opens Book 2 with a short general discussion of the question of "whether sceptics can investigate the pronouncements of the Dogmatists" (*PH* 2.1), in response to Dogmatic allegations that such an investigation is itself inconsistent with sceptical principles (and accusations and counter-accusations of inconsistency, paradoxicality and self-refutation were flung with abandon between the sceptics and their opponents: see "God and causes"). The Dogmatists claim that, in order to take issue with their contentions, the sceptics must apprehend them; but in that case they are unfaithful to their sceptical way (*PH* 2.2–3; "The sceptical slogans" above). Sextus accuses them of trading on an ambiguity in the meaning of "apprehend": "does it merely (a) mean 'think of', without any further affirmation of the reality of things we are making statements about? Or does it (b) involve positing the reality of the things under discussion?" (*PH* 2.4). Meaning (a) is harmless, and perfectly sceptical, and all that the sceptic requires; (b) would indeed be incompatible with scepticism, but no sceptic need be committed to it. As Sextus points out, Dogmatists too are perfectly capable of understanding the content of their opponent's concepts without endorsing them; indeed, if a matter genuinely is under investigation, then no one, whether sceptic or dogmatist, should as yet apprehend it (or claim to) in sense (b) (*PH* 2.4–10). This is a clever and subtle defence, and much more can (and should) be said about it. It is a further question, one beyond the scope of this essay, whether it is not itself subject to further, serious, anti-sceptical assault.

Sextus organizes the succeeding discussion around the canonical Hellenistic division of philosophy into logic (broadly construed to include epistemology), physics and ethics (*PH* 2.13), and he begins with the question of the criterion. Largely as a result of the sceptical developments in epistemology sketched in "The origins of Pyrrhonism" (above), the issue of how to distinguish true from false, real from unreal, had come to dominate philosophy; and this was expressed in terms of a search for the criterion, or standard, of truth.[28] Sextus begins by distinguishing the criterion of truth from that of action (discussed at *PH* 1.21–4: "The sceptical life"), and then notes that the former has "a general, a particular, and a most particular sense" (*PH* 2.15): in the "general sense", a criterion is anything that may be said to judge or discriminate, including for instance the sense-organs; in the "particular sense", a criterion is a measuring instrument "such as the rule or compass"; the "most particular sense" is that of "logical, rather than everyday, criteria, those that the dogmatists employ for determining the truth" (*PH* 2.15), in other words criteria in the philosophical sense, and it is these that will occupy Sextus.[29]

These too are susceptible of further subdivision, into "the agent, the instrument, and the touchstone" (*PH* 2.16: literally "that by which, that by means of which, and that in relation to which"), and Sextus proceeds to treat each of them in turn. But first he asks the general question: is there such a thing as a criterion of truth? His method here is the standard one of discovering a disagreement: some (i.e. dogmatists) say that there is; others deny it (he names one Xeniades of Corinth, as well as Xenophanes, as being of this opinion); while sceptics (of course) suspend judgement (*PH* 2.18). The next stretch of argument is characteristic:

> They will say that this disagreement, then, is either decidable or undecidable. If undecidable, they will *ipso facto* be committed to the necessity of suspending judgement; but if they say that it is decidable, let them say by means of what it will be decided, since we have accepted no criterion, and do not know, but are still investigating, whether one exists. Furthermore, in order to settle the disagreement which has arisen regarding the criterion, we need an accepted criterion by means of which we will be able to settle the dispute; but in order for us to possess an accepted criterion, the dispute regarding the criterion must first be settled. Thus the search for a criterion becomes hopeless, falling foul of the circular mode; and we cannot allow them simply to assume a criterion on the basis of a hypothesis, while if they try to judge the criterion on the basis of another criterion, we force them into an infinite regress.   (*PH* 2.19–20)

Here the Modes of Agrippa are deployed in concert, and, as was noted above ("The Modes of Agrippa"), the Agrippan Modes amount, fundamentally, to the denial of the possibility of there being a criterion. Care is required here, however; the sceptic will not *endorse* that denial *in propria persona*, as *PH* 2.18 reiterates. The function of all sceptical argument is to create (or at least to bring into the open) a dispute; the illusion of a negative dogmatism is generated by the fact that the overwhelming majority of the argument is destructive. After all, the dogmatists already believe their positions – there is no need to argue for them – and common sense itself (although the Sextan sceptic will deny this) is dogmatic. Thus, for instance, the great bulk of the discussion of motion (*PH* 3.64–81) is devoted to arguments against the possibility of motion, but the desired "conclusion" is, as always, suspension of judgement as to whether there is any such thing (*PH* 3.65, 81).

Outlines of Pyrrhonism 2.22–47 deals with the "criterion by which", the agent; the arguments do not require detailed discussion, and are not, in truth, terribly impressive (Sextus argues that we cannot even apprehend "man", since different dogmatic schools offer different definitions of the concept: *PH* 2.23–8). In dealing with the "criterion by means of which" (*PH* 2.48–69), Sextus's strategy is simple: the instrument in question must be either the senses or the intellect, but neither individually, nor taken together, can they fulfil their desired role. The argument regarding the senses largely recapitulates material already detailed by the Ten Modes. As regards the intellect, Sextus first argues against its apprehensibility (*PH* 2.57), but even allowing that we can apprehend it, it still cannot (he claims) function as a criterion, since intellectual judgements too are various and themselves require a criterion for their resolution (*PH* 2.59–60). Further, repeating a strategy already deployed in the course of the Ten Modes, he argues that we should not accept the majority judgement, since majorities are fickle, and in any case no reliable guide to truth; while to prefer the view of one individual on the grounds that they seem cleverer itself requires a criterion, and even if it can be satisfied there is no guarantee that one yet cleverer (but with a different view) may not emerge (*PH* 2.61–2).

The most important arguments concern the "criterion in relation to which", since it is under this rubric that Sextus discusses the Stoic epistemological notion of the cataleptic impression: an impression of a type that is supposed to guarantee the truth of its content. The precise interpretation of the notion is difficult and controversial, but on any understanding, it obviously provides sceptics with a temptingly juicy target, and from Arcesilaus onwards they had happily trained their fire on it.[30] Even if we allow that the notion of an impression is itself apprehensible (*PH* 2.70–71), it cannot serve as a criterion, since it is an internal condition of the cognizer: "the senses do not apprehend external objects, but only, if anything, their own affections" (*PH* 2.72); honey is not the same as my being sweetened. Nor will it do to say that the affections resemble their objects, since there is no independent way of verifying the truth of any such claim (*PH* 2.74). Sextus, like many sceptically minded epistemologists, draws attention to the veil of perception; and supposes (at least for the sake of argument) that it is opaque.[31]

Signs and proof

The theory of signs was equally central to Hellenistic philosophy,[32] and in a sense it is a part of criteriology. A fundamental distinction was made (whether initially by philosophers or empiricist doctors is disputed) between "commemorative" and "indicative" signs. As Sextus says: "Some things, according to the Dogmatists, are self-evident, others non-evident; of the latter, some are (i) totally non-evident, some (ii) temporarily non-evident, and some (iii) naturally non-evident" (*PH* 2.97). Class (i) is that of things universally agreed never to be knowable, "such as whether the number of stars is even"; class (ii) includes things that simply happen at the moment not to be evident, "such as the city of Athens is to me"; while class (iii) is that of things that are intrinsically non-evident, but that, or so the dogmatists allege, can still be apprehended: "things temporarily or naturally non-evident are apprehended by means of signs, the former by way of commemorative, the latter of indicative signs" (*PH* 2.99). It is only against the latter that sceptics train their fire (*PH* 2.102); the former, those in which the signifier (e.g. smoke) "suggests to us the thing associated with it but which is not now perceived" (e.g. fire), is perfectly acceptable to the sceptic (and was a cornerstone of empiricist medicine), although it cannot involve anything as strong as commitment to the truth of the belief that there's no smoke without fire; rather, Sextus describes the process much as Hume does in his psychological account of the causal relation: "we do not fight against ordinary life, but rather go along with it, assenting undogmatically to what it has been persuaded by, while opposing the particular fictions of the Dogmatists" (*PH* 2.102).

The latter include the indicative sign, one that is supposed to license an inference from an evident premise to a non-evident conclusion: "the Stoics ... say that a sign is an antecedent proposition in a sound conditional which is revelatory of its consequent" (*PH* 2.104). One of the Stoics' favourite examples is that the fact of sweating reveals the existence of imperceptible pores in the skin (*PH* 2.240). Sceptics will reject the probativeness of such an inference on the grounds of the second aetiological Mode ("The Modes of Agrippa"); but Sextus also attacks the definition on the grounds that it presupposes an understanding of the conditional and its truth-conditions, which are a subject of dogmatic dispute (*PH* 2.110–12). What he reports, here and in what follows, is of enormous interest and importance in the understanding of ancient logic, but of less import for the history of scepticism (although we will briefly consider the attack on the Stoic notion of proof below). But two of his strategies are worth brief notice. First, he claims that the notion of a sign is relational: a sign is a sign of what it signifies. But if that is the case, Sextus claims, the sign cannot be apprehended independently of what it signifies, and hence it cannot serve to reveal it (*PH* 2.117–20). The objection is fairly easily evaded (although Sextus deploys a congruent argument against the conceivability of causes: "God and causes" below); we may apprehend the *item* that is the sign before we (directly) apprehend the item that it signifies, although once we apprehend it *as a sign* we will then immediately know (or at least believe or accept) that what it signifies obtains.[33] Secondly, he attempts to show that the concept falls foul of circularity. The existence of the indicative sign is controversial, and hence should not be accepted without proof, but proof is itself a type of sign: "but it is absurd to prove what is at issue through something equally at issue, or through itself" (*PH* 2.122).

Outlines of Pyrrhonism at 2.134–92 discusses the question of proof. The target is almost exclusively the Stoics (Aristotelian procedures are subjected to a shorter treatment at *PH* 193–203), and Sextus argues intriguingly that there is an incoherence at the heart of Stoic logic. They reject arguments with redundant premises as invalid, yet a conditional, on their account, is true just in case the antecedent entails the consequent. But in that case the argument-form *modus ponens* (the Stoics' "first indemonstrable") is invalid through redundancy, since the conditional premise "if p then q" may be dropped, and q inferred directly from p.[34] Towards the end of the discussion, Sextus acknowledges a dogmatic counter-objection to the sceptical procedure. The sceptics *argue* against proof: "these arguments are either probative or not probative. If the latter, they cannot show that there is no such thing as proof; but if they are probative, they themselves are led by self-refutation to posit the existence of proof" (*PH* 2.185). Sextus's opponents couch the argument in the following form: if proof exists, proof exists; if proof does not exist, proof exists; but proof either exists or it does not; therefore proof exists" (*PH* 2.186). The dogmatists (presumably Stoics) make use of the inference pattern that would become known to the medieval philosophers as the *lex clavia*: if if not-p, then p, then p. Sextus retorts that *if* the arguments given are sound, then they entail that proof does not exist, and hence it doesn't (*PH* 2.187). He also notes that a crucial conditional in the "proof" ("if proof does not exist, proof exists") cannot be true on any ordinary understanding of the Stoics' truth conditions for conditionals.[35] But he also claims, as he does in other contexts ("Sceptical medicine"), that the "proofs" act like purgative drugs, flushing themselves out along with the noxious opinions they are designed to eliminate, and, he says, this holds for such apparently self-refuting expressions as "nothing is true": "it not only destroys every other proposition, but overturns itself along with them" (*PH* 2.188). The interesting thing, of course, is that Sextus does not suppose its "overturning itself" to entail that it is *false* (and hence that at least one proposition is true). But as Sextus also notes, the sceptics need not commit themselves to the truth of the arguments involved. They work, if they work at all, because the dogmatist is forced to accept both their content and their form. But the sceptic is under no such obligation.

God and causes

The rest of Book 2 is concerned with other logical matters; thus, there is a brief attack on induction (the procedure can be valid only if all possible instances are canvassed, but this is impossible: *PH* 2.204); a longer discussion of definition (*PH* 2.205–12), division (*PH* 2.213–14), part–whole relations (*PH* 2.215–18), genera and species (*PH* 2.219–27); general properties (*PH* 2.228) and sophisms (*PH* 2.229–59). Book 3 turns to physics, and starts with God "the most efficient of causes" (*PH* 3.2). Typically, Sextus points to the divergence of views regarding His (or their) nature (is He corporeal or not, inside or outside the universe?) as reasons for suspending judgement (*PH* 3.3), but he is careful to emphasize that "following ordinary life, we say undogmatically that there are gods, and that we reverence them, and that they are provident" (*PH* 3.2). This is probably more than mere conventional (and prudent) orthodoxy; the undogmatic adherence to the ordinary practices of life is, as we have seen ("The sceptical life"), central to the Pyrrhonian way of life. One particular argument is worth brief mention as being an early instance of a long tradition. God must be either provident or not; if the former (as for instance the Stoics hold), then he must either provide[36] everything or only some things. But if the former there would be no evil in the world; but there is. However if God only provides some things, why these and not others?

> For either he has both the will and the power to provide everything, or else he has the will but not the power, or the power but not the will, neither will nor power. But if he had both will and power, he would have had forethought for everything. But this is not the case for the reasons stated; therefore he does not have both the will and the power to provide everything; but if he has the will but not the power, he is weaker than the cause [which impedes him] …; but that God should be weaker than anything conflicts with our conception of him. But if he has the power but not the will, he will be thought malign.　　(*PH* 3.10–11)

The argument is not particularly elegantly handled, but it is, and remains, a powerful challenge to any over-optimistic theodicy.

The general attack on causation[37] (*PH* 3.13–30) also follows a familiar pattern. Sextus begins by noting the disagreement as to whether causes are material or not, and whether they are causes of processes or states (*PH* 3.13–14). He then constructs a typical sceptical dilemma. That causes exist is plausible, for without them we can make no sense of

> increase, decrease, generation, corruption, change in general, every physical and mental effect, the organization of the universe, and all the rest ... for even if none of these things exists in their real nature, we will say that they appear to us in the way that they are not as a result of some cause. (*PH* 3.17)

Moreover, the alternative is to suppose that everything in the universe is random, but this defies common sense, and the evident order in things (*PH* 3.18), while to deny the existence of causes is self-stultifying; if you do so "for no cause" you will not win credence, but if you offer causes (reasons) for your position, you refute yourself (*PH* 3.19). On the other hand, Sextus deploys arguments against the conceivability of causes that recall those against signs ("Signs and proof"). We cannot, he says, conceive of the cause as a cause before we apprehend its effect; but equally we can only know the effect as the effect of its cause; thus we must know each of them before the other (*PH* 3.20–22). Further, someone who says that there are causes must either do so on the basis of no cause (reason), in which case his pronouncement is unfounded, or on the basis of some cause or other, but this will fall foul of either the Mode from regress or the Mode from circularity Modes (*PH* 3.23–4). Moreover, causes ought to precede their effects in order to bring them about; but if cause and effect are correlative, then they must co-subsist (*PH* 3.25–7). These arguments can be blunted by making the crucial distinction between the nature of the relation itself, and the history of its relata; but such distinctions are sophisticated, and did not come easily to the Greek mind, which was accustomed to treat relations as things.

Physics

The remaining physical topics (elements, bodies, mixture, motion, increase, subtraction and addition, transposition, whole and part, generation and destruction, rest, place, time, and number: *PH* 3.30–167) can be briefly and compendiously

111

treated. Sextus's treatment is the now-familiar mixture of the acute and the embarrassingly bad. He notes the disagreements among the dogmatists: Pherecydes says all is earth, Thales water, Anaximenes air, Hippasus fire – and they can't all be right (*PH* 3.30); and there are endemic (and apparently undecidable) disputes as to whether space and matter are discrete or continuous. We cannot accept all of these incompatible alternatives, but if we are to accept one, we must do so either with or without proof. Surely the latter is unacceptable, but any purported proof must, again for familiar reasons, be subjected to criterial assessment; and the result will be either circularity or regress (*PH* 3.34–6). Moreover, the attack on the concept of causation serves to undermine the coherence of numerous further concepts that apparently rely on it (as many of the list just given evidently do, and see *PH* 3.17). For instance, "some [the Stoics] say that a body is that which can act and be acted upon" (*PH* 3.38); but action is plainly a causal notion, and so subject to the same difficulties which plague that concept. But the notion of body is subject to its own difficulties. It is said to be the complex of three-dimensionality and resistance or solidity (*PH* 3.39), but these concepts themselves are incoherent. And if bodies are defined by their limits, or two-dimensional surfaces, the latter can have no existence other than as the boundary of bodies, so the account is viciously circular (*PH* 3.40–42). At *Outlines of Pyrrhonism* 3.71–81, Sextus retails a series of arguments against motion, some going back to Zeno and the Eleatics, all of which seek to discern incoherence in the concept as it relates to time and space. Where is the moving object? Does it move in the space where it is or where it is not? Not the former, since that space is the same size as the body, leaving no room for movement; but not the latter, since "where it is not it can neither do nor undergo anything" (*PH* 3.71). Equally, arguments against motion are mounted on the assumption that space is either continuous or quantized. If continuous, then the mover will have to perform an infinity of tasks; if quantized, then the ordinary concept of velocity as a ratio between time elapsed and distance travelled breaks down. Sextus's handling of the arguments themselves is not original (although it is concise and acute); what matters, of course, is the conclusion, not that motion *is* incoherent, but "in view of the opposition between appearances and arguments regarding the existence or non-existence of motion, we suspend judgement" (*PH* 3.81).

Ethics

Finally in Book 3 (169–279), Sextus returns to questions of ethics.[38] He repeats some of the examples adduced in the Tenth Mode ("The Modes of scepticism"), but devotes most of his time to dealing with disagreement between philosophers, the conflicts of "dogmatic suppositions", which *Outlines of Pyrrhonism* 1.145 signalled but of which it offered no pertinent examples. First of all, there is disagreement about the real nature of the good:

> all probably agree that the good is useful and choiceworthy … and that it is productive of happiness; but when asked what this actually is, they fall into ceaseless war, some [the Stoics] saying that it is virtue, some [Cyrenaics and Epicureans] pleasure, some freedom from pain [Democritus], and some something else. (*PH* 3.175)

Mere accord as to the analytically entailed properties of the good (that it is choiceworthy) does not amount to substantial agreement, and the same goes for evil (*PH* 3.176). The Stoics defined virtue as the knowledge of what is good, bad and indifferent, but there are reasons to suppose that nothing is by nature good (or bad or indifferent), but only in relation to circumstances and individuals. Fire heats everything, but "none of the supposed goods affects everyone as being good" (*PH* 3.179; cf. 194–239). Here Sextus relies on a general principle, commonly deployed in his arguments, to the effect that if x is F by nature, x must invariably appear to be F (the Modes of Aenesidemus are designed to show that nothing plausibly meets this standard, which is why we suspend judgement). But whatever the truth of the claim in other contexts, it does seem paradigmatically the case regarding questions of value. There is no agreement even as to the appearances in cases of goodness; and no second-order agreement as to their analysis. Thus philosophers differ over whether it is making the appropriate choices of goal, even if they should be frustrated, rather than actual achievement of the goals, that constitutes the good (*PH* 3.183).

The bulk of the remainder of the book is devoted to the question of whether there is an art of living (*PH* 3.188–278), which is of course what dogmatic schools of philosophy purport to teach. Some of the argument turns on technicalities in the definition of an "art" (*technê*): arts should have particular subject matters, but "life" is too general for that (*PH* 3.243–9); equally arts are by definition capable of being taught; but, as Sextus argues, there can be no such thing as teaching (*PH* 3.253–73).

Sceptical medicine

Many of these arguments are of doubtful validity; and some are downright feeble. Sextus himself explicitly acknowledges this at the very end of *Outlines of Pyrrhonism*, when he asks "Why do the sceptics deliberately employ arguments of feeble plausibility?" Not of course to persuade of their truth; they are all deployed in order to establish a *diaphônia* and hence to promote *epochê*:

> The sceptic, being a philanthropist, wishes to cure the Dogmatists' vanity and rashness so far as he can. So, just as doctors prescribe remedies of differing power in the case of bodily complaints ..., so too the sceptic employs arguments of differing strength, using those which are weighty and capable of vigorously the Dogmatists' ailment of vanity against those who are afflicted with a bad case of rashness, and the milder ones where the ailment of vanity is milder and easily cured, and who can be restored by a milder degree of plausibility.
>
> (*PH* 3.280–81)

This curious text has excited much comment. If it is to be taken seriously (and there is no obvious reason not to) it shows at the very least that the Pyrrhonian concept of argument and its role is very different from the norm, certainly the modern norm (although the ancient rhetorical tradition was sometimes inclined to think of argument in terms of main force). But Pyrrhonism, as we saw at the outset, was meant to be a way of life (albeit not one involving some dogmatic "art"). Truth as such becomes irrelevant; tranquillity is everything. This crucial feature of Sextan Pyrrhonism is often lost sight of in modern discussions, and Sextus's text has traditionally served less as a recipe for the tranquil life, and more as a source of arguments to be deployed *in propria persona* to particular positive ends, something that no sceptic could of course countenance. But in order to combat the worst cases of dogmatism, the sceptics had to produce some pretty serious arguments, and some of them have had a profound effect, albeit often as several removes, on the subsequent history of philosophy. If the effect of sceptical arguments against particular positions has usually been to force the proponents of those positions to refine them in order to evade the objections, rather than to make them simply give up and cultivate their gardens, that is perhaps ironic, but it should simply stir the sceptic to produce new, stronger medicine, from which in turn the dogmatists will seek to immunize themselves. The process is open ended, but, after all, the sceptics styled themselves "enquirers", and supposed the enquiry to be completely open ended. In that sense, perhaps, two millennia and more of philosophy have made sceptics of us all.

Notes

1. He is indeed mentioned as an Empiricist in a text wrongly attributed to Galen (*Introduction*, vol. 14, C. G. Kühn (ed.) (Leipzig, 1819–33), 683).
2. *PH* is the standard modern abbreviation of the Greek title of *Outlines of Pyrrhonism*: *Purrhôneiôn Hupotupôseôn*.
3. Barnes has pointed out that "meta-dogmatism" would be a happier description of the position. Sextus also ascribes it (also controversially) to the Academics: *PH* 1.1–4, 1.226–35. On this issue, see Ioppolo (1984); Hankinson (1995: Chs 5 & 6).
4. What to do about Sextus's apparent epistemic preference for the Methodists is a matter of unresolved scholarly controversy; on Methodism itself, see Frede (1982); on Empiricism, see Edelstein (1967) and Frede (1987b, 1988, 1990).
5. Books 7–8 are also known as *Against the Logicians*, Books 9–10 as *Against the Physicists*, and Book 11 as *Against the Ethicists*. Again I follow the standard (albeit flawed) modern practice by abbreviating them as *M* 7–11, from their Latin title *adversus Mathematicos*, but this name should more properly apply only to the treatises of *M* 1–6.
6. Stopper (1983).
7. Hankinson (1995: 58–65); Bett (2000).
8. For an account, see Hankinson (1995: Ch. 5).
9. See Hankinson (1995: Ch. 5); Ioppolo (1984).
10. For one account of this process, see Hankinson (2003); see also Frede (1983).
11. See Hankinson (1995: 116–21) and Brittain (2001).
12. See the excellent, albeit sceptical, account in Barnes (1989).
13. The evidence is largely to be found in the introduction to the summary of his eight-volume *Pyrrhonian Discourses*, compiled by the ninth-century Patriarch of Byzantium Photius in the catalogue of his library (*Bibliotheca* 212); the text is reproduced in Long and Sedley (1987: 71C).
14. As I am inclined to believe: see Hankinson (1995; Ch. 7); Woodruff (1988).
15. This story is developed in detail in Hankinson (1997).
16. "He [the Pyrrhonian] must acknowledge, if he will acknowledge anything, that all human life must perish were his principles universally and steadily to prevail. All discourse, all action, would immediately cease; and men remain in total lethargy, till the necessities of nature, unsatisfied, put an end to their miserable existence" (*Enquiry Concerning Human Understanding*, §XII ii). Hume is wrong (I think) about Pyrrhonism as such; but he sketches the argument with his customary force and vivacity. On the issue of the livability of the sceptical life, see Burnyeat (1980); Hankinson (1995: Chs 17 & 18).
17. There is much debate among scholars about the meaning of this key term in Sextus: for differing views, see Frede (1979) and Barnes (1982). See also Hankinson (1995: Ch. 17).
18. "So-called" because their attribution to Aenesidemus rests on relatively fragile ground (essentially one reference in *M* 7.345), while *Outlines of Pyrrhonism* simply ascribes them to "the older sceptics". At all events, they represent a longish tradition in Pyrrhonism, although both their use and their structure evidently evolved over time; see Woodruff (1988); Hankinson (1995: 155–61).
19. See on this issue (and others related to the Modes) Annas & Barnes (1985); Hankinson (1995: Ch. 9).

20. And this is consistent with the different approaches of Sextus and Diogenes; while the former clearly sought to systematize, and perhaps even expand, the material he inherited from his predecessors, the latter was far more simply a relatively faithful excerpter and copyist. This is all the more striking in that both of them are clearly relying, in large part, on the same material from the same tradition, as can be inferred from the fact that they cite many of the same examples, sometimes in the same language.

21. For an excellent general analysis of the Agrippan Modes and their philosophical power and import, see Barnes (1990a).

22. See Barnes (1990a: 116–19); Hankinson (1995: 189–92).

23. See further Barnes (1983); Hankinson (1995: 213–17).

24. This too is controversial; see Hankinson (1995: 75–85).

25. The plausibility of this claim as a characterization of medical Methodist methodology is extremely controversial; see Frede (1982) for a useful summary.

26. On Heraclitus, Democritus, Xenophanes and other alleged precursors of scepticism, see Hankinson (1995: Ch. 3).

27. On Protagorean relativism and scepticism, see Hankinson (1995: 41–7) and Barnes (1990b).

28. See the essays collected in Huby & Neal (1989).

29. See further Hankinson (1995: 193–200).

30. For a survey, see Hankinson (2003).

31. Sextus offers a much longer treatment of these issues in *M* 7; see Hankinson (1995: 198–200).

32. For a comprehensive recent treatment of the topic, see Allen (2001).

33. See Hankinson (1995: 206–9).

34. For more on this, see Barnes (1980).

35. For they hold that a conditional is true when the antecedent conflicts with the negation of the consequent: but it is hard to see how "proof does not exist" might be held to conflict with "it is not the case that proof exists".

36. "Provide" in the slightly unusual sense of foresee and have care for.

37. For a general discussion, see Barnes (1983); Hankinson (1995: Ch. 12). Sextus himself offers a much longer treatment at *M* 9.195–66.

38. On sceptical ethics, see Annas (1986); Hankinson (1995: Ch. 16).

Bibliography

Allen, J. 2001. *Inference from Signs*. Oxford: Oxford University Press.

Annas, J. 1986. "Doing Without Objective Values: Ancient and Modern Strategies", in *The Norms of Nature*, M. Schofield & G. Striker (eds), 3–29. Cambridge: Cambridge University Press.

Annas, J. & J. Barnes 1985. *The Modes of Scepticism*. Cambridge: Cambridge University Press.

Annas, J. & J. Barnes 1994. *Sextus Empiricus: Outlines of Scepticism*. Cambridge: Cambridge University Press.

Bailey, A. 2002. *Sextus Empiricus and Pyrrhonean Scepticism*. Oxford: Oxford University Press.

Barnes, J. 1980. "Proof Destroyed", in *Doubt and Dogmatism*, J. Barnes, M. F. Burnyeat & M. Schofield (eds), 161–81. Oxford: Oxford University Press.

Barnes, J. 1982. "The Beliefs of a Pyrrhonist", *Proceedings of the Cambridge Philological Society* **28**, 1–29.

Barnes, J. 1983. "Ancient Skepticism and Causation", in *The Skeptical Tradition*, M. F. Burnyeat (ed.), 149–203. Berkeley, CA: University of California Press.

Barnes, J. 1989. "Antiochus of Ascalon", in *Philosophia Togata*, J. Barnes & M. Griffin (eds) 51–96. Oxford: Oxford University Press.

Barnes, J. 1990a. *The Toils of Scepticism*. Cambridge: Cambridge University Press.

Barnes, J. 1990b. "Scepticism and Relativity", *Philosophical Studies* **32** (1988–90), 1–31.

Barnes, J., M. F. Burnyeat & M. Schofield (eds) 1980. *Doubt and Dogmatism*. Oxford: Oxford University Press.

Bett. R. 1986. *Sextus Empiricus: Against the Ethicists*. Oxford: Oxford University Press.

Bett, R. 2000. *Pyrrho, his Antecedents, and his Legacy*. Oxford: Oxford University Press.

Brittain, C. 2001. *Philo of Larissa: the Last of the Academic Sceptics*. Oxford: Oxford University Press.

Brunschwig, J. 1980. "Sextus Empiricus on the *Kritêrion*: The Skeptic as Conceptual Legatee", in *The Question of "Eclecticism"*, J. Dillon & A. A. Long (eds), 145–75. Berkeley, CA: University of California Press.

Burnyeat, M. F. 1980. "Can the Sceptic Live His Scepticism?", in *Doubt and Dogmatism*, J. Barnes, M. F. Burnyeat & M. Schofield (eds), 20–53. Oxford: Oxford University Press (reprinted in Burnyeat 1983).

Burnyeat, M. F. (ed.) 1983. *The Skeptical Tradition*. Berkeley, CA: University of California Press.

Bury, R. G. 1933. *Sextus Empiricus: Outlines of Pyrrhonism*, Loeb Classical Library. Cambridge, MA: Harvard University Press (= *PH*).

Bury, R. G. 1935. *Sextus Empiricus: Against the Logicians*, Loeb Classical Library. Cambridge, MA: Harvard University Press (= *M* 7–8).

Bury, R. G. 1936. *Sextus Empiricus: Against the Physicists, Against the Ethicists*, Loeb Classical Library. Cambridge, MA: Harvard University Press (= *M* 9–11).

Bury, R. G. 1949. *Sextus Empiricus: Against the Professors*, Loeb Classical Library. Cambridge, MA: Harvard University Press (= *M* 1–6).

Edelstein, L. 1967. "Empiricism and Skepticism in the Teaching of the Greek Empiricis School", in *Ancient Medicine*, 195–204. Baltimore, MA: Johns Hopkins University Press.

Frede, M. 1979. "Des skeptikers Meinungen", *Neue Hefte für Philosophie*, **15/16**, 102–29 (reprinted in English in Frede 1987a).

Frede, M. 1982. "On the Method of the So-called Methodical School of Medicine", in *Science and Speculation*, J. Barnes, J. Brunschwig, M. F. Burnyeat & M. Schofield (eds), 1–23. Cambridge: Cambridge University Press.

Frede, M. 1983. "Stoics and Sceptics on Clear and Distinct Impressions", in *The Skeptical Tradition*, M. F. Burnyeat (ed.), 69–93. Berkeley, CA: University of California Press.

Frede, M. 1987a. *Essays in Ancient Philosophy*. Oxford: Oxford University Press (contains all previously cited articles).

Frede, M. 1987b. "The Ancient Empiricists", in *Essays in Ancient Philosophy*, 243–60. Oxford: Oxford University Press.

Frede, M. 1988. "The Empiricist Attitude Towards Reason and Theory", in *Method, Medicine and Metaphysics*, *Apeiron*, supp. vol. 21, R. J. Hankinson (ed.), 79–97. Edmonton:

Academic Printing and Publishing.

Frede, M. 1990. "An Empiricist View of Knowledge: Memorism", in *Epistemology*, Companions to Ancient Thought II, S. Everson (ed.), 225–50. Cambridge: Cambridge University Press.

Hankinson, R. J. 1995. *The Sceptics*. London: Routledge.

Hankinson, R. J. 1997. "The End of Scepticism", *Kriterion* **96**, 7–32.

Hankinson, R. J. 2003. "Stoic Epistemology", in *The Stoics*, B. Inwood (ed.), 59–84. Cambridge: Cambridge University Press.

Huby, P. & G. Neal (eds) 1989. *The Criterion of Truth*. Liverpool: Liverpool University Press.

Ioppolo, A. M. 1984. *Opinione e Scienza*. Naples: Bibliopolis.

Long, A. A. & D. N. Sedley (eds) 1987. *The Hellenistic Philosophers*, Volume 1. Cambridge: Cambridge University Press.

Schofield, M. & G. Striker (eds) 1986. *The Norms of Nature*. Cambridge: Cambridge University Press.

Stopper, M. R. 1983. "Schizzi Pirroniani", *Phronesis* **28**, 267–95.

Woodruff, P. 1988. "Aporetic Pyrrhonism", *Oxford Studies in Ancient Philosophy* **6**, 139–68.

Further reading

The best English translation of *Outlines* is that of Annas & Barnes (1994); still serviceable, and with a facing Greek text, is Bury (1933); and Bury (1935, 1946, 1949) provides similar Greek-English versions of the rest of Sextus's surviving *oeuvre*. Much important work has been done on Sextus and scepticism in the past couple of decades, although much is in the form of scholarly articles in learned journals. For a general account of Greek scepticism, there is Hankinson (1995); more narrowly focused on Sextus is Bailey (2002). Annas & Barnes (1985) provide an exemplarily clear philosophical analysis of the Ten Modes, and Barnes (1990) does a similar job for the Modes of Agrippa. Barnes (1980) analyses the sceptical attack on logic and proof; Annas (1986) deals with sceptical arguments in ethics. On the key epistemological notion of the criterion, see Brunschwig (1980). For the central question of the nature and liveability of the sceptical life, see Burnyeat (1980); the related question of the nature of the sceptical rejection of belief and its coherence are dealt with in Barnes (1982), and Frede (1979); and that of the sense in which scepticism can have a goal, Hankinson (1997).

5

Plotinus

The Enneads

Stephen R. L. Clark

Introduction: text and context

The Enneads of Plotinus (204–70 CE) would, in modern terms, be better entitled *The Collected* [or even *Complete*] *Works of Plotinus, arranged and introduced by Porphyry of Tyre.* By his sometime pupil Porphyry's own account,[1] Plotinus began to write down summaries and expansions of seminar discussion in his early fifties, and continued to write until shortly before his death. Having weak eyes, he could never bear to re-read or revise his work, and his colleagues and students might reasonably have doubted whether every copy had been properly proofread.[2] Thirty years after Plotinus's death, Porphyry produced what then became the definitive edition of the works (wholly superseding the "hundred volumes" of Amelius and the edition of Eustachius). Porphyry chose to ensure that there were precisely 54 treatises, collected in six groups of nine (hence *Enneads*, from the Greek term *ennea*), even if he had to divide continuous stretches of philosophical enquiry (sometimes in mid-sentence), or elevate minor notes into treatises to achieve the number.[3] He also took care to provide the order of writing, as far as he could know it. Later scholars have not always agreed that the Porphyrian order is the best approach to Plotinus, but no better arrangement has achieved canonical status, unless perhaps the Arabic version known as *The Theology of Aristotle*, which carried neo-Platonic thought into the heart of Islam. *The Theology* consists of edited selections from the treatises contained in *Enneads* IV–VI (see Adamson 2003). *The Enneads'* textual tradition is secure; the archetype of the surviving manuscripts, it is agreed, was probably written between the ninth and twelfth centuries, as a faithful copy of the original (see Henry & Schwyzer 1964–82). Influential European translations have included those of Marsilius Ficino into Latin (1492), Thomas Taylor into English (1817), E. Bréhier into French (1924–38), R. Harder into German (1930–37, revised 1956) and Stephen MacKenna into English (1921–30, finished by B. S. Page). MacKenna's is probably still the most widely read English version (an abridged version was published by Penguin (1991), with introductions by Dillon and Henry), but the better English edition is that of Hilary Armstrong, in seven volumes in the Loeb Classical Library (1966–88). It is customary to include a reference to the chronological position of a treatise in giving the reference: thus, *Enneads* I.6 [1] is Plotinus's first known writing, on Beauty, and *Enneads* I.7 [54] his last, on the Primal Good and Other Goods. The titles are Porphyry's. His commentary on his master's work is lost, unless some parts of it are to be found in the Arabic text.

Plotinus himself was born in Egypt in about 204 CE, studied under the philosopher Ammonius Saccas in Alexandria, joined the emperor Gordian's ill-fated expedition against the Persians (being eager to learn about the Persian and Indian philosophical traditions), escaped to Antioch when Gordian was assassinated, migrated to Rome and spent the rest of his life leading philosophical discussions in the Platonic tradition. He died in 270. Discussions often began from readings of Plato, Aristotle, Numenius and the Aristotelian commentators, and rambled thereafter. "Since he encouraged his students to ask questions", Porphyry tells us, "the course was lacking in order and there was a great deal of pointless chatter" (Porphyry, *Life of Plotinus*, 3.37f.: Armstrong 1966–88: 1, 11). Porphyry felt differently about the habit when it was he who was asking questions; to someone who wanted Plotinus to produce a set treatise rather than be always dealing with Porphyry's problems, Plotinus replied that "if we do not solve [Porphyry's] difficulties we shall not be able to say anything at all to put into the treatise" (13.13f.: Armstrong 1966–88: 1, 39). The treatise he wrote in response to those particular difficulties is probably one known to Longinus as *On the Soul*, divided by Porphyry into IV.3 [27], IV.4 [28] and IV.5 [29]. Like other such extended works, it is marked by Plotinus's readiness to consider and reconsider difficulties, within a framework that he had largely established to his satisfaction years before. Porphyry ascribed Plotinus's unwillingness to give details of his ancestry and early life to his "being ashamed of being in a body" (1.2: Armstrong 1966–88: 1, 3), and this judgement – along with familiar aphorisms describing philosophy as "the flight of the alone to the Alone"[4] – suggests to careless readers that Plotinus was an unsociable depressive. It is more likely that *Porphyry* was depressive: he records that Plotinus spotted his condition, and ordered him away from Rome to Sicily to recover. Plotinus himself was more robust. He had, after all, served in Gordian's army, and had some influence in Gallienus's court. If he avoided the public baths or public rituals it was not because he was shy or arrogant. He was trusted to manage the persons and estates of orphans left in his charge, "so his house [actually, the house of an aristocratic Roman widow] was full of young lads and maidens" (9.10: Armstrong 1966–88: 1, 31). He kept his head in the jealous atmosphere of Rome's intellectual cliques. He drew lessons from sculpture, dance and boxing matches, as well as from rumours about Egyptian priests and the works of Plato and Aristotle. "In answering questions he made clear both his benevolence to the questioner and his intellectual vigour" (13.10: Armstrong 1966–88: 1, 39). When he began to suffer from the disease that killed him (whether leprosy or tuberculosis), his friends avoided him, because he was still inclined to greet everyone with a kiss. In character, in brief, he was more sanguine than melancholic, and readier than most philosophers to listen and to learn.

Even though Porphyry may not be the ideal lens through which to see Plotinus, he is nonetheless the best lens we have. Even those scholars who prefer the *chronological* order must acknowledge that we depend on Porphyry for this as well (he divides them, in that mode, into those written before he himself joined Plotinus [1–21], the "superior" treatises written during the years of his stay [22–45], and those written after he had left for Sicily [46–54]). In putting his master's treatises in order he attempted to make them more accessible. The first book deals chiefly with ethical issues, such as beauty, well-being, evils and the wrongness of self-slaughter. The second deals with contemporary physics (the heavens, astrology, substance and sight), culminating in his denunciation of those "gnostics" who chose to despise the physical universe (itself extracted from a larger work distributed by Porphyry into III.8 [30], V.8 [31], V.5 [32] and II.9 [33]). The third deals with further issues about our place in the physical cosmos, providence, eternity and time. The fourth deals with issues about the soul, including its descent into the physical; the fifth with intellect, and its relationship with the intelligible cosmos and "the One". The sixth concludes the course, with detailed and difficult examinations of categories, being and the One. With most authors it would be unwise to treat their work as all of a piece, as though there were a single vision, a single theory, behind everything they wrote or wondered, at whatever time of life and in whatever context. Plotinus, more than most, had established his fundamental theory well before he began to write, and although there are occasional revisions, it seems likely that Porphyry's order represents his thought as well as any, and more easily than some.[5]

On beauty

The Enneads, if they are a single work, are partly Porphyry's creation. If they are instead conceived as merely collected works, their unity is that achieved by a powerful mind at work to unfold a single vision. Sometimes, it is easy to believe that Plotinus intended to address a particular issue in an extended treatise, even if he gave it no title, and left it to his friends and followers to call it *On the Soul* (= IV.3–5) or *On Being* (= VI.1–3). But if he returned to that same topic at some later time, he may not have felt any gap. That, after all, was the gift identified by Porphyry: "even if he was talking to someone, engaged in continuous conversation, he kept to his train of thought" (*Life of Plotinus* 8.12f.: Armstrong 1966–88: 1, 29). So what Plotinus himself counted as a "single work", we cannot say. Maybe it was his entire output, and Porphyry knew better than we how that work should be presented. Nonetheless, Plotinus's written works began with what has been called the treatise on Beauty (I.6 [1]), and this is the treatise that has probably had the widest audience. It deserves close attention, always bearing in mind that *Plotinus* maybe conceived it as a section of a larger work, whether with those he wrote immediately thereafter, or those linked to it by particular topic (as might be *On the Intelligible Beauty* (V.8 [31]), *On Love* (III.5 [50]) and *On What are Evils* (I.8 [51])).

In reading Plotinus it is well to remember that he regards Plato's texts as our best guide in the pursuit of wisdom, but treats that pursuit as something to be followed for oneself, not merely read about. He wishes to ascend by the same route that Plato proposed in his *Symposium*, by attention to Beauty, in its physical, moral and transcendent forms. But whereas Plato seems to suggest that Beauty is one Form among many, Plotinus equates Beauty with the whole array of intelligible reality: *all* the Forms, all really real things, are essentially beautiful. The soul, in experiencing something as beautiful, is turned towards that network of Forms, unified in the intellect. Without its focus on the One, there is no intellect and nothing is understood: that is, the intellect exists only in its turn towards the One, the Good that lies beyond being, which Plotinus variously describes as Beauty or as the transcendent source of Beauty.

"Beauty" translates *to kalon, to kallos* or *he kallone*, and means more than the aesthetic. As in Aristotelian ethics, it includes what we normally translate as "fine", "noble" or even, simply, "right". But Plotinus, like Plato, takes his start from just such beauties as ordinary lovers know, with "wonder and a shock of delight and longing and passion and a happy excitement" (I.6 [1].4). What is it that draws our attention to bodies? "Nearly everyone [that is, the Stoics] says that it is good proportion of the parts (*summetria ton meron*) to each other and to the whole, with the addition of good colour" (I.6 [1].1, 21ff.: Armstrong 1966–88: 1, 235). Edmund Spenser, an Elizabethan Platonist, knew better:

How vainely then doe ydle wits invent,
That beautie is nought else, but mixture made
Of colours faire, and goodly temp'rament
Of pure complexions, that shall quickly fade
And passe away, like to a sommers shade,
Or that it is but comely composition
Of parts well measurd, with meet disposition.
Hath white and red in it such wondrous powre,
That it can pierce through th'eyes unto the hart …
Or can proportion of the outward part,
Move such affection in the inward mynd,
That it can rob both sense and reason blynd?
                    "Hymne in Honour of Beautie": Spenser (1912: 590)

Plotinus's own argument against the Stoic analysis is cooler (although this is not to say that Spenser's questions were not also his: such things could no more engender beauty than life (V.9 [5].5; see Clark 1996)). On the Stoic theory, Plotinus says, nothing simple could be beautiful, and the parts of any whole would not themselves be beautiful. But how could a whole be beautiful, he asks, if the parts are not?[6] And how could we deny that colours themselves, and lightning, and the light of a single star are beautiful? Even a well-proportioned face is sometimes beautiful and sometimes not, so that something other than proportion brings the beauty (in a later treatise he was to add that the ugliest living face is more beautiful than the best proportioned statue; VI.7 [38].22). The beauty of laws, or sciences, cannot rest, he says, in "symmetry", since there can be concord or agreement even between bad ideas. And the beauty of soul, or virtue, has no formula for the mixture of parts or speculations. All these arguments, of course, raise counter-questions, many of which are addressed in later sections of the corpus. In this record of discussion Plotinus moves directly to assert that the soul recognizes bodily beauty (and is repelled by bodily ugliness) at first glance, and that this is because the soul, "when it sees something akin to it or a trace of its kindred reality, is delighted and thrilled and returns to itself and remembers itself and its own possessions" (I.6 [1].2, 9f.). The trace it sees is the presence of a divine formative power, bringing unity out of the parts. "As sometimes art gives beauty to a whole house with its parts, and sometimes a nature gives beauty to a single stone" (I.6 [1].2, 26f.). Art, be it noted, is already being cast as something greater than the imitative skill that Plato reckoned it: "for Pheidias did not make his Zeus from any model perceived by the senses, but understood what Zeus would look like if he wanted to make himself visible" (V.8 [31].1, 39f.). So also the architect sees a house as beautiful because it is, apart from the stones, "the inner form divided by the external mass of matter" (I.6 [1].3, 8). Simple colours are beautiful by the presence of light (and that is why fire is the most beautiful of elements: "it shines and glitters as if it was a form" (I.6 [1].3, 26)). And melodies are beautiful if their formula allows the production of a form (I.6 [1].3, 33).

Beauties beyond the realm of sense are perceptible only to those who have accepted them: "people cannot speak about the splendour of virtue who have never even imagined how fair is the face of justice and moral order; 'neither the evening nor the morning star are as fair'" (I.6 [1].4, 10f.).[7] Those who do see it experience that shock of delight that lovers feel. But why do we call such virtues beautiful? "They exist and appear to us and he who sees them cannot possibly say anything else except that they are what really exists. What does 'really exist' mean? That they exist as beauties" (I.6 [1].5, 18f3.). "Or rather, beautifulness is reality" (I.6 [1].6, 21). "For this reason being is longed for because it is the same as beauty, and beauty is lovable because it is being" (V.8 [31].9, 41). These virtues, Plotinus proposes, reveal the soul's own being. Souls appear ugly when they are impure:

> dissolute and unjust, full of all lusts, and all disturbance, sunk in fears by its cowardice and jealousies by its pettiness, thinking mean and mortal thoughts as far as it thinks at all, loving impure pleasures, living a life which consists of bodily sensations and finding delight in ugliness. (I.6 [1].5, 26ff.)

When souls are purified or conformed to intellect they become form and like God (or possibly "a god").

Why are being, beauty and form equated, and why are only the virtuous, as it seems, to be considered *real*? To modern ears it may seem that beauty can only be superficial, and reality, for all we know, ugly. Beautiful ideas appeal to romantics and the naïve, while sensible people prefer *practical* ideas (that is, ideas that are some use in keeping us alive and happy). To Platonists (and probably to other ancient moralists and metaphysicians) the case is otherwise. Ugliness is a failure of form to master or fully inform the material, and therefore anything ugly is less perfectly what it should or could be, less perfectly informed, less real. The beauty that is the Form, the ideal type, of any visible thing, is attractive to us because (so Platonists suppose) it reminds us of the soul's true home, the soul's own being. Virtue – I shall return to the point below – is the purification of our senses so that we value that transcendent being more than the momentary pleasures of here and now. They are not merely *instrumentally* useful, as if we are to admire virtue only because it leads to earthly prosperity. Earthly prosperity, on the contrary, may be a distraction from what is truly valuable. The sight of beauty starts us on our struggle home.

The Three Hypostases or Fundamental Principles that are later recognized as the Plotinian contribution to metaphysics (namely, the One, the Intellect and the Soul: on which more below) are here given an "aesthetic" introduction. It is life (that is, Soul) that makes things beautiful, or else it is Form (that is, Intellect) that does so, or else this beauty is a grace shed on well-formed, living things by the Good (another label for the One) that lies even beyond being and knowledge (as Plato said: *Republic* 6.509).

> First we must posit beauty which is also the good [that is, what everything desires]; from this immediately comes intellect, which is beauty; and soul is given beauty by intellect. Everything else is beautiful by the shaping of soul, the beauties in action and in ways of life. And soul makes beautiful the bodies which are spoken of as beautiful. (I.6 [1].6, 26f.)

It is important to recall that these are not three distinct "things": the One, after all, isn't "a thing" at all, but rather the fundamental principle on which all things depend, as facets of the single coherent system that is Intellect. Soul, in turn, does not grasp anything other than reality, but does so in a piecemeal, perspectival, linear way. Everything owes its experienced being to Soul, and to Intellect, and to the One.

Our ascent back towards the Good "which every soul desires" involves our stripping off (I.6 [1].7, 6f.), or travelling homewards, after Odysseus's allegorical example (I.6 [1].8, 18f.; see V.9 [5].1, 21f.),[8] or polishing our internal statue (I.6 [1].9, 8f.). We may desire it as good even if we have not seen it, but "he who has seen it glories in its beauty and is full of wonder and delight" (I.6 [1].7, 16f.).

> All our toil and trouble is for this, not to be left without a share in the best of visions ... A man has not failed if he fails to win beauty of colours or bodies, or power or office or kingship even, but if he fails to win this and only this. (I.6 [1].7, 34f.)

All those lesser things are only traces or reflections or reminders of our true country (I.6 [1].8, 17f.), and our route to it is by becoming virtuous (or beautiful) ourselves. The Good we seek is "in a loose and general way of talking" the primary beauty, but strictly we should say that "the place of the Forms is the intelligible beauty, but the Good is That which is beyond" (I.6 [1].9, 40).

A proper reading of this treatise inevitably leads onwards; all the other treatises could in a way be considered footnotes or appendices to explain Plotinus's concepts. But the treatise also stands on its own, and has influenced poets, artists and philosophers in Europe and Islam.

Ontology and therapy

Plotinus's version of the Platonic ascent employs many of Plato's own techniques. The first is simply to engage with other theorists, and suggest that their preferred hypotheses don't fit the facts of our experience and ordinary judgement. The Stoics are wrong about beauty because more things are reckoned beautiful – even by them – than their theory allows. In other treatises he similarly argues that, for example, soul cannot be produced entirely from unliving elements (IV.9 [8].5), or that the intellect cannot be separated from the objects of its thought (for if it were, we could never know that our *impression* of the truth was actually true: V.3 [49].5, 23ff.). But argument, or discursive thought in general, is not the goal, nor does it start from wholly neutral premises. Plotinus, like other antique philosophers, desires a system that will make sense of, and assist, the way of life with which he is identified. How could the world as a whole be inanimate, or ruled by chance, if we are alive and purposive? How could we be confined to virtual imaginings of a world we cannot ever know directly, if there is to be any point in the pursuit of truth? How could intelligent thought itself be vindicated except in something that transcended ordinary divisions? How could we even affirm our own delight in beauty unless beauty itself were real? The intellectual enterprise depends on our believing (truly) in the significance of (for example) mathematical beauty, and in an attainable reality that is yet other than our own immediate experience. The possibility of continuing with it depends in turn on our being able to trust other eyes than ours, to recognize each other as fellow-travellers rather than as prey or parasites. And none of this will do us any good unless we have some actual way of changing our minds and characters, which is not done by argument alone.

The founding fathers of modern science were often Platonists, and despite the fashion for supposing that "science" somehow supports materialism, there are still scientists willing to agree with Plotinus (see Malin 2001). No "law of nature" (being of the form, "if *A* then *B*") can ever explain why anything exists at all or "what breaths fire into the equations". It follows that there is either no explanation for the brute reality (and existence is, at bottom, merely "as it happens") or the explanation must lie in something transcending "intellect and being" (which Plato and Plotinus call the Good, or else the One). It is not only *existence* that needs explanation: so also does the fact that what there is is intelligible. The cosmos, to be a genuine *cosmos*, must be the expression of an unchanging intellect: a house, as it were, that is "apart from the stones, the inner form divided by the external mass of matter, without parts but appearing in many parts" (I.6 [1].3, 8f.). And the cosmos, finally, must be alive in all its parts (where could life come from but the living?). Serious attempts to think through what a cosmos entirely stripped of explanation, unity or real identities must be like make the presumed "success" of science impossible. Vocal materialists, trading on their expertise in particular scientific disciplines but without any good account even of those disciplines, should not be allowed to claim the scientific high ground. Working scientists, in practice, admit the significance of beauty; not every seemingly "beautiful" theory is true, no doubt, but that is because the cosmos has better taste! Ugly theories are rejected long before experiment disproves them. Plotinus at least attempted to make sense of things, and of our insight into them. This does not prove him right, but at least suggests that his arguments should be taken seriously.

Plotinus also followed Plato in using metaphors and stories to awaken insight or confirm a conviction, and to speak of something that, in its nature, cannot be entirely formalized.

> Intellect also, then, has one power for thinking, by which it looks at the things in itself, and one by which it looks at what transcends it by a direct awareness and reception, by which also before it saw only, and by seeing acquired intellect and is one. And that first one is the contemplation of Intellect in its right mind, and the other is Intellect in love, when it goes out of its mind 'drunk with the nectar'; then it falls in love, simplified into happiness by having its fill, and it is better for it to be drunk with a drunkenness like this than to be more respectably sober. (VI.7 [38].35)

Considered in one way, Plotinus, like other systematic thinkers, offers an ontology (for which see especially V.1 [10]). At the pinnacle is the First Hypostasis, the One or the Good: wholly indescribable, and the source of all things. Sprung from it is the Second Hypostasis, the Intellect, containing the intelligible cosmos and the many forms of beauty. From this in turn springs the Third Hypostasis, the Soul, whose nature is to experience what the Intellect unchangeably knows, from every possible vantage point. The Soul exists as every soul, including the World Soul from which the natural order takes its beginning. That order is a reflection in space and time of the intelligible world. Individual souls leap downwards into nature, some further into unknowingness than others. At the far limit of the cosmos is mere matter, having no real being of its own: a painted corpse (II.4 [12].5, 18) incapable of generating any novelty and yet the bare condition for all material being. Matter as such is wholly imperceptible, "bound in a sort of beautiful fetters, as some prisoners are in chains of gold" (I.8 [51].15, 25f.).[9] Each of us has a choice: to descend still further down the ladder of Soul or to attempt to climb back up to the Intellect and the One. Climbing up should be no real hardship since that part of our Soul most closely tied to Intellect has not descended; there is a part of each of us that has not consented to the world of generation and decay, and returning there is indeed a return home. Travelling the other way will lead to lower and lower incarnations, as the dramatist, so to speak, assigns less arduous roles to failed actors (III.2 [47].17, 45f.).

It is not unnatural or unreasonable that many readers have interpreted Plotinus as suggesting that the material or phenomenal world is an error, that the material world exists because the Soul has fallen. It is perhaps the very similarity of his own doctrine to the gnostics' (so called) that leads him to write so fiercely against those who thus despise the world. "What other fairer image of the intelligible world could there be?" (II.9 [33].4, 26). But the treatise on Beauty stands for all: bodily beauties should not be denied, but also should not become the sole attractors. What is at issue for Plotinus is the attitude we take to the world and to ourselves, which offers a different reading of his text than the ontological. It is likely enough that he did indeed suppose that the structure of the All was as his text suggests: the One, the Intellect and the Soul are the primary hypostases. Soul is distributed into the World Soul and us lesser souls; Nature (the whole array of phenomenal reality that arises in the life of the World Soul) is the image of the Intelligible, and Matter is as much beyond reason as the One. Despite the scorn that moderns often express for dualists, there is no reasonable objection to the sort of dualism that the ancients offered: there is a real distinction between the phenomenal worlds we ordinarily experience, and the real world that outlasts and explains them all. In *my* world, there are nearer and more distant regions, containing entities more or less opaque to my immediate understanding. *My* world is not the same as *the* world, and the conflict between Plotinus and the materialists is not that he was dualist and they were not. On the contrary, they were and remain more dualist than he, in that the *material* world is expressly divided from the ordinarily *experienced* world that is our starting-point. For Plotinus, the real world that outlives and contains us is the *intelligible* world, unified in an Intellect to which we have access. The "real world" imagined into being by materialists is one that we can never know, devoid of colour, meaning and identities. The real intelligible cosmos contains Soul as well as Forms, and we can learn more of it, even from our present bodily condition, just because we are not alien to it. The real world is not the imagined world that would be without Soul, but rather the interwoven whole containing all the points of view there are. In Armstrong's words:

> Plotinus's divine mind [which is also the totality of intelligible being] is not just a mind knowing a lot of eternal objects. It is an organic living community of interpenetrating beings which are at once Forms and intelligences, all "awake and alive", in which every part thinks and therefore is the whole; so that all are one mind and yet each retains its distinct individuality without which the whole would be impoverished. And this mind-world is the region where our own mind, illumined by the divine intellect finds its true self and lives its own life, its proper home and the penultimate stage on its journey, from which it is taken up to union with the Good.
>
> (Armstrong & Markus 1960: 27)

It is not "the view from nowhere" that has authority, but the view from everywhere. What traps us in illusion is the wish to have things our own way. Plotinus's account of the fall of individual souls is that "as if they were tired of being together, they each go to their own" (IV.8 [6].4). But they exist as individuals before their fall, and so does the world of nature. It is right that they should take their part in animating this great image, wrong that they should forget their real situation (see IV.3 [27].12–13).

> When we look outside that on which we depend we do not know that we are one, like faces which are many on the outside but have one head inside. But if someone is able to turn around, either by himself or having the good luck to have his hair pulled by Athena herself, he will see God and himself and the all ... He will stop marking himself off from all being and will come to all the All without going out anywhere. (VI.5 [23].7, 9f.)

The "inward turn" is not a turn *away* from company. It is when we recall the *real* world in which we live that we can have companions; concentrating instead on the sensory and sensual phenomena that we do *not* share with others is to lose them. Treating those companions as merely material is also to lose them; their reality is as souls, and not only stuff.

Even what we think most "material" is not *only* stuff. It is true that an artist may sculpt a stone into beauty. Such a stone "will appear beautiful not because it is a stone – for then [another, unsculpted] stone would be just as beautiful –

but as a result of the form which art has put into it" (V.8 [31].1, 13f.). But there is a beauty also in unsculpted stone (I.6 [1].2, 27), since "nature" is at work there too.

> The growth and shaping of stones and the inner patterning of mountains as they grow one must certainly suppose take place because an ensouled forming principle is working within them and giving them form; and this is the active form of the earth, like what is called the growth nature in trees. (VI.7 [38].11, 24ff.)

"A manifold life exists in the All and makes all things, and in its living embroiders a rich variety and does not rest from ceaselessly making beautiful and shapely living toys" (*Ennead* III.2 [47].15, 31f.).[11]

The stars above us are also living; it may be, indeed, that they are the appearances of our own higher selves, and their visible beauty a reminder of that part of us that has never consented to sin.[12] They do not control us, and certainly don't cause us to do wrong (see II.3 [52]). If astrological prediction or description works it is only because "all things are filled full of signs" (II.3 [52].7, 12), since there is a single power at work throughout the cosmos, and every part of it carries traces of every other. "All things are filled full of life, and, we may say, boiling with life. They all flow, in a way, from a single spring" (*Ennead* VI.7 [38].12, 23f.; see also III.3 [48].7, 10ff.). The life that works through the All, making and remaking images of the eternally real, does not need to *plan* its action. It has no blueprints, nor any instrumental attitude. Plotinus's "Providence" is not that of popular religion. Stags don't have antlers, have not been "given" antlers, for their protection, but simply because that sort of being requires them (VI.7 [38].10). Being a stag is a particular form of Beauty, made multiply visible for and by the soul. What Soul perceives piecemeal and from particular perspectives, Intellect contains whole, including what to us is past or future (see VI.7 [38].1, 48f.). That whole in turn exists as the revelation or epiphany of the transcendent One, the only way that Intellect can grasp the One and the only adequate revelation of its power.

This account of reality as a living, united whole, bound together by magical sympathies, and constantly recreating itself as an image of the eternal, may seem very distant from the sort of natural reality that our modern experts admire. There are at least *analogies* between the neo-Platonic universe and the one revealed or posited by science, and maybe modern scientists owe more than they will usually admit to the renaissance of this ancient wisdom. It is true that Plotinus's astronomical problems, for example, are not ours: how is it that the stars and planets circle the earth forever, and are they compounded of all the elements or only fire (see II.2 [14] and II.1 [40])? But in his rejection of the fifth Aristotelian element, the ether, he laid down that the heavens are moved according to the same laws as the earth. And in rejecting astrological and literally demonic theories of illness, he asserted the helpful principle that the *causes* of disease are to be identified by the *cures* (II.9 [33].14, 21).

In one sense, Plotinus's ontology is entirely "naturalistic", but in another, it is not. It is not a neutral description of a world divorced from value, and the way to verify or secure it is not neutral either. Indeed, we may conceive his account as a set of recipes for living a better, clearer, more companionable life rather than (or as well as) straight ontology. In Rappe's words,

> decoding these texts involves seeing them as something like meditation manuals rather than mere texts. The non-discursive aspects of the text – the symbols, ritual formulae, myths, and images – are the locus of this pedagogy. Their purpose is to help the reader to learn how to contemplate, to awaken the eye of wisdom. (Rappe 2000: 3).

Rather than begin with the One, we should begin, as Plotinus advises, with the Soul.

> Let every soul, then, first consider this, that it made all living things itself, breathing life into them, those that the earth feeds and those that are nourished by the sea, and the divine stars in the sky; it made the sun itself, and this great heaven and adorned it ... And heaven, moved with an everlasting motion by the wise guidance of soul, becomes a "fortunate living being" and gains its value by the indwelling of soul; before soul it was dead body, earth and water, or rather the darkness of matter and non-existence and "what the gods hate", as a poet says. (*Ennead* V.1 [10].2, 1ff., 24ff.)[13]

Note that it is not – or not only – a single creative agent, animating the whole of Nature (that is, the World Soul) that does this, as though Plotinus was describing a single creative event (Plotinus, after all, did not suppose that the cosmos had any actual beginning[14]). The point is rather that *every* soul is the maker of its world: without our soul's illumination there is nothing but "the darkness of matter and non-existence", or James's "black and jointless continuity".

> We may, if we like, by our reasonings, unwind things back to that black and jointless continuity of space and moving clouds of swarming atoms which science calls the only real world. But all the while the world

we feel and live in will be that which our ancestors and we, by slowly cumulating strokes of choice, have extricated out of this, like sculptors, by simply rejecting certain portions of the given stuff. Other sculptors, other statues from the same stone! Other minds, other worlds from the same monotonous and inexpressive chaos! My world is but one in a million alike embedded, alike real to those who may abstract them. How different must be the worlds in the consciousness of ant, cuttlefish or crab! (James 1890: 1, 288f.)

That black and jointless continuity is as imaginary as matter itself, not the real origin of things, but it can stand in for the totality from which we construct our own particular worlds. Having made our worlds we may be fascinated by its parts, forgetting the beauty that inspires it. Simone Weil's aphorism is to the point:

It may be that vice, depravity and crime are nearly always, or even perhaps always, in their essence, attempts to eat beauty, to eat what we should only look at ... If [Eve] caused humanity to be lost by eating the fruit, the opposite attitude, looking at the fruit without eating it, should be what is required to save it. (Weil 1956: 1, 121)

What we are to do is recall the "pure Intellect ... the true life of Kronos, a god who is fulness and intellect" (V.1 [10].4, 8f.).[15] Whereas as souls we inevitably experience things in a linear and piecemeal fashion, intellect is all things, all together. And we see the world as intelligible, or even its parts as intelligible, in so far as we see them unified. To see the world aright – that is, to see it happily – we must, as it were, look through the sensible, to the underlying Forms. The One itself is seen only under the guise of the intelligible Beauty that contains us all: that is, to see the world aright we need to focus our intellectual eyes beyond it, rather as puzzle pictures resolve themselves into a proper picture instead of a waste of coloured dots when we look through them, focusing either "on infinity" or on some image reflected in the glass of the picture.

   Among the images and spiritual exercises that Plotinus offers is that of the Intelligible Sphere.

Let there be in the soul the shining imagination of a sphere, having everything within it ... Keep this, and apprehend another in your mind, taking away the mass: take away also the places, and the mental picture of matter ... calling on the god who made that of which you have the mental picture, pray him to come. And may he come, bringing his own universe with him. (V.8 [31].9, 8ff.)[16]

132

But this particular abstract exercise is perhaps of less interest to most of us than the simple operations of ordinary love. Learning to be lovers is a lifelong enterprise, a gradual awakening from greed and ignorance to get some sense of our beloved's own real being. "No eye ever saw the sun without becoming sun-like, nor can a soul see beauty without becoming beautiful" (I.6 [1].9, 30f.; see Plato *Republic* 6.508b3).

The ethical dimension

Those who classify Plotinus as a "mystic", or at least as a contemplative philosopher, sometimes conclude that he has little to tell us about the ordinarily moral (O'Brien 1964: 19). This is only even partly plausible on a conception of morality that confines it to our outward dealings with other human beings. This is not what it once was. Hadot points out that the later treatises especially, written while Plotinus faced his death, concern themselves with how to live well and decently. Plotinus certainly thought that the gods transcended civic virtue (I.2 [19].7), and that action was a sort of weakness, a failure, in a way, to live up to contemplative virtue. Doing the right thing depends on being able to see the right (see V.1 [10].11: justice and beauty need to be possessed by intellect as standards for discursive reasoning), and perhaps to see that nothing more is needed. At the very least, like Aristotle, Plotinus thought that a truly courageous person would not actually want to display courage, since that depends on there being wrongs to resist or even wars to fight (VI.8 [39].5). "Pity would be no more, if we did not make somebody poor" (Blake 1966: 217),[17] unless "pity" is also a name for a better condition that does not need to act. Virtues are purifications (I.2 [19].4f.), and action here in the world should issue from those virtues. Plotinus is robust in this, and doesn't advise rebellion either for slaves or for citizens. Rebellion, after all, doesn't change anything much even when it succeeds. What is of more importance is to focus on what really matters, and not to think oneself injured simply by the ordinary mishaps of this life. Bullies will get their karmic reward, and those whom they bully should face up to them. Tyrants rule by the weakness of their subjects (III.2 [47].8), and "the law says those who fight bravely, not those who pray, are to come safe out of the wars" (III.2 [47].32, 36f.). But the point is not *just* to "stand up and fight", but to know what one is fighting for, and what threats are unreal (most, he thinks, are no more than children's bogeys (I.4 [46].8)). Being tortured is very unpleasant (for the outer self), but it happens because too many people regard it as a threat sufficient to turn them away from right-doing. Remembering that the inner self is not affected (at the least, one is no worse a person for being tortured) ensures that tyrants can no longer get their way so easily by threatening this.

Contemplation is to be preferred to action, but it does not follow that what is done (or not done) is of no account. Porphyry records Plotinus's fury when specious arguments were offered for the thesis that pupils should have sex with their master, if the master wished it (*Life of Plotinus*, 15.7ff.: Armstrong 1966–88: 1, 43). "He refused to take medicines containing the flesh of wild beasts, giving as his reason that he did not approve of eating the flesh even of domestic animals" (*Life of Plotinus*, 2.4: Armstrong 1966–88: 1, 5). He looked after the property of the orphans left in his care, in case they turned out not to be philosophers (*Life of Plotinus*, 9.14: Armstrong 1966–88: 1, 31). He dissuaded Porphyry from suicide.[18] In short, he reasoned his way to understanding what to do, or not do, and, on Porphyry's account, maintained that way. Nor did he avoid the larger issue: what is the source of the law? That Minos (VI.9 [9].7) brought the laws down from his colloquy with Zeus may be a historical claim, but it is expressly also an allegorical one (see also Plato, *Laws*, 1.624). And Plotinus wanted to found a city, not just a university with support staff (*Life of Plotinus*, 12.4: Armstrong 1966–88: 1, 37)! How would it have been governed? Not necessarily by an inspired few (who are *very* few), although the Delphic Oracle claimed Plotinus was one such:

> often, when your mind was thrusting out by its own impulse along crooked paths the Immortals raised you by a straight path to the heavenly circuits, the divine way, sending down a solid shaft of light so that your eyes could see out of the mournful darkness.
> (quoted by Porphyry, *Life of Plotinus*, 22.35ff.; see also 23.17ff.)

Plotinus describes how, in the absence of such inspiration, an assembly can move to a correct or more correct decision (VI.5 [23].10), by consensus. Each of us is only one face or facet of the truth, and so can learn from others.

Plotinus concludes from this same fact that it would be wrong to make cities only out of equals; cities, like the world itself, need all sorts and ranks of creatures (III.2 [47].11, 13ff.). A little alarmingly, to our taste, he is also willing to consider that

> there is no accident in a man's becoming a slave, nor is he taken prisoner in war by chance, nor is outrage done on his body without due cause, but he was once the doer of that which he now suffers; and a man who made away with his mother will be made away with by a son when he has become a woman, and one who has raped a woman will be a woman in order to be raped.   (III.2 [47].11, 13ff.)

At the same time (and in the very same treatise), Plotinus suggests that "we should be spectators of murders, and all deaths, and takings and sacking of cities, as if they were on the stages of theatres" (III.2 [47].15, 44f.). Such things are no more than children's games: "one must not take weeping and lamenting as evidence of the presence of evils, for children, too, weep and wail over things that are not evils" (III.2 [47].15, 61). The whole is beautiful, or as beautiful as it could be, despite or even because of its evil-seeming parts, "just as the public executioner, who is a scoundrel, does not make his well-governed city worse" (III.2 [47].17, 87f.).

Beauty is woven, in this world, from brighter and darker threads, and there is no prospect of making a new "better" world (II.9 [33].5, 24f.). "In this city [of the world] virtue is honoured and vice has its appropriate dishonour, and not merely the images of gods but gods themselves [the stars] look down on us from above" (II.9 [33].9, 19ff.). At the same time, there is another world than this, and we must make our way there without despising this one.

> It does no good at all to say "Look to God", unless one also teaches how one is to look ... In reality it is virtue which goes before us to the goal and, when it comes to exist in the soul along with wisdom, shows God; but God, if you talk about him without true virtue, is only a name. Again, despising the universe and the gods in it and the other noble things is certainly not becoming good ... For anyone who feels affection for anything at all shows kindness to all that is akin to the object of his affection, and to the children of the father that he loves. But every soul is a child of That Father.
>
> (II.9 [33].15, 33–16.10).

Every soul, in fact, is Aphrodite.[19]

> When it is there [that is, in the intelligible realm] it has the heavenly love, but here love becomes vulgar; for the soul there is the heavenly Aphrodite, but here becomes the vulgar Aphrodite, a kind of whore. And every soul is Aphrodite ... The soul then in her natural state is in love with God and wants to be united with him; it is like the noble love of a girl for her noble father. (VI.9 [9].9, 28ff.)

The Delphic Oracle and Porphyry conclude their account of Plotinus's life with the expectation that he has gone to be a companion of those who "set the dance of immortal love".[20] "There the most blessed spirits have their birth and live a life filled full of festivity and joy; and this life lasts for ever, made blessed by the gods." Modern materialists are bound to consider that a dream, and reckon that *this* life is all that we can realistically expect. Plotinus, conversely, reckons that such materialists are themselves asleep (III.6 [26].6, 65f.). But even if he were wrong to think that life here is an image (or occasionally a caricature or parody) of life There, his dream may still be needed.

> Our country from which we came is There, our Father is There. How shall we travel to it, where is our way of escape? We cannot get there on foot; for our feet only carry us everywhere in this world, from one country to another. You must not get ready a carriage, either, or a boat. Let all these things go, and do not look. Shut your eyes, and change to and wake another way of seeing, which everyone has but few use. (I.6 [1].8, 22ff.)

That "other way of seeing" relies on argument and imagery, but also on a virtuous intention. At the very least *The Enneads* are a record of a serious attempt at understanding both science and virtue, and a significant influence on later theorists and poets from Augustine to Yeats.

Notes

1. Porphyry (232–*c*.306 CE) was Phoenician by birth, and himself the author of writings "against the Christians", which have not survived, and *On Abstinence from Killing Animals*, which was the first and for centuries the only work of a professional philosopher to argue for an animal-friendly vegetarianism (see Clark 2000).
2. That indeed was what Longinus thought of the copies Amelius had sent him (Porphyry, *Life of Plotinus*, 19f.: Armstrong 1966–88: 1, 53ff.; all quotations are from this translation).
3. Since the only other "Enneads" are the groups of nine Egyptian gods known, for example, at Memphis or Heliopolis, it may seem that Porphyry had some esoteric reference in mind; if he did, we don't know what it was. On the possible connections between Egyptian and neo-Platonic doctrine, see Iversen (1984).
4. Plotinus, *Enneads*, VI.9 [9].11, 51 (Armstrong 1966–88: 7, 345 prefers "escape in solitude to the solitary"). This is the phrase with which Porphyry elected to close *The Enneads*, although the treatise is the ninth in chronological order. The reference is to the 51st line of the eleventh paragraph of the ninth treatise in Book VI. Plotinus's own last words, apparently, were: "Try to bring back the god in you to the divine in the all" (Porphyry, *Life of Plotinus*, 2.26f.: Armstrong 1966–88: 1, 7).
5. Those imagining themselves to be short of time may perhaps still profit from examining only the first book. MacKenna found those treatises "the dreariest and least tempting of his wares" (MacKenna 1991: xviii), but the judgement is a puzzling one, not least because MacKenna chose *On Beauty* (*Ennead* I.6 [1]) as the first to translate.
6. Either he later changed his mind (see below), or this is, as is quite likely, part of an

argument in process. It is unwise to infer Plotinus's "own opinion" from passing remarks or even apparently compelling arguments. *The Enneads* are a record of debate, even if there is an underlying, unchallenged, framework.

7. Euripides fr 486 Nauck, cited from Aristotle *Nicomachean Ethics* 5.1129b28f. See also *Ennead* VI.6 [34].6, 40), where Plotinus calls justice "an intellectual statue".

8. *The Odyssey* recounts Odysseus's travel homewards, his failures and escapes from those who would kill or hinder him. Like other Greek heroes he was often taken to stand for all humanity, and his adventures with the Lotus-eaters, the Cyclops, Circe the witch, Calypso the goddess and so on were given allegorical interpretations (see Lamberton 1992).

9. Interestingly, the One also is strictly imperceptible, and holds beauty as a screen before itself (I.6 [1].9, 39). All that sense or intellect can ever perceive is form; the difference is in the way we see. Looking "down" towards matter, we see rubble; looking "up", to the One, we see order.

10. The reference is to an episode in Homer's *Iliad* (I.197f), in which Athena (the goddess of good sense) recalls Achilles from a murderous rage.

11. This is Plotinus's defence against the charge that the world is too full of killings to be admired. Killings, he says, are only transformations of one thing into another, or steppings aside so that others can take the stage. Without these exchanges "there would be a barren absence of life".

12. *Ennead* III.4 [15]. 6, 19f., after Plato *Timaeus* 41d6ff.; see Julian of Norwich (1966: 118): "in every soul to be saved is a godly will that has never consented to sin".

13. Citing Homer (*Iliad* 20.65), who uses the phrase of Hades (that is, of the Unseen).

14. See *Ennead* II.9 [33].4. This is one of the issues on which "pagan" and Christian Platonists most often disagreed, although the content of their disagreement is not altogether clear.

15. Plotinus interprets the archaic sequence of Ouranos, Kronos and Zeus as an allegory of the One, Intellect and Soul: Kronos is etymologized as *koros*, satiety, or *kouros*, son, and *nous*, intellect; Zeus as *zen*, to live (see V.1 [10].7).

16. Dillon (1986) confirms that the exercise has its effects.

17. From "The Human Abstract" (*Songs of Experience*); see also Aristotle (*Nicomachean Ethics* 10.1178b7ff.).

18. See *Enneads* I.9 [16]; cf. I.4 [46].7–8. Armstrong (1, 320) very oddly remarks that since I.9 [16] was written before Porphyry joined Plotinus "it cannot represent the arguments Plotinus used to discourage Porphyry from suicide" (*Life of Plotinus*, 11). It is true that Plotinus does change tack a little between I.9 [16] and I.4 [46], which concedes that there will be occasions when suicide is at least permissible (when it is impossible to live well in slavery, or one's pains are entirely too much to bear), although not obligatory.

19. Aphrodite was the Greek goddess of love, two of whose aspects (*Ourania* and *Pandemos*) were allegorized by Plato in his *Symposium*, as the "heavenly" and the "vulgar" Aphrodite respectively. Mythologically, Aphrodite was either the child of Ouranos or the child of Zeus. Plotinus takes her to be the child of Zeus, which is to say that each individual soul, including the World Soul herself, is an instance of the one original Soul.

20. "... *khoron sterixan erotos athanatou*" (Porphyry, *Life of Plotinus*, 23.36f., after 22.54ff.). The words are not Plotinus's, but still Plotinian: "*sterizein*" means "to establish, or set firm", but what is thus established is a *dance* (cf. II.9 [33].7, 36f. on the fate of the tortoise who does not manage to range itself with the movement of the dance).

Bibliography

Adamson, P. 2003. *The Arabic Plotinus: A Philosophical Study of "The Theology of Aristotle".* London: Duckworth.

Armstrong, A. H. (trans.) 1966–88. *Plotinus, The Enneads.* Loeb Classical Library, London: Heinemann.

Armstrong, A. H. 1967. "Plotinus", in *The Cambridge History of Later Greek and Early Medieval Philosophy*, 195–268. Cambridge: Cambridge University Press.

Armstrong, A. H. & R. A. Markus 1960. *Christian Faith and Greek Philosophy.* London: Darton, Longman & Todd.

Atkinson, M. J. (ed.) 1983. *Plotinus' Ennead V.1.* Oxford: Oxford University Press.

Blake, W. 1966. *Complete Writings*, G. Keynes (ed.). Oxford: Clarendon Press.

Brisson, L. & J. F. Pradeau 2002. *Traités 1–6.* Paris: Flammarion.

Clark, G. (trans.) 2000. *Porphyry: On Abstinence from Killing Animals.* London: Duckworth.

Clark, S. R. L. 1996. "Body and Mind", in *The Cambridge Companion to Plotinus*, Lloyd Gerson (ed.), 275–91. Cambridge: Cambridge University Press.

Corrigan, K. 2002. *Reading Plotinus: A Practical Introduction to Neoplatonism.* Ashford, OH: Purdue University Press.

Deck, J. N. 1995. *Nature, Contemplation and the One.* New York: Larson Publications.

Dillon, J. 1986. "Plotinus and the Transcendental Imagination" in *Religious Imagination*, J. P. Mackey (ed.), 55–64. Edinburgh: Edinburgh University Press; reprinted in J. Dillon, *The Golden Chain* (Aldershot: Variorum Press, 1990), 58ff.

Dufour, R. 2002. *Plotinus: A Bibliography* 1950–2000. Leiden: Brill.

Gerson, L. (ed.) 1996. *The Cambridge Companion to Plotinus.* Cambridge: Cambridge University Press.

Gerson, L. 1994. *Plotinus.* London: Routledge.

Hadot, P. 1993. *Plotinus: The Simplicity of Vision*, M. Chase (trans.). Chicago, IL: University of Chicago Press.

Henry, P. & H.-R. Schwyzer 1964–82. *Plotini Opera.* Oxford: Clarendon Press.

Iversen, E. 1984. *Egyptian and Hermetic Doctrine.* Copenhagen: Museum Tusculanum Press.

James, W. 1890. *The Principles of Psychology.* New York: Macmillan.

Julian of Norwich 1966. *Revelations of Divine Love*, C. Wolters (trans.). Harmondsworth: Penguin.

Lamberton, R. 1992. *Homer the Theologian: Neoplatonist Allegorical Reading and the Growth of the Epic Tradition.* Berkeley, CA: University of California Press.

Lloyd, A. C. 1990. *The Anatomy of Neo-Platonism.* Oxford: Oxford University Press.

MacKenna, S. (trans.) 1991. *Plotinus: The Enneads*, J. Dillon (ed.). Harmondsworth: Penguin (an abridged edition of the original 1956 Faber edition).

Malin, S. 2001. *Nature Loves to Hide.* New York: Oxford University Press.

Miles, M. 1999. *Plotinus on Body and Beauty.* Oxford: Blackwell.

O'Brien, E. (trans.) 1964. *The Essential Plotinus.* Indianapolis, IN: Hackett.

O'Meara, D. 1993. *Plotinus: An Introduction to the Enneads.* Oxford: Clarendon Press.

Rappe, S. 2000. *Reading Neo-Platonism: Non-discursive Thinking in the Texts of Plotinus, Proclus and Damascius.* Cambridge: Cambridge University Press.

Rist, J. 1967. *Plotinus: The Road to Reality.* Cambridge: Cambridge University Press.

Spenser, E. 1912. *Poetical Works of Spenser*, J. C. Smith & E. de Selincourt (eds). Oxford: Oxford University Press.

Wallis, T. 1992. *Neo-Platonism*. London: Duckworth.
Weil, S. 1956. *Notebooks*, A. F. Mills (trans.). London: Routledge & Kegan Paul.

Further reading

For modern translations of *The Enneads*, it would be best to read A. H. Armstrong's translation for the Loeb Classical Library (London: Heinemann, 1966–88). S. MacKenna's translation, edited by John Dillon (Harmondsworth: Penguin, 1991; an abridged edition of the 1956 Faber edition), is more readily available, but a lot more difficult to follow.

Alternative introductory selections include Elmer O'Brien's *The Essential Plotinus* (1964: I.6 [1], V.9 [5], IV.8 [6], VI.9 [9], V.1 [10], V.2 [11], I.2 [19], I.3 [20], IV.3 [27], III.8 [30]). Dominic O'Meara's short *Introduction to the Enneads* (1993) selects passages for discussion from throughout the corpus. Luc Brisson and J. F. Pradeau have produced a French translation and commentary on "the first six treatises" (counting chronologically); namely, I.6 *On Beauty*, IV.7 *On the Immortality of the Soul*, III.1 *On Destiny*, IV.2 *On the Essence of the Soul*, V.9 *On Intellect, Forms and Being*, and IV.8 *On the Descent of the Soul*. Other modern introductions to Plotinus's thought include Armstrong's (1967), Corrigan's (2002), Deck's (1995), Gerson's (1994), Miles's (1999) and Rist's (1967). A detailed bibliography of recent work has been produced by Richard Dufour (2002), and is kept up to date at http://rdufour.free.fr/BibPlotin/Anglais/Biblio.html (accessed Oct. 2004).

6

Augustine

City of God

Christopher Kirwan

Introducing the man and the work

Augustine is one of the most influential authors who have ever existed; perhaps only Aristotle has had more effect through his writings on the development of Western culture. That does not in itself make Augustine a fit subject for a volume concerned with philosophy; but I shall try to show that in fact he does qualify to be counted among the philosophers, in our narrow contemporary Anglophone understanding of the word, even though his place among them is not in the premier division (he did not lack the aptitude, I believe, but he did lack the training, and the time).

The reason why Augustine can be counted as one of our founding philosophers is that among the voluminous writings that survive from him (more words than from any other ancient author) many contain discussion of what in our tradition are instantly recognizable as philosophical problems, conducted at an instantly recognizable standard of step-by-step reasoning: put otherwise, he has a place in the line of succession that stretches to us over 25 centuries from Parmenides and Socrates in the fifth century BCE. Within the collection of these philosophy-rich works stands, perhaps pre-eminently, *City of God*. In a later section I shall outline its structure; but first let us see how it came to be written, who was the man who wrote it, and in what ways that man, although mainly famous for non-philosophical reasons, nevertheless ranks among the philosophers.

We have to imagine ourselves in the summer of 410 CE, and the month of August. Augustine, a citizen of the Roman Empire, who would soon come to be revered among western Christians as "saint" and "doctor", was nearly 56 years old and had been bishop for 14 years of Hippo Regius (now Annaba, Algeria), a maritime North African city in the province of Numidia. In that month the city of Rome was sacked by a Gothic army under Alaric. Although famine and atrocities were rife and widely reported, Alaric, himself a Christian (of the persuasion loosely called "Arian" in the West), respected the major Christian sanctuaries of the city, which already included old St Peter's amongst other shrines. In any case, Rome had been expecting trouble since 140 years before, when the emperor Aurelian had provided it with walls, still today partly standing. For all that, the shock in 410 CE was great. Rome was *the* imperial city; it had been secure for *eight* centuries, since Gaulish raiders destroyed most of it around 396 BCE. It had long been the centre of a vast and moderately peaceful Empire. Although no longer the seat of imperial government, which had become split (since 330 CE) between Constantinople – "new Rome" – in the east and (since 404 CE) Ravenna in the west, Rome retained all its old glory and prestige, nourished by nearly 1,200 years of history, by magnificent buildings dating from the first to the fourth centuries (some impressive to this day), by old noble families who often still clung to their pagan past, and by a bishop (it was Innocent I at the time) whose office was already held in high regard, especially in the West, by reason of the tradition of its foundation by Peter, the "rock" on whom Jesus had promised to build his church (Matthew 16:18–19). After the sack refugees flocked to nearby Africa. If only for that reason a response was called for. Augustine preached sermons on the topic. A major theme was to rebut accusations that the disaster was due to neglect of the old pagan gods.

People could hardly fail to notice that Rome's disaster coincided with the Christianization of the Empire. Christianity had been tolerated and indeed favoured for a century, but the process of establishing the new religion became serious only 19 years before the sack, when an edict of Theodosius I (Codex Theodosianus 16.10.10, 391 CE) effectively put other worship under a civil ban. From that date action proceeded steadily; in 399 CE, for example, commissioners had arrived at Carthage in Africa to oversee destruction of its pagan temples (*City* 18.31.2). This then was the generation, coinciding with Augustine's ministry, in which for the first time all classes in the Empire found themselves under government pressure to show allegiance, or at least deference, to the Christian church.

Augustine is historically important because he saw this new opportunity and was eager and competent to grasp it. Various of his writings testify to his musing on the proper place of Christians in these "tempora Christiana" and, more widely, on God's design in bringing mankind up to, and henceforward onwards from, the dispensation newly prevailing throughout the known world. Every reflective person in the Empire, looking back over the past four centuries, would now recognize the same historical progression: Jesus the Galilean, having passed his earthly life in what had then recently become a corner of the Roman Empire, had sent forth apostles; and thanks to that Empire their evangelical work seemed to be approaching completion at last. What, asked Augustine, should one make of it? And how should one see the broader scene of human history into which such amazing events had entered? There are hints that he had been maturing his response to these questions before 410 CE (*Cat. Rud.* 19.31, *Gen. Lit.* 11.15.20). The sack of Rome provided an occasion for putting the response into words.

Who was the man who used this occasion? He was, above all, a controversialist, fond of argument, rational in using it, and adept at using it in writing against whatever he saw as error; and at the same time he was a convinced and unwavering Christian, and burdened with the administrative and pastoral cares of episcopal office. His life can be told briefly. Born in 354 CE, he had grown up in a heavily Christian region. His mother Monica was a Christian, his father Patricius not. Patronage from a neighbour in his inland home town of Thagaste (now Souk-Ahras in Algeria) helped to secure him a traditional education in grammar and literature that would have been recognizable in Cicero and Virgil's day four centuries earlier, and that was still designed to equip a boy for a career – by this time wearisome but still honourable – as a leading citizen of the Empire or of some city within it (but unlike most literary westerners before him he was never at ease with Greek; *Conf.* 1.13.20). After schooling, Augustine attended university at Carthage, once the centre of Rome's chief enemy but long since re-established as metropolis of the western half of the north African seaboard. At first he led an unrestrained life there, joining a fraternity called the Smashers and frequenting indecent theatrical festivals (he will deprecate them obsessively in *City of God*, e.g. 2.4, 2.26.2); but soon he settled down with a concubine and a son by her, and attached himself to the Manichees, a rigorist sect whose theology and cosmology differed strikingly from that of mainstream – as he himself would come to say, "Catholic" – Christianity. After nine years of Manichaean allegiance Augustine fell out with the sect and, by now a self-employed professor of rhetoric, moved to Rome and in 384 CE to Milan, where the western imperial government then temporarily sat. At Milan he was introduced to a group of Christian Platonists, who owed their philosophical outlook to the third-century Greek-speaking pagan philosopher and contemplative Plotinus. At the same time he felt the force of the local bishop Ambrose, a man of serious political power and lasting doctrinal influence on western Christianity. This was the ambience in which Augustine, after much hesitation and in a scene made famous in his *Confessions* (8.12.29), embraced the Christian message of Paul (Romans 13:13), including its call to chastity (with a marriage in prospect his concubine had already been dismissed – but replaced; the marriage was abandoned; his teenage son remained with him, but died a few years later). He returned to Thagaste and there set up a semi-monastic community for the study of philosophy. But soon, on a visit to the African coast in 391 CE, he was seized by the Catholic congregation at Hippo and pressed to accept ordination, first as presbyter and after 396 CE as sole bishop. He served in that office until his death 34 years later in 430 CE.

His writings had begun before ordination: philosophical works, mainly influenced by his education and by Platonism. But from 391 CE the character of his published output changed, as he quickly took his place as the chief Catholic apologist in Africa, and before long as a spokesman of Empire-wide reputation. His opponents were threefold: the Donatists, adherents of an African schism dating from the Great Persecution before Constantine I's "peace of the church" in 313 CE, and more numerous in Hippo than Catholics; his old coreligionists the Manichees; and later, beginning to engage him only after some of *City of God* had already been written, the British-born charismatic Pelagius, who had fled from Rome before Alaric's sack, dispersing disciples and controversial doctrine (see "Free will", below). Amid and as part of the polemical writings Augustine had also, notably, found time to compose his *Confessions* (late 390s), a self-examination addressed publicly to God. Readers of *City of God* can easily see that he was a born teacher, perhaps especially in his splendid digressions and elaborations (e.g. on the perfect number six, *City* 11.30; on why it is that when dead we are not dying, although when asleep we are sleeping, *City* 13.9–11; on the exact longevity of the patriarchs, *City* 15.10–14; on the demonstration he had witnessed of a magnet, *City* 21.4.4).

The development of his thought cannot be charted here, beyond saying that it became more sombre as his biblical knowledge, his experience of his flock, and the Empire's troubles deepened.

Augustine's Bible was the "Old Latin", a set of variable and uncoordinated translations from two sources: for the Old Testament, from the Greek Septuagint, itself a translation from Hebrew started in the third century BCE (Augustine comments on it at *City* 8.11, 18.42–4), which in some parts differs markedly from the texts that are today received by both Jews and Christians; and for the New Testament, from the original Greek. In both Testaments the Old Latin came to be superseded during Augustine's lifetime by the version, now known as "Vulgate", made from the original languages by his irascible but scholarly contemporary Jerome (?331– 420 CE); and as the composition of *City of God* progressed, Augustine seems to have become increasingly willing to prefer Jerome's text (see the discussions at *City* 15.10–14, 18.42–4, 20.21ff., 22.29.2). Scholarship since the Renaissance has made sundry further changes, generally minor (e.g. to the numeration of the Psalms; see note 2). Augustine's biblical canon is the same as that of modern Christians – including the Apocrypha, although by his day Jews no longer admitted it (*City* 17.20.1, 18.36; his own use of the word "apocrypha" at *City* 15.23.4 refers to different intertestamental texts).

He kept copies of his writings, and in 426–7 CE surveyed 93 of them in a work called *Retractationes* (i.e. "Reviews": the Latin "retractare" means "re-treat", not "retract"). We also possess more than 300 of his letters – or in some cases letters addressed to him – on themes theological, political and pastoral (we really see the man there); and about 550 sermons, out of several thousand that he is reckoned to have preached, all apparently extempore but recorded by shorthand writers present in church, usually at Hippo or Carthage. At the time of his death the western half of the Empire was in what turned out to be terminal decay. A tribe of Vandal invaders, Christian but "Arian", who had crossed the Rhine and then Gaul and Spain and the strait of Gibraltar, was besieging Hippo, which fell to them shortly afterwards. Seemingly Augustine's library was sent abroad soon after his death – perhaps also his body, which is claimed by Pavia in Italy. Experts reckon that the earliest surviving manuscript of *City of God*, Veronensis 28 containing books 11–16, was written in Africa in the early fifth century (O'Daly 1999: 275; could it be his own library copy?—it cannot be an autograph, because he dictated, *Ep*. 139.3). The Vandals' rule in Africa lasted until they were ousted by Belisarius under the eastern emperor Justinian in 533 CE; but that recovery gave way to Arab conquest after 698 CE, since when the region has been in Moslem hands save for a period of French colonial rule. Hardly anything remains of Roman Hippo.

In western Christendom Augustine's writings have never ceased to command respect and attention. *City of God* comes about seventh in the list of our earliest printed texts (Subiaco 1467; see Drobner 2000: 19). The Reformation and Counter-Reformation were, in their theological aspect, to a remarkable extent a dispute about Augustine's doctrines (Luther had been an Augustinian friar). Today the bibliography in the *Revue des études augustiniennes* lists more than 300 items per annum (Drobner 2000: 19).

Access to his writings is not altogether straightforward (see Bibliography for the abbreviations that follow). Everything known in the late seventeenth century (so excluding some sermons and letters subsequently identified in scattered libraries) was splendidly edited by the Benedictine monks of St Maur (Paris 1679–

1700), and is reprinted in PL; and for much, there are better modern texts in CCL and CSEL. The Cetedoc Library of Christian Latin Texts (Louvain, www.fltr.ucl. ac.be/publications/cetedoc), the Augustinus-Lexicon (Würzburg, www. augustinus.de) and Past Masters (Charlottesville VA, www.nlx.com) all claim to offer the complete works on CD-ROM, in one edition or another. Modern trans-lations are not complete: BA is quite extensive (in French, with text); in English there are various particular works, also various series on the "Fathers" such as ACW, FC, LCC, NPNF and, aiming at completeness on Augustine himself but not yet including *City of God*, AHI (also available on CD-ROM and by subscrip-tion on line: www.nlx.com). In addition, many of the passages I cite are translated in Dyson (2001). The division of his works into "books", an ancient custom, is his own; but the division into chapters and in some cases sections of chapters was probably made later.

Augustine as a philosopher

"Philosophers" enter *City of God* as adversaries at book 5, and later he speaks of "[the] philosophers, against whose misrepresentations [calumnias] we are defending the city of God" (*City* 13.16.1). Sometimes he mocks them (*City* 18.24), especially for disagreeing among themselves (*City* 18.41.1). But he knows that philosophy does not have to be hostile to the gospel message.

The extent of his own philosophical formation is not known to us. He had read Aristotle's *Categories* (in Latin translation, *Conf.* 4.16.28); there are plenti-ful signs of his knowledge (secondary, but so is our own) of the Stoic tradition that had been vigorous for many centuries down to about 200 CE; and no one can doubt the debt that he incurred during his Italian years to the more recently revived Platonism. Before that crucial experience he had already composed one work, *De Pulchro et Apto* [On the Beautiful and the Fitting], but it is lost. Every one of his writings that we possess comes from the 44 years during which he was a thinking Christian, and the dominant themes after his ordination are pastoral and doctrinal. So where is the philosophy?

In *City of God* he was to write, with seeming approval: "men philosophise for no other reason than to be happy [nulla est homini causa philosophandi nisi ut beatus sit]" (*City* 19.1.3).[1] This quotation tells us something, but not much. It tells where he got his conception of philosophy from, for the sentiment comes from the Roman antiquarian Varro (see below) and beyond question Varro will have got it from Socrates and Plato. It tells us also that, in this classical tradi-tion, "philosophy" was seen as not merely a way of enquiry but a way of life (for a vivid sketch see Brown (1995: 34–8)). On the other hand, we have to look further if we are to see whether Augustine's works contain philosophy in *our* sense of the word. Although for himself he ceased to claim membership among "philosophers" early in his Christian career, we with our different perspective ought not to agree. Scattered through many of his works can be found both of the two marks of our discipline: (i) method and (ii) topic.

(i) When in philosophical vein, he explicates questions when necessary, and answers them with arguments, occasionally formal (e.g. *City* 2.13), and with critique of opposing arguments. The quotations in this chapter will give a little of the flavour. However, readers must beware that Augustine is not willing to question the veracity of the Bible, in which he finds plenty of obscurity but never falsehood (*City* 18.41.1); reason may supplement its authority (e.g. *City* 19.1.1, 21.2), but can never override it.

(ii) As for topic, Augustine makes useful, sometimes notable, contributions to all of the following: scepticism, the nature of time, minds and bodies, free will and determinism, ethical principles (e.g. spirituality; and the rash-seeming admonition to "love, and do what you will", *Ep. Joh.* 7.8), consequentialism (he is against it, see Kirwan (1999)), philosophy of language (in which he advances well beyond the travesty presented by Wittgenstein, see Kirwan (2001)), ideal-ist metaphysics (he follows the Platonists, not the Stoics). Many of these topics get an airing in *City of God*, which unintentionally goes some way towards furnishing a compendium of his contributions to the discipline. My aim in this chapter is to comment on the various parts of that contribution in *City of God*, the nuggets in a greater whole that is best regarded as itself exceeding the bounds of philosophy, the work's overall purpose being to reject the pretensions of paganism and to define the place of Christian men and women in history and society. On that grand theme I shall offer only oblique comment in what follows.

The sources, title, and structure of *City of God*

The document on which Augustine mainly relies is, of course, the Bible. Paul's letters are central. But *City of God* is also peppered with commentary on classi-cal writers, for Augustine the "ancients [veteres]". The most important are fellow Latin authors: Varro, antiquarian, 116–27 BCE, all works lost to us; Cicero, statesman and philosopher, 106–43 BCE, most works surviving for us; Sallust, historian, *c.*86–35 BCE, some works surviving; and Virgil, poet, 70–19 BCE, all major works surviving. Among philosophers he also refers to Plato (mainly *Timaeus*), Aristotle, the Stoics Zeno (335–263 BCE, works lost) and Chrysippus (*c.*280–207 BCE, works lost), and some others, all Greek; but his main attention is on the more recent authors Apuleius (a fellow African, writing in Latin, b. *c.* 123 CE, works surviving), Plotinus (Greek but available to Augustine in Latin translation, works surviving), and Plotinus's editor and biographer Porphyry (232/3–*c.*306 CE, also Greek but also available to Augustine in translation, works now largely lost). These last three, although pagan, were "Platonists" and, as such, thinkers towards whom, because of his conversion history, Augustine was disposed to show serious respect; Porphyry in particular, "most learned of the philosophers though sharpest critic of Christianity" (*City* 19.22), had come close to Augustine's theology. He also owes something to the writings of the Hellenizing Jew Philo (*c.*20 BCE–*c.*50 CE, Greek, works surviving), who had influenced Ambrose. In *City of God* 15–18 he makes use of the *Chronica* of Eusebius (Bishop of Caesaria, *c.*260–*c.*340 CE), known to him and to us in Jerome's Latin adaptation. *City of God* 21 appears to draw on the elder Pliny, encyclopedist (23/4–79 CE, Latin, works surviving).

We cannot tell exactly by what stages *City of God* grew. Already in a sermon preached probably in 410 CE Augustine had given careful reasons to his congregation (he always liked to give reasons, but as simply as possible to simple people) for thinking it "false, what they say of our Christ, that he is Rome's destroyer, and that the gods of stone and of wood were her protectors" (*Serm.* 105.9.12). Probably he started on the "huge work" (*City* 22.30.6) in 412 CE, and it was finished by 426 CE, four years before his death. Its early books are addressed to a high Roman official Marcellinus, to whom Augustine had adumbrated the project in a letter of 412 CE (*Ep.*138).

Our MSS give the title as *De Civitate Dei contra Paganos*. "City of God" comes from Psalm 86/87:3.[2] Augustine contrasts two cities, one of God or heavenly, the other earthly, which are intermingled among living men until the General Resurrection. The idea of a city (civitas, *polis*) defined not by location but by the allegiance of its citizens (*City* 1.15.2) probably begins with the Stoic Chrysippus, and is mentioned by Cicero and others (see references in Schofield (1991)). The psalmist's city of God had been Jerusalem, and in Christian times John the Divine had pictured a new Jerusalem coming down out of heaven at the last days (Revelation = Apocalypse 21:2). Augustine exploits this image of development from an Old to a New Covenant; but he follows various precursors in repositioning the new city among living Christians (contrast Hebrews 13:14), at the same time eschewing the triumphalist vision, which may have tempted him earlier, that the city of God can be identified with an earthly Christian regime such as the Empire had become (see Markus 1988: 33–44); rather, its citizens remain "pilgrims" here (peregrini, literally "resident foreigners" – an idea already in Philo, see Schofield (1991: 77 n.26), cf. Hebrews 11:13), and do not even coincide with the church (e.g. *City* 15.1.2, 18.23.2, where Abel and the Sibyl are admitted; *City* 1.35, 21.25, where some of the baptized are excluded – your city depends on your chief love, *City* 14.28). *Contra Paganos* is not in the title used by Augustine himself in his review at *Retractationes* 2.69. It indicates the work's polemical purpose rather than its intended readership, which is likely to have been mainly Christian; Marcellinus was a Christian, and pagans appear in it as "they" not "you".

There is not space to give a summary here of the contents of the work. Its structure is well explained by Augustine himself at the end of book 10:

> Of these [first] ten books, the first five [1–5] have been written against those who think that the [Roman] gods should be worshipped for the sake of the good things of life, the second five [6–10] against those [philosophers] who hold that worship of the gods should be preserved for the sake of the life that is to come after death. Next therefore, as we promised in the first book, I shall set out, so far as I receive divine help, what I think needs to be said about the origin [11–14], the progress [15–18] and the due ends [debitis finibus, 19–22] of the two cities that, as we have said, are interwoven and mixed up together in the present age.
>
> (*City* 10.32.4; cf. *Ep.* 1A, *Retract.* 2.69.1)

Throughout runs the message that pagan gods – existent, but better called demons (cf. Psalm 95/96:5) – are mischief-makers who lack even inferior dominion; Rome's early disasters prove their impotence (he never explains why it was otherwise with Israelite disasters). For book 3, readers need a modest background knowledge of republican Roman history (see e.g. Hornblower and Spawforth 2003: "Rome (History) *1*"), and for books 15–18, of the Old Testament story (see e.g. Metzger and Coggan 1993: "Genesis, Book of" and "Israel, History of").

Homicide, war and suicide: *City* 1.17–27

Using the authority of the Bible, Augustine starts from the Commandment "You shall not commit murder" (Exodus 20:13, Deuteronomy 5:17, tr. New English Bible). Many translations of the Hebrew original have preferred "kill" to "murder", and they include Augustine's Latin version "non occides", "you shall not kill" (so too the Vulgate). Despite this word, Augustine was confident that the ban is restricted to the killing of human beings, homicidium, and he mocks Manichaean idiots who imagine that it protects bushes (*City* 1.20). Furthermore he regards homicidium as in general a sin (peccatum, an ordinary word for wrongdoing), and sins must be intentional (e.g. *Du. An.* 12.17, *Lib. Arb.* 3.18.50; cf. Exodus 21:13, Numbers 35:16–29, Deuteronomy 19:4–5).

The Commandment is unqualified. How, then, is it consistent with the Hebrew Bible's accounts of God's unremitting support for Israelite bellicosity? Augustine believes that there is no inconsistency. From his reading of the scriptures he concludes that intentional killing of human beings is permitted when it is done under *authority* (*C. Faust.* 22.70);[3] for in that case, he argues, the killer is no more than a prop (adminiculum, *ibid.*; cf. "minister", *Quaest. Hept.* 6.10), who "does not himself kill" (*City* 1.21). But what about the authority? There are two kinds: divine and human. The former was at work when, for example, Abraham set out to kill his son Isaac at God's command (Genesis 22:1–18, *City* 1.21); the latter gives a general justification to the work of soldiers (*C. Faust.* 22.75) and executioners (*City* 1.21, *Lib. Arb.* 1.4.9; cf. Genesis 9:5–6). Such is the doctrine. It invites two questions: (i) how do we identify an authority's commands; and (ii) whence comes the authority's right to license homicide?

(i) Augustine admits that there can be doubt, even in the Bible, whether God has issued an "express command applicable to a particular person at a given time" (*City* 1.21). But concerning human authority he is relaxed. It is a matter of "enacted law" (*ibid.*), either imperial, or "political" in the original sense of belonging to a *polis* (civitas, city). Soldiers, says Augustine, "are not guilty of homicide under any law of their city" (*City* 1.26; cf. *Ep.* 47.5). Moreover, the powers of civil legislators are extensive (see "Political authority" below).

(ii) God's authority comes from himself; that is the starting-point of Augustine's monotheism (preponderant good must flow from a divine command, even if those who are commanded cannot discern it, *City* 5.21, 20.2). Human authority devolves from God, on to the existing regime (Proverbs 8:15, *City* 5.19). For Augustine offers no political blueprint; in letters no less than sermons his pleas for amendment concern individuals (*Ep.* 138.2.10, *City* 2.19), never, I think, institutions. "There is no power [potestas]," Paul had written, "that is not from God ... consequently anyone who rebels against a power, rebels against God's ordinance" (Romans 13:1–2, quoted e.g. at *Ep.* 93.6.20). Augustine is willing to accept this – as so much else – of Christianity's inheritance from Judaism.

The authority delegated to rulers may nevertheless be abused, and Augustine has things to say on good rulers (*City* 5.24–6). How will good rulers proceed in the matter of homicide? Augustine, well aware of the commonplace that no other animal is so aggressive as man (*City* 12.23/22[4]), has been treated from Gratian (twelfth century) onwards as founder of the Christian theory of just war (on which see, for example, Barnes (1982)). His main contribution, in fact, was to join others in repudiating earlier Christian pacifism (*Epp.* 138.2.13, 189.4–6). But in commenting on the book of Joshua (*Quaest. Hept.*, e.g. 4.14, 6.10) he does give some casual guidance about the conduct of war (in later language "ius in bello"); and concerning the justification for going to war ("ius ad bellum") one text declares that "just wars are customarily defined as those which avenge wrongs" (*Quaest. Hept.* 6.10; cf. *City* 19.7, *C. Faust.* 22.74), suggesting that the proper purpose of war – apart from self-defence (*City* 3.10) – is (collective) punishment (Langan 1984, Dyson 2001: Ch. 4). As to civil punishment, the arrival of Christian emperors had had little impact on Roman criminal procedures and penalties, beyond abandonment of crucifixion. Augustine deplores cruelty (he is fascinated, for example, by the legend of Regulus's horrible death, *City* 1.15.1), but he accepts judicial torture and execution; such things are "necessities" (*City* 19.6; cf. *Ep.* 189.6 on the "necessity" of war), although he often makes particular pleas for leniency (e.g. *Ep.* 133.1). It is central to his theodicy that human suffering can always be explained as just punishment for sin, including the "original" sin with which we are all born, as "sinners not in ourselves but in our origin [non proprie sed originaliter peccatores]" (*City* 16.27) by transmission from Adam's disobedience (see "Evil and the will" below).

Is suicide banned under the sixth Commandment? There are several reasons why Augustine's Christian contemporaries might have thought not. In Graeco-Roman culture it attracted little hostility, and many thinkers, especially Stoics, commended it as a rational response to certain afflictions or dangers (e.g. Diogenes Laërtius 7.130; Plotinus, *Enneads* 1.4.7.43, but contrast 1.9). The Bible is hardly less indulgent: although there may be no general "command or permission of it" in the "canonical books" (*City* 1.20), it is equally true that (the Commandment apart) "there is not a single text of scripture which prohibits it" (Hume 1985: 588 n.); indeed a number of suicides are recorded by biblical writers without censure and in some cases with seeming approval (e.g. Samson, Judges 16:23–31). Thirdly, suicides consent to their death, and many since Aristotle (*Nicomachean Ethics* 1136b13) had been attracted to the principle that no one can be wronged willingly. Finally, the deaths of Christian martyrs, hugely honoured in penal times and including many whose grandchildren might still be alive in the early fifth century, had sometimes come close to self-killing. This last consideration was especially topical in Augustine's Africa, because of the presence there of Donatists, who had latterly become the object of imperial persecution. The history of these people cannot be told here; what matters is that in their rancorous and often violent conflict with Catholics some of them continued to exercise a penchant for martyrdom, in excesses that were now sometimes indisputably suicidal (*Corr. Don.* 3.12).

The Donatists may have had some effect in forming Augustine's attitude to suicide. At any rate he stood against it; and it is due to him more than anyone that Christian morality stands against it still. His doctrine was simple: self-killing (he did not use the word "suicida", which is first attested in a pamphlet of the twelfth century, see Murray (1998: 38)) is homicide; sometimes, in the Bible at least, it is authorized by God (he implausibly cites Samson, *City* 1.21); otherwise, it is a sin. In killing herself, what did Lucretia do? she murdered an innocent person (*City* 1.19.2). Judas Iscariot's suicide (Matthew 27:3–5), although execution of a criminal, was unauthorized (*City* 1.17).

In 410 CE, stories came to Africa that Roman nuns had taken their own lives in order to avoid rape by some among the pillaging Goths; and this is the occasion of Augustine's careful treatment of the subject in book 1 of *City of God*. He does not consider the defence that the victim of a suicide consents. He looks at the suicides' motives. The nuns acted in order to avoid rape. But "no one can be stained by someone else's sins" (*Ep.* 93.10.36); so being raped is no sin (*City* 1.18.1). Perhaps a suicide acts in order to escape adversity (*City* 1.22), or out of despair (*Serm.* 353.3.8), or as the ultimate protection against lapse into future sin (*City* 1.27). Those too are bad motives.

Political institutions: *City* 5

Most scholars now agree that, despite the worthy "great book" tradition of some university courses in philosophy or politics, *City of God* is not an essay in political theory or political philosophy (but see TeSelle (1991) for a measured recent response to this view). Nevertheless, the work does contain a certain political or, one might say, anti-political theory, an insidious one, which may even have damaged political reconstruction in the Dark Ages of the post-Roman West: it is the theory that institutions are unimportant. "What does it matter," Augustine asks, "under what rule a man, soon to die, lives, provided that those who rule do not compel him to infringe duty and justice [ad impia et iniqua non cogant]?" (*City* 5.17.1). This seems to be an abrogation of hopes he had expressed elsewhere (e.g. *Mor. Cath.* 1.30.63, *Ep.* 155.10) that the Christian Empire would be – as in the Byzantine East it became – a monitor of morals and doctrine. Certainly the sentiment is a world away from Plato's *Republic*, and from the classical idea that it is a city's business to make its citizens good (e.g. Aristotle, *Nicomachean Ethics* 1180b25). For Augustine, the value of a political system is merely coercive (*Ep.* 153.6.16). It is not a value to be despised: "so long as the two cities are intermingled, we too take advantage of [utimur] the peace of Babylon", i.e. Rome (*City* 19.26); indeed, Christians have a duty to assist in civil administration (*City* 19.6). But there is no place in his scheme for projects of political reform. Against rulers who command what God forbids, the right response is to defy them and accept the consequences quietly, as did the martyrs (*Serm*. 62.5.8, *Ep*. 185.2.8). In heaven, all "sovereignty and human sway [principatus et potestas humana]" (*City* 19.15) will disappear. See Markus (1988: especially Ch. 4) for a seminal treatment; also generally Dyson (2001).

Political authority: *City* 19

Augustine does not discuss, either in *City of God* or elsewhere, the sources and limits of political authority, beyond the Pauline claim that rulers' powers are "from God" (Romans 13:1). But he does reveal a conception of the nature of such authority. It is that of a "dominus".

The word "dominus" was in traditional and habitual Latin use, often respectfully but sometimes censoriously, of anyone who dominates; it was used, for example, of masters in relation to their slaves (Latin "servi"). Augustine betrays no anxiety about the institution of slavery (again following Paul, e.g. Colossians 3:22; see Garnsey 1996: Ch. 11); its prime cause is sin, and as punishment for sin it preserves the natural order (*City* 19.14–15). He seems to see a similarity between the slave–master relation and that of citizen to governor or emperor (see Markus 1988: appendix B; Weithman 2001). Citizens are not actually slaves, of course: they cannot be bought or sold. On the other hand, slaves too had rights under Roman law, were sometimes accorded trust and influence, and sometimes looked forward to freedom; the word "servant" better conveys the status of many of them. Augustine agrees with Cicero that commonwealths, res publicae, must be founded on "concord" (*City* 19.24); yet within them a dominus had all powers unless constrained by law (cf. *City* 1.17), a very different conception from "no powers unless conferred by some sort of consent". That was the mindset in 410 CE; and it must have been reinforced for Christians by the choice of "dominus" to render the New Testament Greek "*kurios*", "the Lord", used of Jesus, and also to render "*kurios*" in the Septuagint, Hebrew "*adonai*", "the LORD", used of the Israelite God in place of his unutterable name. In Augustine's Bible God's followers are often spoken of as his "servi" (standardly "servant" in English translations, e.g. 2 Samuel 7:5, Romans 1:1), and this "metaphor" (Garnsey 1996: Ch. 14) was exploited by Augustine.

Within such a mindset, it is no surprise that the virtue of obedience is much on display in Augustine's works. Yet naturally he demands that dominatio be properly exercised and, like anyone else, he can sometimes deprecate it, as when he gleefully seconds Sallust's complaint that already in ancient days Rome had succumbed to "lust for lordship [libido dominandi]" (*City* 1 pref., 3.14.2, 19.14). The besetting vice of rulers is haughtiness or pride (superbia, *City* 1 pref., 19.14); "leaving justice aside, what are kingdoms but extended gangs of robbers?" (*City* 4.4).

Following age-old male pretension (contrast the reality portrayed by ancient dramatists), Augustine holds that the "servitude" owed to males by females is natural, even though aggravated by the Fall (*Gen. Lit.* 11.37.50 on Genesis 3:16). However, in sexual obligations there is *absolute* equality (e.g. *Serm.* 354A.4).

Creation and time: *City* 12

Augustine sees a problem about *beginning*, a "very difficult question" (*City* 12.22/21.1). The dominant opinion among ancient philosophers (despite apparent dissent in Plato's *Timaeus*, noted at *City* 12.13/12) had been that the world – *cosmos*, mundus – had no beginning in time, and against that view Jews and Christians alike had long been obliged to struggle in defence of the biblical doctrine of creation. The Bible contains two accounts, Genesis 1–2:3 (the six-day story) and Genesis 2:4–3:24 (Adam and Eve and the Fall). Augustine was fascinated by them. We shall see something of his treatment of the Fall under "Evil and the will". As regards creation itself he gave most attention to Genesis 1–2:3, making it the subject of no fewer than five examinations, one of them in *City of God* books 11 and 12.

According to his method, argument is not needed in support of Genesis (although *Conf.* 11.4.6 had earlier provided one, as perhaps does *City* 11.4.1), but only in reply to the objections of "philosophers" against it. He aims to show merely, as one passage has it, that "no necessity compels us, therefore, to think that the human race did not have a beginning in time from which it started to exist" (*City* 12.21/20.3). The objections that he considers in pursuit of that aim I shall divide into three.

(a) God is immutable. But if creation happened at any particular time,[5] God must have decided to do what he had previously been content not to do, thus randomly changing his mind. Augustine responds that a will to change is not a change of will: it is possible to effect a new act with a will (voluntas) or deliberation (consilium) that is not new but has existed even from eternity (*City* 11.4.2, 12.15/14, 22.2.1). Biblical references to God's repenting what he had done (e.g. Genesis 6:6 repenting of the creation of man) have to be explained away (*City* 17.7.3).

(b) God is Lord, Dominus. So he must always have had creatures to dominate. Augustine's response hinges on his Leibnizian and anti-Newtonian belief that times require change (*City* 11.6, 12.16/15.1), unargued but inherited from Plato, Aristotle, Philo Judaeus and the weight of ancient tradition; and it reveals his conviction, equally unargued in *City of God* (but see the *locus classicus* at *Conf.* 11.12.14–11.13.15), that times themselves were created by God, who is therefore outside time (*City* 12.26/25). His discussion, which relies on results in the previous book 11, starts by confessing, "my thoughts about this are many, and must be many because I cannot discover the one that is true, whether it is one among mine or something else that happens not to have occurred to me" (*City* 12.16/15.1). He concludes that if the angels were created on the first day, they can be as old as time, and hence God can have had creatures to dominate at all *times*, even if not through all eternity.

(c) At *City* 12.13/12 Augustine confronts the claim – it is Stoic, but seemingly adopted by certain Platonists – that past events return endlessly in cycles (circuitus temporum) and "nothing is new under the sun" (Ecclesiastes 1:9, *City* 12.14/13.2). On this view, the world had no beginning. Augustine starts by noting that the cycle theory conflicts with other Christian doctrine besides belief in creation, for example that Christ died *once* for our sins (*City* 12.14/13.2) and that the saints will enjoy eternal life (*City* 12.20/19). He considers an argument of the "philosophers" at *City* 12.18/17.1: God is never idle; he cannot form new plans; he cannot form infinite plans (knowledge of the infinite is impossible); so he must endlessly repeat himself. Augustine's response is robust; in particular he argues that creation does not imply that God was idle beforehand, for there was no beforehand (*City* 11.5; cf. *Conf.* 11.13.15).

The difficulties raised by God's being outside time are beyond the scope of this chapter, but four further remarks about Augustine's treatment of times are in order. (i) He notes, in effect, that if you bring it about that something happens at a given time, it does not follow that your bringing it about occurs at that same time – nor perhaps at any time: God "in affecting temporal things, is not affected in a temporal way [temporalia movens temporaliter non movetur]" (*City* 10.12, cf. 22.9, Kirwan 1989: 176–9). (ii) He shares a widespread conception of God's *knowledge* of temporal things: past and future are alike "present" to him (*City* 11.21, cf. Boethius, *Consolation of Philosophy* 5.6.59–72); however, he does not make the mistake of inferring God's timelessness from this conception. (iii) As is normal in Latin, Augustine mainly uses the word "tempus" for a stretch, not a point, of time (the Greek "*chronos*" is always so restricted). (iv) *Conf.* 11.14.17–28.38 contains his famous examination of the question "Quid est tempus?", best understood as "What is a time?" rather than "What is time?" (there are no articles in Latin). (See Kirwan 1989: Chs 8–9.)

Evil and the will in Augustine's doctrine of the Fall of Man: *City* 12–14

Greek philosophers had variously devised quite rich vocabularies to account for conflicts of will. But Augustine, in his psychology of action, was largely content with the one simple verb "velle" and its cognate noun "voluntas", both of which I translate "will". In this he follows Paul's postulation in Romans 7: 14–25 of a divided will (cf. Zerlina's "Vorrei e non vorrei" in Mozart's *Don Giovanni*), sometimes developing it in surprising ways: for example, "the will commands that there should be a will, not another one, but itself", yet "what commands is not [a] full [will], which is why what it commands does not occur" (*Conf.* 8.9.21). The curious opinion that Augustine "discovered" the will is presumably to be understood as claiming (disputably) that in texts such as this he gave voluntas a new role or a new prominence (see Kahn 1988). Whatever its prominence, he shares with the classical pagan tradition the view that there is some conceptual link between the will to do something and the understanding (intellectus) that to do it is good or right. Lapses from the "ordered agreement of knowledge [cognitio] and action" (*City* 19.13–14) are to be blamed on the weakness, not absence, of a consenting will. Sinners fail to discern correctly what has value (virtue is "ordering of love", *City* 15.22), which is a kind of lack of understanding, a false consciousness ("being ignorant of God's justice", *City* 18.32), although the failure may itself be wilful ("we can say that every sin is a lie [mendacium]", *City* 14.4.1).

Conflicts of will are consequent on the Fall. Owing to Adam's disobedience, we his progeny disobey our own wills (*City* 14.15.2); and reintegration – as in Aristotelian "virtue" – should be our aim (*Serm.* 30.3.4). In one notable case, erection of the penis (never so called, but often alluded to in *City* 13, and relentlessly examined in the second half of *City* 14), males' very bodies disobey their wills; for erection is not even subject to the will, as it was for Adam, and as any decent person would wish it still to be (*City* 14.16). In paradise insemination could have been achieved without lust and even without defloration (*City* 14.26).

The Fall of Man had been central to Augustine's theology from early days, because it was the point at which his Catholic faith diverged most plainly from Manichaeism. Manichees, scorning the Old Testament, believed that men had been created by an evil power and that sinfulness was their natural state. But Catholics must accept that God created everything and that everything he created was "very good" (Genesis 1:31). The evil in our world – Augustine never denies its existence – is often useful (e.g. *City* 18.51.1). But when it is not, it must result from the bad will of God's creatures, the inheritance from our progenitor's disobedience in eating the forbidden fruit. Three questions arise, all of which get some consideration in *City of God*.

(a) Why did Adam sin? Answer: he was loyal to Eve, who was led astray by the serpent, who was the instrument of the Devil (*City* 14.11.2). But what caused the Devil, part of the first-day creation of angels, to become a deceiver? *City* 12 gives Augustine's argument: an "efficient" cause of the first evil would, impossibly, have to be good (*City* 12.6); but such a cause is not needed; we can no more expect to find the cause of defects or failures than to see darkness or hear silence; in so far as they are defects, Augustine obscurely concludes, "they have deficient causes" (*City* 12.7). The idea behind this label may be that things just naturally go downhill if God does not sustain them (cf. *City* 22.22.2). An earlier but fuller treatment is in *Lib. Arb.*; and for criticism see Scott (1995: 216–28).

(b) Opponents had put the question: why did God make creatures who not only possessed free will but also (as he foreknew, *City* 14.11.1) would exercise it in such a disastrous way?

> God, they say, should have made man of such a nature that he would have no will [nollet omnino] to sin. Now I grant that a nature that has no will to sin is a better nature. (*Gen. Lit.* 11.7.9)

But, Augustine goes on, a nature that is able not to sin but does sin is good too. *City of God* explains:

> In and through [such creatures] he was able to exhibit both what their fault [culpa] merited and what his grace bestowed, [so that] with himself as creator and disposer no perverse disturbance by offenders could pervert the right order of things. (*City* 14.26)

As a later age would say, the fault was fortunate (felix culpa), making space for redemption by the Christ through grace. Augustine's doctrine of grace is his most important contribution to Christian theology, but it was mainly developed in response to Pelagius and is not a central theme of *City of God*.

(c) How can Adam's sin account for apparently unmerited suffering, for example of infants (and, one might add, of non-human animals, but they are not treated in *City of God*)? Augustine's response is his doctrine of original guilt (originalis reatus, e.g. *Simp.* 1.2.20): from Adam we all of us inherit an "infirmity of flesh ... great enough to be penal" (*Pecc. Mer.* 1.37.68). The first half of *City* 13 encapsulates the doctrine, but Augustine's case for it is scattered in other works. (See Kirwan 1989: Chs 4, 7.)

Free will: *City* 5.9 and 5.10

In two very interesting chapters Augustine examines whether free will is compatible with (a) foreknowledge (praescientia), specifically God's foreknowledge, (b) fate, and (c) necessity. His discussion, although not always easy to follow, is cogent on (a) and (b).

(a) Cicero's *De Divinatione* (surviving) and perhaps *De Fato* (partly surviving) are the starting points. To divine is to foretell the future from god-sent signs. Cicero, says Augustine, had argued against divination on the ground that if all human acts can be foreknown, "nothing is in our power and there is no decision of the will" (*City* 5.9.2). Augustine replies that the religious mind "chooses both of the two", namely free decision of the will (liberum voluntatis arbitrium) and foreknowledge of the future. The latter is made necessary for Christians not by divination and astrology, which are indeed spurious, but by Old Testament prophets, and God: prophecy is "clearer than light", and "one who does not have foreknowledge of all the future is surely not God" (*City* 5.9.2; cf. *Lib. Arb.* 3.2.4). As for free decision, "we do by our own will whatever we feel and know is done by us not without our willing" (*City* 5.9.3). It follows that something must be wrong with the reasoning of Cicero, that "great and learned man" (*City* 5.9.2). Augustine sets out the reasoning (very much in his own terms – he anticipates here the modern philosopher's habit of "reconstruction"). He concedes without argument that one cannot foreknow a fact without tracing "the ordained [certus] order of its causes". ("Certus" is a difficult word: does it mean "ordained", or "known", or "fixed"? – notice that all these properties can change with time.) But causes include those that are "voluntary"; and "our wills themselves are in the order of causes that is certain to [?ordained by] God and contained in his foreknowledge" (*City* 5.9.3; cf *Lib. Arb.* 3.3.8, "[God] also foreknows the [human] power"). There is nothing therefore to prevent foreknowledge of freely willed acts. (Of course, God does not strictly speaking *fore*know, if he is outside time; but that snag rarely troubled Augustine.)

(b) Cicero's discussion had introduced the Stoic notion of fate ("fatum"; Greek "*heimarmenê*", allotment). Augustine cuts through this complication efficiently, by means of a dilemma. Some people, he says, "call by the name of fate the connexion and sequence of all causes, by which everything happens that does happen" (*City* 5.8); and these people include the Stoics, Cicero's target (*City* 5.9.4, cf. Cicero, *De Divinatione* 1.55.126). In that Stoic sense of the Latin word, everything that is caused is indeed fated, but fate, like foreknowledge, is no threat to free will. Augustine toys with the idea that the Stoic sense might conform with a derivation (favoured by modern etymologists) of "fatum" from "fari", "to say", making it mean something like "what is ordained". Nevertheless he is firm that the ordinary sense of the word in his own day ("usitato more", *City* 5.9.4) is different, applying only to things whose happening "is outside the wills of God and men, by an ordering that is necessary" (*City* 5.1). If fate in that ordinary sense were universal, free will would indeed be an illusion; but in fact that sort, at least as peddled by the charlatan astrologers who are the ostensible target of *City* 5, does not exist at all.

(c) Necessity cannot be banished so easily (nor therefore can *all* aspects of fate, according to Augustine's own initial definition at *City* 5.1). *City* 5.10 confronts the question whether necessity in its turn is to be feared by a defender of human free will. Once more Augustine's response is by way of a distinction ("distinguere", *City* 5.10.1):

> If [on the one hand] our necessity is spoken of as what is not in our power but effects what it can even if we will it not to, for example the necessity of death, it is clear that our wills, by which life is conducted rightly or wrongly, are not subject to [sub] such necessity; for we do many things that we would certainly not do if we willed not to.
>
> (*City* 5.10.1)

If, on the other hand, necessity is defined as when we say "it is necessary that something be as it is, or happen as it does", that does not interfere with liberty or make things subject to necessity: for example, God's "power is not lessened when it is said that he cannot die, or be deceived" (*ibid.*).

On this discussion of necessity I offer two comments. (i) The words in which Augustine defines his second sort of necessity could be understood as introducing a class of conditional (sometimes called "de dicto") necessities: the necessity that a thing happens-if-so-and-so-happens. His final example, "it is necessary that when we will we will by free decision", is certainly of the conditional type. The other examples, however – all concerned with God's powers – exhibit simple or absolute (so-called "de re") necessity: the necessity that a thing happens. The difference between these two is a strangely elusive one, that has had to be rediscovered several times during the history of philosophy and is still missed by some commentators; and I know no text of Augustine which proves that he understood it. (ii) More probably the distinction that Augustine intended in *City* 5.10 is between simple necessity as compulsion and simple necessity as immunity. The latter does not remove a power but does, as Augustine admits, remove a possibility. He is on highly contentious ground in his implication that, for example, the impossibility of God's dying leaves God *free* in any decision of his will to remain alive (cf. *C. Sec. Jul.* 6.11, *Corr. Gr.* 12.33; and the "ultimate" human freedom at *City* 22.30.3). It could do so, if "what occurs voluntarily, even if it occurs necessarily, still occurs freely", a conception of free will – so-called "liberty of spontaneity" – that, although condemned by the Vatican in 1567 (Denzinger & Schönmetzer 1965: no. 1939), was defiantly ascribed to Augustine by his seventeenth-century Roman Catholic champion Jansen (Jansen 1652: part 3, 6.6; cf. *Gr. Chr.* 1.13.14, "liber facit qui libens facit"). However, there is dispute whether Jansen got Augustine right, because various other texts seem to tell a different story.

To sum up this section: *City of God* contributes to Augustine's treatment of free will but does not fully illuminate it. On the one hand, as we have just seen, the philosophical enquirer needs to know better how Augustine understood the notion of free decision of the will, on which others of his treatises, early and late, are a vital source (in one sense, he concedes, "decision of the will is truly free [only] when it is not [as since the Fall we all are] the slave of faults and sins", *City* 14.11.1; and habits make necessity, e.g. *Conf.* 8.5.10). And on the other hand, his really serious confrontation with the question whether free will is compatible with *causation* came not so much from the ideas of Cicero and the Stoics as from his own contemporary Pelagius, whose views tending to restrict God's role in shaping human deeds provoked Augustine during his last decade into a campaign of condemnation and a flood of passionate polemics. It would be out of place to comment here on the Pelagian controversy, beyond saying that both of the original disputants seem to have adopted extreme positions between which there is logical space, and that part of the issue remains open among philosophers today – science replacing God, and usually under the counsel-darkening label "determinism". (See Kirwan 1989: Ch. 6.)

Scepticism: *City* 11.26

> In the matter of these truths the arguments of the Academics are no terror, when they say, "What if you are deceived?" For if I am deceived, I am [si fallor, sum]. For anyone who is not, surely cannot be deceived; and because of this I am, if I am deceived. Because, therefore, I am if I am deceived, how am I deceived <in thinking> that I am, when it is certain that I am if I am deceived? Because, therefore, I who was deceived would *be*, even if I were deceived, it is beyond doubt that I am not deceived in that I know myself to *be*. (*City* 11.26)

At Rome in 383 and 384 CE, long before *City of God*, Augustine had been troubled by the scepticism purveyed in Cicero's *Academica* (parts of which survive); and after that trouble was cured by his Platonist acquaintances at

Milan, he composed *Contra Academicos*, the first of his surviving works. The Academics of its title had been sceptics, whose views dominated the Platonic Academy at Athens for a long period after the death of its very differently minded founder (they saw themselves rather as followers of Socrates). From the third century BCE these Academics engaged in controversy with the rival Athenian school of Stoics, who had invited sceptical challenge by incautiously adopting a very strict criterion of knowledge (which they called a "criterion of truth"). Surviving evidence of the criterion's wording is indirect, and suggests, unsurprisingly, that amendments were tried out as the debate progressed and as different Stoics took part in it. What concerns us, however, is not the Stoic doctrine but Augustine's conception of it. In *Contra Academicos* he calls it "Zeno's definition", referring to the Stoic founder. Unfortunately his formulations there are neither constant nor very clear, but they tend towards a demand of *infallibility*: you know only what you cannot be wrong in believing. Against the Academics, then, Augustine appears to have set himself the heavy task of showing that people do have infallible beliefs.

When, near the end of his life, he came to review his works in *Retractationes*, he wrote of *Contra Academicos*, "My purpose was to rid my mind, with the strongest reasoning I could, of the arguments of those who cause many to despair of finding truth ... For these arguments were also influencing me" (*Retract.* 1.1.1). Evidently the purpose was achieved. But it may be that as the years passed he had become less satisfied with the reasonings of *Contra Academicos*; at any rate, it was only later that he spotted the possibility of finding infallibility among beliefs about *himself*. The new idea develops gradually in several passages of his writings (esp. *Ver. Rel.* 39.73, *Du. An.* 10.13, *Trin.* 10.10.14, *Trin.* 15.12.21), and finds its tidiest form in *City of God*'s demonstration that "sum", "I am", is a belief that nobody could hold about themselves erroneously. (See Kirwan 1989: Ch. 1.)

The demonstration is also Descartes's: not what Descartes presented himself as doing, concluding to "sum" from the premise "cogito", but what he actually did in *Meditation* 2, concluding to "this proposition, *I myself am, I myself exist*, whenever it is put forward by me or conceived in my mind is necessarily true" from the premise "there is no doubt that I myself also am, if [a deceiver of supreme power and cunning] is deceiving me" ("ego etiam sum, si me fallit"; Descartes 1964–76: vii 25). Descartes was using an argument at least twelve centuries old (in our surviving record there is, I believe, no serious claimant earlier than Augustine). What is perhaps interesting about Augustine in this history, and not particularly creditable to him, is that his youthful worries about scepticism appear to have been allayed from the moment that he was satisfied that he knew *something*. Descartes was to be much more ambitious, aiming to rebuild "all the sciences amassed together" (Descartes 1964–76: x 184; and see Matthews 1992: esp. 29–34).

Augustine's analytical views on knowledge (scientia, actualized as under-standing, intellectus) and belief (the verb is "credere", the noun usually "fides", faith, there being, unfortunately, no Latin noun cognate with "credere") do not come to the surface in *City of God*. He thought, like the Platonists, that the latter is an inferior but often unavoidable substitute for the former (*City* 11.2).

The highest good: *City* 19

In ancient moral philosophy it had been a commonplace (for better or worse) that the question "How should one live?" is equivalent to the question "How is one to be happy [beatus, *eudaimôn*]?" In *City* 19 Augustine proceeds to expound the Christian conception of happiness.

Happiness is the highest good (summum bonum), that is, "the culmination [finis] of our good for the sake of which other things are desirable and which is itself desirable for its own sake" (*City* 19.1.1, echoing Aristotle, *Nicomachean Ethics* 1094a18–19). We all want it (e.g. *Conf.* 10.20.29), but how is it to be iden-tified? Varro had computed $3 \times 2 \times 2 \times 2 \times 2 \times 2 \times 3 = 288$ possible answers, and had given his own verdict in favour of a combination of virtue with goods such as health, to be enjoyed by both oneself and one's "friends", in a life mixing the "leisurely" pursuit of cultivation (otium) with its contrast, public business (negotium, *City* 19.1–3). All very high-minded and conventional.

But the Christian ideal is quite different. According to Christians, says Augustine, the summum bonum is eternal life, to be attained by "living rightly" (*City* 19.4.1). Then alone will there be peace, the culminations of goods (*City* 19.11). So far as we are happy on earth "we are made happy by hope" (*City* 19.4.5; cf. *Serm*. 19.4). The "Salem" in "Jerusalem" means peace (*City* 19.11). "The peace of all things is the tranquillity of order" (*City* 19.13.1; order is a key Augustinian concept, but not much examined in *City of God*).

This vision of the afterlife leaves open the question why happiness in the present world should not be counted as at least the temporal *part* of the summum bonum. Augustine's answer in *City* 19 is a curious one: it cannot be counted at all, because earthly goods are so often denied to men, virtue is so often a struggle (*City* 19.4.3), tortures and injustices abound (*City* 19.6), we fear the ruin or perfidy of our friends (*City* 19.8) – and so the book goes on in a sombre catalogue of human woes (cf. *City* 22.22.4, "the near-hell of this miserable life"). Although he has no time for the Stoic reply that such evils do not affect happiness (*City* 19.4.4), the puzzle remains why he should think that the *rarity* of earthly happiness counts against its *value* when, however rarely, it is attained.

Perhaps the solution can be found in an earlier passage, where he had acceded to the thought that:

> the soul is certainly not happy even in the times when it is said to be happy, if it foresees its own future misery and disgrace [turpitudo]; while if it does not foresee the coming disgrace and misery, but counts on being happy forever, it is happy in a false over-confidence [falsa opinione], which is as stupid a thing as could be said.
>
> (*City* 11.4.2, cf. 12.14/13.1, 12.21/20.2, *Mor. Cath.* 3.5)

Here Augustine demands a great deal: you cannot be happy if unhappiness lies in store for you, since then you must be either anxious or deluded (why not happy in a false over-confidence? because happiness for the ancients – beatitudo, *eudaimonia* – was not a feeling but a state, of whose presence or absence its owner might be unaware). So earthly miseries destroy *all* earthly happiness (cf. *Retract.* 1.2, amending an earlier more cheerful view).

Souls and bodies: *City* 19.3

Every animal ("animal" is also the Latin word) has a soul (Latin "anima"); even the little ones such as feed on corpses have little souls, animulae (*City* 19.12, using the word that the emperor Hadrian had chosen in the moving poem of farewell to his own soul). Animals are animated bodies ("corpora animata"; *City* 13.24.4). Men are among the animals, differentiated from the rest as mortal and rational (*City* 9.13.3). The human soul is sometimes distinguished as an anim*us*.

"A man himself is constituted out of a soul [animus] and a body [corpus]" (*City* 8.8). God is different: he is not a body, because he created souls, which are superior to bodies (*City* 8.5; the theory of causation as propagation appears to be at work here); and seemingly he does not have a soul (*City* 8.5), doubtless because one of his persons is the Holy Spirit, and the spiritual is higher than the animal (cf. 1 Corinthians 15:46; both the Latin nouns in fact connote breath, cf. *City* 5.9.4, as do their Greek equivalents).

But how are a man's body and soul related? Varro had put the question, and had sought by means of analogies to explain three possible answers, which Augustine reports as follows (emphasis mine):

> Is the soul [anima] alone the man, so that his body is to him as a horse is to a *horseman* (for a horseman is not a man and a horse, but a man

alone, said to be a horseman because of being related to a horse in a certain way)? Or is the body alone the man, being related to the soul in a certain way, as a *drinking-cup* is to a drink (for what is said to be a drinking-cup is not the cup and the drink it contains together, but the cup alone, which is so because it is designed to hold a drink)? Or are neither the soul alone nor the body alone but both together the man, soul and body each being one part, while the whole is constituted out of both of them so as to be a man, as we call two yoked horses a *pair* (though whether you take the right or the left part of the pair, and however it is related to the other one, we do not say that that one is a pair, but only the two together)? (*City* 19.3.1)

Thus there are three ways of being "constituted out of" a body and a soul: (1) as a soul using a body; (2) as a body "containing" a soul; and (3) as a whole in which a body and a soul are parts. Varro's question could be applied to all animals, but Augustine asks it only about men. Unfortunately, though, he does not answer it. At *City* 19.3.1 he tells us that Varro had chosen (3); and in the closely parallel passage of an earlier work he had annoyingly commented that his own purpose there made adjudication unnecessary (*Mor. Cath.* 4.6). A dialogue of Plato's, perhaps the origin of Varro's idea, has Socrates argue for (1) (Plato, *Alcibiades I*: 130), and Gilson thought that this is "in keeping with Augustinism's deepest tendencies" (Gilson 1961: 45; and see *City* 22.29.6 on "wearing" resurrection bodies). Aquinas read *City* 19.3.1 as "commending" Varro's choice of (3) (Aquinas, *Summa Theologiae* 1a.1.75.4.2); and in support of this O'Daly cites *City* 13.24.2 (O'Daly 1987: 56 n.152). I myself have argued, perhaps wishfully, in favour of Augustine's acceptance of (2) (Kirwan 1990). Two things, I think, stand out: (i) he was not a Cartesian dualist, if that involves believing that, for us men, bodily characteristics belong *not* to ourselves but *only* to our bodies (for example he knows that orthodoxy demands that Jesus *himself* was fixed to the cross); and (ii) he always felt that the manner of association of souls and bodies is puzzling (*Ep.* 137.7.11, *Gen. Lit.* 3.16.25, *City* 21.10.1).

At the General Resurrection, all men will recover their bodies (1 Corinthians 15:35–44; Augustine defends this view at *City* 13.16–20). But meanwhile the dead survive without bodies, as souls (*City* 13.19, 21.10.2) or perhaps as tenuous soul-vehicles (*Ep.* 13.2, 158.5; O'Daly 1987: 75–9). Since all we men have bodies in one or another of Varro's ways, it follows that during this waiting-time we will not properly speaking be men (*City* 13.24.2, *Mor. Cath.* 4.6); so that a man's being a man is like a child's being a child, not necessary to his or her (continued) existence. Augustine accepts this consequence (*Trin.* 8.6.9).

Notes

1. "Homo" denotes the species; I shall continue to translate it as "man", even though that imports an English ambiguity from which Latin – unlike modern Romance languages – is happily free. The Latin for a male of the species is "vir".
2. I.e. 86 in the numeration of the Septuagint, Augustine, and the Vulgate, 87 in the modern Jewish and Protestant numeration.
3. So hitting (by accident? or obscure tradition?) on what I am told is the true meaning of "*ratsach*", the word in the Hebrew text: intentional unauthorized homicide.
4. There are divergent chapter numerations in this part of book 12.
5. Augustine accepts the calculation in Eusebius' *Chronica* that the creation happened 6,000 years ago, but he notes that the calculation does not matter (*City* 12.13/12).

Bibliography

Editions containing City of God *and other works of Augustine cited*

BA   *Œuvres de saint Augustin*, with French translation, Bibliothèque Augustinienne (Paris and Bruges: Desclée De Brouwer, 1936–).

CCL   *Corpus Christianorum, Series Latina* (Turnhout: Brepols. 1953–).

CSEL   *Corpus Scriptorum Ecclesiasticorum Latinorum* (Vienna: Tempsky, 1866–).

D&K   *Sancti Aurelii Augustini Episcopi De Civitate Dei Libri XXII*, 4th edn, B. Dombart & A. Kalb (eds) (Leipzig: Teubner, 1928–9). (Reprinted Stuttgart: Teubner, 1981.) The standard modern edition of *City of God*, text reprinted in CCL 47–8.

Loeb   *Saint Augustine: The City of God against the Pagans*, 7 vols, text and facing translation by various hands, Loeb Classical Library (London: Heinemann/ Cambridge, MA: Harvard University Press, 1957–72). The only edition with text and English translation together.

PL   *Patrologiae Cursus Completus, Series Latina*, J.-P. Migne (ed.) (Paris: Garnier frères, 1844–55). Reprints Maurist edition of Augustine's works (Paris, 1679–1700). Omits a number of sermons and letters recovered more recently.

English translations containing City of God *and other works of Augustine cited*

ACW   *Ancient Christian Writers: The Works of the Fathers in Translation*, J. Quasten & J. C. Plumpe (eds) (Westminster, MD: Newman Press, 1946–).

AHI   *The Works of Saint Augustine: A Translation for the 21st Century*, J. E. Rotelle (ed.) for Augustinian Heritage Institute (Brooklyn, NY: New City Press, 1990–).

Bettenson   *St Augustine: City of God*, H. Bettenson (Harmondsworth: Penguin, 1984).

BW   *Basic Writings of Saint Augustine*, with introduction and notes by W. J. Oates (New York: Random House, 1948).

Dyson   *De Civitate Dei*, R. W. Dyson (Cambridge: Cambridge University Press, 1999).

FC   *Fathers of the Church*, L. Schopp, R. J. Deferrari *et al.* (eds) (Washington, DC: Catholic University of America Press, 1947–).

LCC   *Library of Christian Classics* (London: SCM, 1953–).

Loeb   see *Editions* above

NPNF   *A Select Library of the Nicene and Post-Nicene Fathers of the Christian Church*, first series 1886–8, P. Schaff (ed.) (reprinted Grand Rapids, MI: Eerdmans, 1971–80).

Works of Augustine cited (and approx dates of composition), with editions and, after the semi-colons, translations and their volume numbers

C. Acad.   *Contra Academicos* (386 CE)
    PL 32, CSEL 63, CCL 29, BA 4; ACW 12, FC 5, M. P. Garvey (Milwaukee, WI: Marquette University Press, 1957), P. King (Indianapolis, IN: Hackett, 1994).

C. Faust.   *Contra Faustum Manichaeum* (397–9 CE)
    PL 42, CSEL 25.1; NPNF 4.

C. Sec. Jul.   *Contra Secundam Juliani Responsionem, opus imperfectum* (429–30 CE) (Julian of Eclanum had taken up the cudgels for Pelagius.)
    PL 45, CSEL 85.1 books 1–3; AHI 1.25.

Cat. Rud.   *De Catechizandis Rudibus* (399 CE)
    PL 40, CCL 46; ACW 2, NPNF 3.

City   *De Civitate Dei* (*City of God*) (c.412 –c.426 CE)
    PL 41, CSEL 40, D&K = CCL 47–8, BA 33–7; Dyson, Bettenson, Loeb, NPNF 2, FC 8, 14, 24, BW 2 (part).

Conf.   *Confessiones* (*Confessions*) (397–401 CE)
    PL 32, CSEL 33, CCL 27, BA 13–14, J. J. O'Donnell (Oxford: Clarendon Press, 1992), J. K. Ryan (New York: Doubleday, 1960, with English tr.); LCC 7, NPNF 1, FC 21, BW 1, AHI 1.1, R. S. Pine-Coffin (Harmondsworth: Penguin, 1961), H. Chadwick (Oxford: Oxford University Press, 1991).

Corr. Don.   *De Correctione Donatistarum* (417 CE)
    = *Ep.* 185; PL 33, CSEL 57; NPNF 4.

Corr. Gr.   *De Correptione et Gratia* (426 CE)
    PL 44, CSEL 92, BA 24; NPNF 5, FC 2, AHI 1.26.

Du. An.   *De Duabus Animabus contra Manichaeos* (392–3 CE)
    PL 42, CSEL 25.1, BA 17; NPNF 4.

Ep.   *Epistulae*
    PL 33 (omitting some recent discoveries), CSEL 34, 44, 57, 58, 88, CCL 47 (1*–29*), BA 46B (1*–29*); NPNF 1 (large selection), FC 12, 18, 20, 30, 32, 81, AHI 2.1 (1–99), J. H. Baxter (Loeb Classical Library, London: Heinemann/Cambridge, MA: Harvard University Press, 1980) (selection).

Ep. Joh.   *Tractatus in Epistulam Johannis ad Parthos* (407–415 CE)
    PL 35; LCC 8, NPNF 7, FC 92, M. T. Clark, *Augustine of Hippo: Selected Writing*, Classics of Western Spirituality (London: SPCK, 1984).

Gen. Lit.   *De Genesi ad Litteram* (401–14 CE)
    PL 34, CSEL 28.1, BA 48–9; ACW 41–2, AHI 1.13, J.H. Taylor (New York: Newman Press, 1982).

Gr. Chr.   *De Gratia Christi et de Peccato Originali contra Pelagium* (418 CE)
          PL 44, CSEL 42, BA 22; NPNF 5, BW 1.

Lib. Arb.   *De Libero Arbitrio* (388, 391–5 CE)
          PL 32, CSEL 74, CCL 29, BA 6; ACW 22, LCC 6, FC 59, C. M. Sparrow
          (Charlottesville, VI: University of Virginia, 1947), A. S. Benjamin & L. H.
          Hackstaff (New York: Bobbs-Merrill, 1964), T. Williams (Indianapolis, IN:
          Hackett, 1993).

Mor. Cath. *De Moribus Ecclesiae Catholicae* (387–9 CE)
          PL 32, CSEL 90, BA 1; NPNF 4, FC 56, BW 1.

Pecc. Mer. *De Peccatorum Meritis et Remissione, et de Baptismo Parvulorum* (411 CE)
          PL 44, CSEL 60; NPNF 5, AHI 1.23.

Quaest. Hept. *Quaestiones in Heptateuchum* (420 CE)
          PL 34, CSEL 28.2, CCL 33; no English translation(?)

Retract.   *Retractationes* (426–7 CE)
          PL 32, CSEL 36, CCL 57, BA 12; FC 60.

Serm.   *Sermones*
          PL 38–9, 46 (omitting some recent discoveries), CCL 41 (50 Old Testament
          sermons, incl. some not in PL), *Sermones post Maurinos Reperti*, G. Morin
          (ed.) (Rome: Vatican, 1930), *Sermones Selecti*, C. Lambot (ed.) (Utrecht:
          Spectrum, 1950), *Vingt-six sermons au peuple d'Afrique*, F. Dolbeau (ed.)
          (Paris: Études augustiniennes, 1996; from a manuscript discovered at Mainz);
          AHI 3.1–11, selections in: NPNF 6, ACW 15, FC 11, 38, P. T. Weller (St
          Louis, MO: Herder, 1959), Q. Howe (London: Gollancz, 1967).

Simp.   *Ad Simplicianum de Diversis Quaestionibus* (395–6 CE) (Simplician succeeded
          Ambrose as bishop of Milan.)
          PL 40, CCL 44, BA 10; LCC 6 (book 1).

Trin.   *De Trinitate* (399–419 CE)
          PL 42, CCL 50, 50A, BA 15–16; FC 45, AHI 1.5, S. McKenna (Cambridge:
          Cambridge University Press, 2002), books 8–15.

Ver. Rel.   *De Vera Religione* (390 CE)
          PL 34, CSEL 77, CCL 32, BA 8; LCC 6, D. Robinson (New York: Bobbs-
          Merrill, 1958).

Secondary literature

Aquinas, Thomas 1964–81. *Summa Theologiae*. London: Eyre & Spottiswoode (text and
    English translation). [Composed *c*.1270.]

Aristotle 1894. *Ethica Nicomachea*, I. Bywater (ed.), Oxford Classical Texts. Oxford:
    Clarendon Press. Many translations as *Nicomachean Ethics*. [Composed late 4th century
    BCE.]

Barnes, J. 1982. "The Just War", in *The Cambridge History of Later Medieval Philosophy*, N.
    Kretzmann, A. Kenny & J. Pinborg (eds), 771–84. Cambridge: Cambridge University
    Press.

Boethius, Anicius Manlius Severinus 1973. *The Consolation of Philosophy*, in *The Theological
    Tractates*, E. K. Rand & S. J. Tester (eds and trans.), Loeb Classical Library. London:
    Heinemann/Cambridge, MA: Harvard University Press. [Composed *c*. 523 CE.]

Brown, P. R. L. 1995. *Authority and the Sacred: Aspects of the Christianisation of the Roman World*. Cambridge: Cambridge University Press.

Cicero, M. Tullius 1959. *De Divinatione*, in *De Senectute &c.*, W. A. Falconer (ed. and trans.), Loeb Classical Library. London: Heinemann/Cambridge, MA: Harvard University Press. [Composed 44 BCE.]

Codex Theodosianus 1971. *Theodosiani Libri XVI cum Constitutionibus Sirmondianis*, T. Mommsen (ed.). Dublin and Zürich: Weidman (first edition Berlin: Weidman, 1904–5). Translated as *The Theodosian Code and Novels*, C. Pharr, New York: Greenwood Press 1952. [Issued 438 CE.]

Denzinger, H. & A. Schönmetzer (eds) 1965. *Enchiridion Symbolorum, Definitionum et Declarationum de Rebus Fidei et Morum*, 33rd edition. Barcinone and elsewhere: Herder.

Descartes, R. 1964–76. *Œuvres de Descartes*, rev. edn, C. Adam & P. Tannery (eds). Paris: Vrin. *Meditations* translated in *The Philosophical Writings of Descartes*, vol. 2, J. Cottingham, R. Stoothof & D. Murdoch. Cambridge: Cambridge University Press. [*Meditations* first published 1641.]

Diogenes Laërtius 1925. *Lives of the Philosophers*, R. D. Hicks (ed. and trans.), Loeb Classical Library. London: Heinemann/Cambridge, MA: Harvard University Press. [Composed *c.*200 CE.]

Drobner, H. R. 2000. "Studying Augustine: An Overview of Recent Research", in *Augustine and his Critics: Essays in Honour of Gerald Bonner*, R. Dodaro & G. Lawless (eds), 18–34. London: Routledge.

Dyson, R. W. 2001. *The Pilgrim City: Social and Political Ideas in the Writings of St Augustine of Hippo*. Woodbridge: Boydell Press. [Contains extensive passages in translation, not only from *City of God*.]

Garnsey, P. 1996. *Ideas of Slavery from Aristotle to Augustine*. Cambridge: Cambridge University Press.

Gilson, E. 1961. *The Christian Philosophy of Saint Augustine*, L. E. M. Lynch (trans. from 3rd French edn, 1949). London: Gollancz.

Hornblower, S. & A. Spawforth (eds) 2003. *The Oxford Classical Dictionary*, 3rd edn. Oxford: Clarendon Press.

Hume, D. 1985. "Of Suicide", in *Essays, Moral, Political, and Literary*, 577–89. Indianopolis: Liberty Fund. Also in *Hume on Religion*, R. Wollheim (ed.), 251–62 (London: Fontana, 1963); and elsewhere. [Published 1777.]

Jansen, C. O. 1652. *Augustinus*. Rouen: Berthelin. [Published 1640.]

Kahn, C. H. 1988. "Discovering the Will: from Aristotle to Augustine", in *The Question of "Eclecticism": Studies in Later Greek Philosophy*, J. M. Dillon & A. A. Long (eds), 234–59. Berkeley, CA: University of California Press.

Kirwan, C. A. 1989. *Augustine*, The Arguments of the Philosophers. London: Routledge.

Kirwan, C. A. 1990. "Augustine on Souls and Bodies", in *Logica, mente e persona*, A. M. Alberti (ed.), 207–41. Florence: L. S. Olschki.

Kirwan, C. A. 1999. "Avoiding Sin: Augustine against Consequentialism", in *The Augustinian Tradition*, G. B. Matthews (ed.), 183–94. Berkeley, CA: University of California Press.

Kirwan, C. A. 2001. "Augustine's Philosophy of Language", in *The Cambridge Companion to Augustine*, E. Stump & N. Kretzmann (eds), 186–204. Cambridge: Cambridge University Press.

Langan, J. SJ 1984. "The Elements of St Augustine's Just War Theory", in *Journal of Religious*

Ethics **12**, 19–38. Reprinted in *The Ethics of St Augustine*, W. S. Babcock (ed.), 169–89 (Atlanta, GA: Scholars Press, 1991).

Markus, R. A. 1988. *Saeculum: History and Society in the Theology of St Augustine*, rev. edn. Cambridge: Cambridge University Press (1st edn 1970).

Matthews, G. B. 1992. *Thought's Ego in Augustine and Descartes*. Ithaca, NY: Cornell University Press.

Metzger, B. M. & M. D. Coggan (eds) 1993. *Oxford Companion to the Bible*. Oxford: Oxford University Press.

Murray, A. 1998. *Suicide in the Middle Ages, vol. 1: The Violent Against Themselves*. Oxford: Oxford University Press.

O'Daly, G. J. P. 1987. *Augustine's Philosophy of Mind*. London: Duckworth.

O'Daly, G. J. P. 1999. *Augustine's City of God: A Reader's Guide*. Oxford: Clarendon Press.

Plato 2001. *Alcibiades I*, N. C. Denyer (ed.). Cambridge: Cambridge University Press. Translated in *Plato: Complete Works*, J. M. Cooper (ed.), D. S. Hutchinson (trans.) (Indianapolis, IN: Hackett, 1997). [Composed early 4th century BCE.]

Plotinus 1966–88. *Enneads*, A. H. Armstrong (ed. and trans.), Loeb Classical Library. London: Heinemann/Cambridge, MA: Harvard University Press. [Composed 253–70 CE.]

Schofield, M. 1991. *The Stoic Idea of the City*. Cambridge: Cambridge University Press.

Scott, T. Kermit 1995. *Augustine: His Thought in Context*, New York: Paulist Press.

TeSelle, E. 1988. "Toward an Augustinian Politics", *Journal of Religious Ethics* **16**, 87–108. Reprinted in *The Ethics of St Augustine*, W. S. Babcock (ed.), 147–68 (Atlanta, GA: Scholars Press, 1991).

Weithman, P. J. 2001. "Augustine's Political Philosophy", in *The Cambridge Companion to Augustine*, E. Stump & N. Kretzmann (eds), 234–52. Cambridge: Cambridge University Press.

Further reading: a very short selection

Brown, P. R. L. 1967. *Augustine of Hippo: A Biography*, London: Faber & Faber.

Chadwick, H. 1986. *Augustine*, Past Masters. Oxford: Oxford University Press.

Wills, G. 1999. *Saint Augustine*. London: Weidenfeld & Nicholson.

7

Anselm
Proslogion

John Marenbon

In many general histories of philosophy, Anselm's role is that of inventing the so-called Ontological Argument for the existence of God, which occupies about two pages in Chapters 2 and (some say) 3 of his *Proslogion*. The remaining 300 or so pages of close argument that make up his philosophical and theological writings are largely ignored, including the rest of the *Proslogion* itself. One purpose of this essay is to right that imbalance, at least as far as the *Proslogion* is concerned. The other chapters of the *Proslogion* are full of exciting philosophical discussion, on topics as varied as omnipotence, justice and eternity. Both Anselm's aims and his originality are obscured when the focus is concentrated on two brief chapters at the beginning of the book. Yet it would be a mistake to ignore entirely the special status of the Ontological Argument. It is not an accident that the shape of its reasoning has fascinated philosophers down the generations, and Anselm himself gave it special weight by including with the *Proslogion* the criticisms of this argument made by a contemporary, Gaunilo, a monk of Marmoutiers, along with his own replies to them.

Anselm's times and the background to the *Proslogion*

Anselm, who was born in 1033 and died in 1109, lived on the eve of one of the most brilliant periods of Western philosophy. Between about 1110 and 1160, thinkers such as Abelard, William of Conches and Gilbert of Poitiers, working in Paris and other schools in the north of France, the area where Anselm had spent much of his life, would produce a body of serious and innovative work in logic, semantics, metaphysics, ethics and (what would now be called) philosophy of religion. Their intellectual background and framework were hardly different from Anselm's. The pattern for study was provided by the seven liberal arts, which led on to the study of Christian doctrine, but the four mathematical arts of the quadrivium (arithmetic, geometry, music and astronomy) tended to be ignored in favour of the three arts of language: grammar, logic and (less important) rhetoric.

Since Latin was the language of ecclesiastical and intellectual life, and it was no one's mother tongue, grammar was the gateway to all further study. But the subject also extended to considering semantics and related philosophical questions (cf. Fredborg 1988), and the study of classical authors, who included not merely poets, such as Virgil and Horace, but the few ancient and late ancient non-logical philosophical texts in common circulation, the most important of which were Plato's *Timaeus*, in an incomplete Latin translation by Calcidius, and the *Consolation of Philosophy* by Boethius (*c.* 524). Anselm clearly knew the *Consolation* well, although the *Timaeus*, central to much twelfth-century philosophy, seems not to have interested him.

Logic loomed even larger than grammar in the eleventh- and twelfth-century curriculum. Only two logical works by Aristotle himself were known, the *Categories* and *On Interpretation*, along with the Introduction (*Isagoge*) by Porphyry, which had been part of the Aristotelian curriculum since late antiquity. But Aristotelian syllogistic and other post-Aristotelian branches of logic were known through monographs by Boethius. Anselm dedicated only one, shortish dialogue (probably from shortly after 1087, but Southern (1990: 65) dates it 20 years earlier) exclusively to logic and semantics, the *De grammatico*, where he asks: into which Aristotelian category does a grammarian fit? "Grammarian" designates its referent in virtue of a quality, his knowledge of grammar; but every grammarian is a man, and every man is a substance. And so is *grammaticus* a substance or a quality? Whether this dialogue is designed to teach students basic principles of logical argumentation (Adams 2000: 108–112) or can be seen rather as a critique of Aristotle (Marenbon, forthcoming), it shows well how Anselm resembles his twelfth-century successors in having a cast of mind shaped by the study of logical and semantic problems. In this respect, indeed, he is the first of a series of medieval thinkers who, for better or worse, resemble very closely in their approach and methods, although not in their aims and presuppositions, contemporary analytical philosophers.

During Anselm's lifetime, his namesake, Anselm of Laon, was beginning the process, starting out from Biblical exegesis, of systematizing Christian doctrine, a process that would establish theology as a formal discipline in the schools. But in Anselm's own day, theology was not an established academic subject. In general, the study of Christian doctrine consisted either in commentary on the Bible, or in response to particular events, such as the appearance of doctrines considered heretical. For example, Anselm's teacher, Lanfranc, engaged in a vigorous debate with Berengar of Tours over the Eucharist (cf. Holopainen 1996: 44–118). There was, therefore, no school tradition into which Anselm's discursive theological writings can be fitted. His model, above all in terms of form, was the great Church Father, Augustine (cf. Southern 1990: 71–87). He was also much influenced by Boethius's short theological treatises (*Opuscula sacra*), which provided an example of bringing the language and distinctions of logic to bear on problems in Christian doctrine.

Before the *Proslogion*

Although Anselm was in his mid-forties by the time he composed the *Proslogion* (1077–78), it was one of his first writings. Early in his twenties he had turned his back on his native Aosta, a North Italian Alpine town, and had come to study under Lanfranc at Bec, a monastery in Normandy. In 1060 he himself became a monk of Bec, and was made Prior in 1063. Very soon after he had finished the *Proslogion*, Anselm became Abbot, and from then on – even more so after 1093, when he succeeded Lanfranc as Archbishop of Canterbury – his life was as occupied by ecclesiastical administration and politics as by intellectual concerns. Yet it is from these last three decades of his life that the greater part of his small but concentrated philosophical and theological work derives: dialogues and treatises on, among other subjects, free will, truth, trinitarian theology, the Incarnation and divine prescience and predestination. From the time before the *Proslogion* there can be dated with certainty only some of his *Prayers* and *Meditations*, some letters and the *Monologion* (1075–76). Although the affective, unargumentative language of the *Prayers* and *Meditations* may seem to separate them sharply from Anselm's philosophical work, the *Proslogion* itself takes the form of a meditation (as does the *Monologion*). Its opening chapter – a "stirring up of the mind to contemplating God" – is four times the length of the chapter that follows, presenting what came to be known as the Ontological Argument, and the book ends with three more chapters in a meditative rather than argumentative vein. Are these sections simply to be ignored by historians of philosophy? I shall suggest nearer the end of my discussion that they are essential to the rationale of Anselm's project.

The connection between the *Monologion* and the *Proslogion* is more straightforward. The *Proslogion* is presented explicitly as a development of the project begun in the earlier work. What is that project? Anselm announces it very clearly in Chapter 1 of the *Monologion*:

> Suppose someone did not know – either because he had not heard or because he did not believe – that there is one nature, the highest of all things that are, who is alone sufficient for himself in his eternal happiness, and who through his omnipotent goodness grants and brings about that all other things are something and that they are in some way well, and the many other things that we believe to be necessarily the case about God and his creation: I think that, to a great extent, if he were modestly intelligent, he could persuade himself of them by reason alone. (13:5–10)[1]

Anselm then proceeds to give arguments to show that there is indeed one thing that is the best and "greatest" of all things that are. Other things are not only good and great through this thing; Anselm argues that it is also through this one same thing that other things are something at all. The following chapters add to this minimal characterization of God by explaining how he made all things from nothing, by considering the ways in which the ordinary language of predication (as set out in Aristotle's *Categories*) does and does not apply to him, and by showing how he is three, Father, Son and Holy Spirit, and yet one. Anselm makes many assumptions that, to most modern readers are patent and unacceptable, but he does not intentionally base any of his argumentation on authority, although he assures his readers that all he says will be found in Augustine.

The plan and aim of the *Proslogion*

At the very beginning of the *Proemium*, Anselm explains that after he had finished writing the *Monologion*,

> having it in mind that it had been made up by putting together many arguments, I began to ask myself whether perhaps one argument could be found, which required no argument other than itself in order to prove itself, and which would on its own be sufficient to establish that God truly is, that he is the highest goodness, which requires nothing else, and which all things require in order to be and be well, and whatever we believe about the divine substance. (93:4–9)

The *Proslogion*, then, will differ from the *Monologion* by presenting *one* argument rather than putting together a number of different arguments. But what is this single argument? From the description given, it needs to show not just that God exists, but that he is truly, and that he has various attributes, such as supreme goodness, self-sufficiency and the other central attributes according to Christian doctrine – the same aim as in the *Monologion* except that the Trinitarian attributes are excluded. Even a first glance at the *Proslogion* shows what Anselm must have had in mind. Almost at the very start of the argumentative part of the book, Anselm introduces the idea that we believe God to be "something than which nothing greater can be thought" (*aliquid quo nihil maius cogitari posit*, 101:5).

The whole treatise is structured around this formula, and it provides an argumentative structure that is repeated again and again in Chapters 1–15. In each case, Anselm argues that, given the meaning of this formula, the thing that satisfies it (which he has already stated we believe to be God) must:

- exist in reality and not just in the intellect (Chapter 2);
- exist in such a way that it cannot be conceived not to exist (Chapter 3);
- be the maker of all things from nothing, and just, true and happy (Chapter 5);
- be capable of sensing, omnipotent, compassionate, impassible and not a body (Chapter 6);
- be uncircumscribed by place and time (Chapter 13);
- be greater than can be thought (Chapter 15).

The pattern of reasoning is very straightforward, except in the first case. Underlying it is the argument that, if God is something than which nothing greater can be thought, then he must have any attribute *A* that has the following property: that it is such that what lacks *A* is less than can be thought. An attribute *A* has this property just in case it is better to be *A* than not to be *A*; we might (although Anselm does not use this word) call such attributes "perfections". So, for example, in Chapter 5, Anselm argues first that God is "that highest of all things, alone existing through itself, which made all other things from nothing" on the grounds that "Whatever is not that is less than can be thought. But this cannot be thought with regard to [God]. For what good can be lacking from the highest good, through which everything is good?" (S104:13–15).

Anselm then goes on to affirm that God is "just, true, happy and whatever *it is better to be than not to be*". God, that is to say, must have every perfection. This simple principle, which might be labelled "God's Necessary Perfection" is also used in Chapter 6 and in Chapter 13 (where it is put in terms of what it is greater or less great to be). The principle of God's Necessary Perfection had already been used in the *Monologion* 15, where it is explained more fully and given some of the necessary qualifications (*A* must not be a relative attribute, and *A* must be considered in isolation; it may well, for instance, be better to be just and not wise, than wise and not just, but in isolation it is better to be wise than not to be wise). The difference is that, in the *Proslogion*, the principle is derived from the affirmation that God is something than which nothing greater can be thought, which is also used to establish that God exists and how he exists, whereas in the *Monologion* it is a separate argument.

The "one argument" of the *Proslogion* is, therefore, not just the reasoning of Chapters 2 and 3, which came to be called, centuries later, the Ontological Argument. It is either the whole of the argumentation based on the power of the idea that God is something than which nothing greater can be thought, or – and more probably – when Anselm speaks of "one argument" he means the formula itself, "that than which nothing greater can be thought" (see Holopainen (1996: 133–45) for a thorough discussion). It was the power of this formula that, as he himself (S93:10–19) recounts, Anselm discovered suddenly one night after an obsessive search for the "one argument" he required. Anselm may in fact have been recollecting a form of words he had read in an ancient Roman writer, Seneca (Southern 1990: 129; cf. Gersh 1988: 273 and further references there), but it was still a discovery, in the sense that Seneca showed no awareness of the formula's importance and power. The argumentative sections after Chapter 15 are more loosely related to the formula, drawing out further, less obvious characteristics of that than which nothing greater can be thought. I shall try to explain in due course (see below, p. 186) why Chapter 15 acts as a turning point.

The argument of Chapter 2

Now it is time to turn to the famous argument in Chapter 2. First, there is a point about Anselm's vocabulary, which is often overlooked but has some important ramifications. In propounding the argument, he uses two verbs with close, but different shades of meaning: *cogito* (translated here as "think") and *intelligo* ("understand"). The most important difference between them is that *cogito* means "think" in a broad sense, so that I might well, in a fantasy, *cogito* that Cambridge is far bigger than London. By contrast, *intelligo*, at least usually, indicates cognitive success, so that, arguably, it would be wrong to say that I *intelligo* that Cambridge is much larger than London, or that something that exists does not exist (see Gaunilo, *Reply 7*: "according to the proper usage of this word, false things cannot be understood [*intelligi*]" (129:12–13); but cf. Anselm, *Reply 4*, 133:24–9).

The argument takes the form of a *reductio ad absurdum*, with the Fool of the Psalms (Psalms 14:1 and 55:1) proposing the premise that, in the end, will be negated: "The Fool says in his heart, God does not exist" [*non est Deus*]. Anselm continues by claiming that when the Fool hears me saying "something than which nothing greater can be thought", he understands what he hears and so "what he understands is in his intellect, even if he does not understand that it exists". Anselm then goes on to illustrate his contrast between understanding something and understanding that it exists. He refers to a painter, who thinks out in advance what he is about to paint, and so has it in his intellect, although he does not understand it to exist until he has painted it. After reaffirming that "something than which nothing greater can be thought" is in the Fool's intellect, Anselm gives the nub of his argument:

> And for certain that than which nothing greater can be thought cannot exist in the intellect alone. For if it is in the intellect alone, it can be thought to exist also in reality (*in re*), which is greater. If therefore that than which nothing greater can be thought is in the intellect alone, that than which nothing greater can be thought is that than which something greater can be thought.

Anselm's train of reasoning seems to be the following:

(1) God is something than which nothing greater can be thought. [Premise]

(2) If someone understands an expression "*a*", then *a* exists (*est*) [Premise]
in his intellect.

(3) The Fool understands "something than which nothing [Premise]
greater can be thought".

(4) Something than which nothing greater can be thought exists [2, 3]
in the Fool's intellect.

(5) Something than which nothing greater can be [Premise for *reductio*]
thought does not exist in reality.

(6) An implicit premise, asserting in some way that existence in
reality is a great-making property: see below.

(7) If that than which nothing greater can be thought exists in the
intellect and not in reality, then something can be thought
greater than it, namely, that than which nothing greater can be [6]
thought existing in reality also.

(8) Something can be thought that is greater than that than [4, 5, 7]
which nothing greater can be thought.

(9) That than which nothing greater can be thought is that than [8]

175

which something greater can be thought.

(10) It is not the case that something than   [Negation of 5, by indirect proof]
which nothing greater can be thought
does not exist in reality.

(11) God exists in reality.   [1, 10]

Steps (2), (6) and (7) call for further comment. Anselm can hardly mean, in (2), that when someone, for instance, understands "lion", there is literally a lion in his intellect. The example he gives, of the painter who conceives his picture mentally before he paints it, is rather a special case, because both the mental picture and the physical one are images of the same thing. What Anselm means in (2) depends on his broader semantic views, which were adapted from Augustine's *De Trinitate* and Boethius (especially his second commentary on Aristotle's *On Interpretation*). In the *Monologion* (Chapters 10 and 33), he suggests that spoken words naturally produce inner "words" in the mind of the hearer, "words" that are envisaged sometimes as concept-like, sometimes as images. It is because of the close resemblance between these concepts or images and the things of which they are concepts or images that we are able to think about things other than ourselves:

> Whenever the mind wishes to think truthfully, either through the imagination of the body or through the reason, it tries to express so far as it can its image [i.e. the image of what it is thinking] in its own thinking. The more truly it makes it, the more truly it thinks of the thing itself ...   (Chapter 33, 52:15–19)

The next problematic step in the argument is one that Anselm does not explicitly state. When he puts forward (7), he is taking it for granted that existing in reality is somehow great-making, but he does not make it clear how strong a claim he wants to make (Oppy 1995: 9–10, gives a list of the possibilities). Summarizing Anselm's argument, Gaunilo (125:8–9: "... and if it is in the intellect alone, *whatever* also exists in reality would be greater than it ...") takes him as proposing

(6a) Whatever exists in reality as well as in the intellect is greater than anything which exists in the intellect alone.

But (6a) raises some obvious objections: is a cancer, or a sin, greater (in Anselm's sense) because it exists in reality? Anselm only needs something much weaker, and easier to defend, for the purposes of his argument, such as

(6b) Something than which nothing greater can be thought is greater if it exists
in reality and the intellect than if it exists in the intellect alone.

Yet even this, weakest formulation has to meet the objections of those who deny
that existence can be a great-making predicate at all. They are twofold: that
existence is not a predicate (at all); and that, even if it is a predicate, existence is
not great-making.

Kant's contention that "to be" is not a "real predicate" (*Critique of Pure
Reason* A598B/B626), although once widely considered a fatal objection to
Anselm's argument, has been rejected as vague and unconvincing by a number
of recent philosophers who have looked at it closely (Oppy 1995: 130–51, 299–
316 for bibliography). Kant's slogan does, indeed, contain an important truth.
Whatever is predicated is predicated of a subject, and so that subject has, in some
sense, to exist before any predications can be made of it. If, then, I say "*a* exists",
what I am doing may be better described as saying that *a* is a subject for predication, than as making a predication (of existence) of *a*. But Anselm, who would
no doubt have acknowledged this truth as readily as Kant, frames his argument
so that something than which nothing greater can be thought is first shown to
exist in some sense: that is to say, in the Fool's intellect. Anselm then asks
whether what, as it has been granted, exists in the intellect, also exists in reality.
This procedure seems to be parallel to that in which, for instance, I have a mental
image of a particular building in certain street, but I do not know whether it is
something I have dreamed up or not, and I go and check out whether it exists in
reality. What objection can be brought to it on grounds of logic?

When Kant goes on in his critique to say that the real contains no more than
the possible – a hundred real pounds contain no more coins than a hundred
possible ones – he seems to be raising the second problem. Whether or not
existence is a predicate, it is not great-making. One response to this line of
objection is that, in the Platonic way of thinking Anselm knew from Augustine
and Boethius, it is usual to think of existence in degrees: the better a thing, the
more truly it exists. No doubt Anselm was influenced by this tradition in his
easy, indeed implicit, acceptance of the idea that existence is great-making, but
this claim can be accepted without the complications of the Platonic apparatus.
Kant himself admits that the real existence of the hundred thalers does make a
difference to his financial position, and there does seem to be an obvious sense
in which, for at least some things that are themselves of a sort to be valuable –
and, most obviously, for that than which nothing greater can be thought –
existing in reality adds value or greatness.

The real problem with Anselm's argument lies in (7). Consider what is said
to be the case in (4): that than which nothing greater can be thought is in the

Fool's intellect; that is to say, there is an image or concept there of that than which nothing greater can be thought (just as there is an image or concept in the painter's intellect of the painting he is going to produce). Although the Fool denies in (5) that there is anything in reality that corresponds to it, the content of this image or concept is that than which nothing greater can be thought existing in reality (it is not as if the Fool had heard and understood the expression "the understanding of that than which nothing greater can be thought". In (7) it is contended that something greater than what is in the Fool's intellect can be conceived: that than which nothing greater can be thought existing in reality too. But in what sense can this latter be conceived? Certainly, the opponent can take the view that – contrary to the Fool's contention – the image is of something that *does* exist in reality, but this would just be to offer an unargued assertion. What is in the Fool's intellect – as an image or concept – is itself already that than which nothing greater can be thought *in reality*; there is no room to posit something greater than it, and so generate a contradiction, by adding the great-making predicate of existence in reality. Indeed, granted Anselm's implicit premise at (6), there *is* a special characteristic of that than which nothing greater can be thought that distinguishes it from other concepts, but it is not that inspection of it shows that it must be instantiated. Rather, it is not a concept about which one could coherently affirm that it is instantiated but only in the world of fiction or make-believe. It makes perfectly good sense to say that my concept of Santa Claus is instantiated, but in the world of imagination, children's stories and the venal fantasies promoted by marketing executives, not in reality. It would, by contrast, be incoherent to claim that the Fool's concept of that than which nothing greater can be thought is instantiated, but only as (for example) a mythical being. If it were a mythical being, then (granted (6)) it would not be that than which nothing greater can be thought. What I need to say, if I wish to propose that many people, wrongly, hold that that than which nothing greater can be thought exists, is that many people say that there exists something that they describe wrongly as that than which nothing greater can be thought, but which *would* be that than which nothing greater can be thought *if* it existed, which it does not.

More on God's existence: Chapters 3, 4 and 15

Anselm ends Chapter 2 by affirming that "without doubt that than which nothing greater can be thought exists, both in the mind and reality" (102:2–3). When he begins Chapter 3 by saying that "This indeed so truly is, that he cannot be thought not to be" (102:6–7), he is clearly *not* beginning a fresh argument for the existence of that than which nothing greater can be thought, but adding a further qualification – or rather, an intensification – to what has already been established. The argument here is straightforward:

(12) That which cannot be thought not to exist is   [Premise]
     greater than that which can be thought not to exist.
(13) That than which nothing greater can be thought   [Premise for *reductio*]
     can be thought not to exist.
(14) That than which nothing greater can be thought   [12, 13]
     is not that than which nothing greater can be thought.
(15) That than which nothing greater can be   [not-13, by indirect proof]
     thought cannot be thought not to exist.

This argument is clearly valid, but it remains unclear what exactly it claims.

According to most modern interpreters, since (15) states in other words that the non-existence of God is inconceivable, this argument shows that God does not merely exist, but he exists *necessarily*, and this necessity is often explained, in modern re-workings, in terms of possible worlds: God exists at every possible world (see e.g. Malcolm 1960; Plantinga 1974). There is good reason, however, to reject such a reading, even if it is presented not as a literal interpretation, but as a working-out, with tools that Anselm himself lacked, of his underlying meaning. In his *Reply* to Gaunilo, Anselm makes it clear what he understands by (15). That than which nothing greater can be thought does not fail to exist at any place or any time, and this is an essential feature of it: if there were some time or some place at which it did not exist, then something greater than it could be thought (Reply I, 131:18–132:2). Anselm, then, thinks of possibility in terms of a single way that things happen along the line of time, and so talk of alternative possible worlds is certainly misleading. And there is good reason to avoid interpreting Anselm's conceivability in terms of possibility altogether. In Chapter 15, Anselm argues that that than which nothing greater can be thought is that which is greater than can be thought; otherwise something greater than it can be thought. This view seems undeniable: if x is greater than can be thought and y is not greater than can be thought, then x is greater than y. If, as the modern interpreters hold, being able to be thought – conceivability – means possibility, then what is greater than can be thought and so cannot be thought, being inconceivable, is by this interpretation therefore impossible.

Even when read as he intended it, there is a serious difficulty raised by Chapter 3, which Anselm indeed notices himself. In Chapter 2, he had quoted from the Psalm that "The Fool says in his heart, God does not exist": how could the

Fool say this in his heart, if that than which nothing greater can be thought, God, cannot be thought not to exist? It is very well for Anselm to quip that the reason why the Fool said to himself something so obviously untrue is that he is, indeed, a fool (103:9–11). He needs to explain how it was possible for the Fool to have such a thought at all. He does so by distinguishing between two different senses of "think" (*cogito*) (and of "say in one's heart", which he considers to mean exactly the same):

> A thing is thought in one way when the word (*vox*) which signifies it is thought, and in another way when that itself which is the thing is understood (*intelligitur*). In the first way, God can be thought not to be, but not at all in the second. No one, indeed, who understands that which God is, can think that God does not exist, even should he say these words in his heart, whether or not they have any outer meaning.
> (103:16–104:2)

Although this distinction apparently answers the difficulty, it actually opens up even more problems. In Chapter 2, Anselm had said that the Fool understands (*intelligit*) what he hears – that is to say "that than which nothing greater can be thought" – and what he understands is in his intellect (*in intellectu eius*). As explained, this seems to mean, given Anselm's semantics, that the Fool forms an image or concept in his intellect, the content of which is that than which nothing greater can be thought. But now Anselm is saying that all the Fool is doing is thinking the words "that than which nothing greater can be thought" without understanding the thing itself that they mean. This revision might seem to rescue the argument from the charge of invalidity due to (8) not in fact following from (4), (5) and (7). But how can the Fool now be said to "understand" these words, since understanding words, for Anselm, involves forming an image or concept of the thing that the words ultimately signify? Anselm, it seems, should not have claimed that that than which nothing greater can be thought was in the Fool's intellect at all. Perhaps, as subsequent developments will indicate (see below, pp. 190–91), he himself came to think so.

God's attributes: omnipotence, justice and mercy

For the moment, however, Anselm moves on to using – as explained above – the Principle of God's Necessary Perfection, derived from his formula, to establish the various attributes of God, such as that he is the creator of all things and that he is just, true, happy, omnipotent and compassionate. The ease with which he is able to accomplish this end should not be allowed to obscure its historical importance. Anselm is, here and in the *Monologion*, the great pioneer of perfect-being theology: the type of theology that attempts to learn about God by considering how he must be, given that he is omni-perfect. The tradition was continued by many of the great medieval theologians, including Aquinas and Scotus, and more recently by Leibniz and many contemporary philosophers of religion. Although Anselm had predecessors, notably Augustine and Boethius, no one had gone about the enterprise in this single-minded, direct way before him.

Anselm recognized, just as his distinguished successors in perfect-being theology would find, that many difficulties arise because an omni-perfect being will, it seems, have various attributes that are at first sight incompatible either with others of his attributes, or with other truths about God. Anselm's treatment of such problems shows him even more clearly as a pioneer: boldly identifying them, but not always arriving at adequate solutions. In Chapter 7, Anselm considers the problem of how it is true both that

(16) God is omnipotent.
(17) There are many things that God cannot do.

The Principle of God's Necessary Perfection entails (16) very obviously, but also (17), since God, being perfect, cannot lie or be corrupted. And (17) is also true (105:10–11) because even an omnipotent God cannot make the true false, or undo what has been done. Anselm's solution is to argue that (17) is not in fact true, because whenever sentences of the form "God cannot φ" are true, their negative verbal form is misleading. Whenever someone "is able" to do what does not benefit him and what should not be done, it is through lack of power rather than power; it is not that he is able, but that because of his lack of power something else can be done to him. Anselm gives as a parallel a sentence like "This person is sitting just as that one is doing", where "doing" is used to refer to a state of not doing anything. This linguistic analysis is ingenious, and it does seem to explain why "God cannot be corrupted" is compatible with (16), but the case is harder with regard to his inability to lie, and his powerlessness to change what is true to false or undo the past does not seem to be covered at all.

In Chapters 8–11, Anselm enters into a long discussion about the apparent paradoxes over God's justice and his *misericordia*. The first problem is how divine impassibility can be reconciled with God's *misericordia*. This problem arises because the usual meaning of *misericors* is not "merciful" (although this is how the translations usually render it) so much as compassionate: to be *misericors* means to feel something in sympathy with the person who is suffering. Anselm's answer is that, when God shows us *misericordia*, we feel its *effect*

– that is to say, we feel what it does, because we are spared punishment – but God does not feel any *a*ffect (106:11–12): he is not affected by any sort of feeling and so his impassibility remains undisturbed. Does this answer mean that God is not, in fact, compassionate? Certainly, on an Aristotelian view of compassion (*Rhetoric* 1385b), he is not, because for Aristotle it is part of the definition of being compassionate that a person might expect the evil that undeservedly afflicts the object of his pity to befall him or a friend of his too. But Anselm certainly did not know Aristotle's views on compassion, whereas he may possibly have come across those of an ancient writer who would be closer to his way of thinking in this area. Seneca, a Stoic, describes (*De clementia* II.5.i) *misericordia* as the vice of the small-minded, precisely because it involves suffering and the loss of tranquillity. The *misericordia* Anselm attributes to God would be a compassion purged of this affective element that makes Seneca reject it.

Even once Anselm has explained how it is to be understood, as a sparing of sinners from deserved punishment, God's *misericordia* – which I shall now translate as "mercy", since the English word fits this conception of it – still presents a very serious problem. How is it compatible with God's justice? One might take the view that just punishment simply is punishment that takes proper account of mercy: that, for example, the battered wife who kills her husband and is given a fairly short prison sentence is at once being justly and mercifully treated, because a longer sentence would not merely have lacked mercy, but would have been unjust. Anselm looks at the matter differently. There is a certain punishment that, in justice, the wicked deserve for what they have done; mercy requires that they do not receive their deserved punishment. The problem is particularly acute for Anselm, because the punishment in question is eternal damnation and, if it is remitted, the sinner will instead be given eternal life in heaven: a stark contrast, to say the least, and one that was even more dramatic in the eleventh century, before the development of the doctrine of purgatory, than it would be a couple of centuries later (Le Goff 1990). No wonder Anselm poses himself (Chapter 9, 107:1–3) anxiously the question, "From where, then, O good God, O good for the good and for the wicked, do you save the wicked, if this is not just and you do nothing which is not just?", and he is tempted at first to answer that it is because God's goodness is incomprehensible.

In fact, Anselm does think he can give something of an explanation. God is merciful, he says (108:5–7), because he is supremely good. But he is supremely good because he is supremely just. Therefore, he is merciful *because* he is supremely just. At first, this argument seems to make the paradox only more acute, since both of the following statements seem to be true (cf. Chapter 10, 108:4–25):

(18) It is just that God punishes the wicked.

(19) It is just that God spares [i.e. does not punish] the wicked.

The air of paradox can be removed, however, if the proper qualifications explaining in what way it is just in each case are inserted into (18) and (19). They should be rewritten, Anselm explains (108:27–109:1), as:

(20) It is just, because it accords with their deserts, that God punishes the wicked.

(21) It is just, because it befits his goodness, that God spares the wicked.

Anselm is able to summarize this distinction and link it to what he had argued before about *misericordia* and impassibility by saying that "in the same way as, in sparing the wicked, you are just with regard to yourself and not with regard to us, so you are merciful (*misericors*) with regard to us and not with regard to yourself" (109:1–2). This comparison, however, throws into relief the weakness of Anselm's position. It *is* plausible that some quality, not exactly what one would usually mean by compassion but within the general semantic range of *misericordia*, can be explained entirely in terms of what the *misericors* does to others, not what he feels. By contrast, it seems to be an essential part of what it means for a reward or punishment to be just that there is the correct relationship between it and the actions or intentions of the person rewarded or punished.

In any case, even allowing the distinction between justice with regard to us and with regard to God, Anselm's answer runs into an immediate difficulty, because he certainly does not believe that God saves all the wicked. At the beginning of Chapter 11, he admits that it is also just with regard to God that he punishes the wicked, because God is so just that no more just can be thought (109:10–11). And so Anselm has to agree that it is just with regard to God both when he punishes and when he spares from punishment. There is no contradiction here, he says (109:17–19), because

(22) Only what God wills is just, and what he does not will unjust

and so

(23) It is not just to save whomever God wills to punish, and it is not just to damn whomever God wills to spare.

Now (23) follows from (22), but what does (22) mean, and on what basis does Anselm propose it? At first sight, (22) appears to be an assertion of voluntarism:

justice is established by God's will, and there is no explanation for why something is just or unjust beyond the fact that God willed or did not will it. But (22) need not be read in this way. It could mean merely that the classes of just things and those willed by God have the same extension, and that any thing that is not just is unjust. This reading is preferable, because Anselm holds that God himself is just – "so just that no more just can be thought" – but God would not be just if to be just meant merely to be willed by God. Anselm is not asserting the dependence of moral values on an arbitrary divine will, but refining his account of the relationship between God's goodness and his justice suggested by (21). From (21), it might appear that God's sparing the wicked is just because it is in accord with his goodness; goodness would, then, be the supreme value, and divine justice would be adjusted according to it. But now Anselm explains that God's mercy derives from his justice, because it is just that God should be good in a way that includes sparing wicked people (109:19–20).

Making justice the highest of all values, beyond even goodness, is an unusual move, and pursuing its ramifications through Anselm's work would lead far beyond the confines of this discussion of the *Proslogion*. Yet Anselm has still left unanswered the main question he faces: why does God choose this sinner for salvation, and leave that one for damnation? This question is even more important than it might seem, because, according to Christian doctrine, since the Fall we are all born as sinners and without God's grace are unable to live well, and so the underlying question is really: why is this person saved, and that one damned? It may well be this background that stopped Anselm from making any attempt to explain God's choices by reference to gradations of wickedness and extenuating circumstances. Anselm is in no doubt that where, as here, perfect-being theology meets revealed Christian doctrine, its conclusions must be shaped and qualified by revelation, and so he is content to declare that God's choices about *which* wicked people he spares or damns are beyond comprehension.

Time, eternity and the hidden God

Anselm discusses God's relation to time and eternity at some length in Chapter 13 (along with his relation to place) and Chapters 18–21. It may not seem, at first, that he is tackling any special difficulty here. Unlike the discussion of justice and mercy, Anselm does not present these chapters as an anguished internal debate in which he strives to explain the seemingly inexplicable. Yet there is, just below the surface, a very difficult problem. God, of course, is eternal, but what is meant by divine eternity? There are two obvious answers. God may be eternal because he has existed and will exist for ever; his duration has no beginning or end. Let us call this sort of eternity "perpetuity". Or God may be eternal because he is not in time at all. We might call this type of eternity "time-lessness". The two conceptions of eternity seem to be sharply distinct, since a perpetual being exists at every time, whereas a timeless being exists at no time.

There is a widespread view among historians of philosophy that most medieval Christian thinkers up to and including Aquinas conceived of divine eternity as timelessness. They trace this tradition back, especially, to Boethius's *Consolation of Philosophy*. There an explicit distinction is made between perpetuity and God's eternity, which is said to be – in a definition that became classic in the Middle Ages – "the whole, perfect and simultaneous possession of unending life". Many commentators take Boethius here to be talking about eternity as timelessness, and it is common to place the *Proslogion*'s discussion within this tradition. It is possible, however, to take a different view (Marenbon 2003: 136–7). Boethius's eternity is certainly not mere perpetuity, but it is not at all clear that he would have denied that temporal statements such as "God has been just" and "God will be merciful" are true. The language of duration he uses to describe eternity, and his conception of it as God's way of living, make it hard to imagine that he thought of it as simply timeless. The *Monologion* (20–24) makes it very clear that Anselm, more than anyone, recognized that there are good reasons for conceiving God's eternity as perpetuity and good reasons also for not thinking of it as temporal in the ordinary way. He argues, first (20), that God exists at every time, since his existence is required for the existence of anything else. But then he shows (21) that God cannot exist in time at all, because if he did so, he would have temporal parts, whereas God has no parts. Anselm's solution is to say that God exists in time (or, better he thinks, "with time") but is not bounded or measured by it, and so he has no temporal parts.

In the *Proslogion*, however, Anselm writes about God that: "You ... were not yesterday nor will be tomorrow, but yesterday and today and tomorrow you are. Rather, you are not yesterday nor today nor tomorrow, but without qualification you are outside all time" (Chapter 19, 115:11–13). There is certainly a change of emphasis in this passage from what he had said a couple of years earlier, but Anselm is saying *not* that divine eternity is timelessness, but just that God is "outside" time. He still recognizes, just as in the *Monologion*, the need to assert in some way God's perpetual existence.

In Chapter 13, where the subject is first raised, Anselm is treating God's relations with place and time in parallel. His point here, which follows neatly on the view of divine eternity presented in the *Monologion*, is that whatever is "in some way enclosed by time or space is less than what the law of place or time does not restrict" (110:12–13). God therefore is "everywhere and always", he is "uncircumscribed and eternal". Anselm has to add some explanation as to how

God's uncircumscribedness – God is "as a whole everywhere at the same time" (*simul ubique totus*, a traditional formula for divine omnipresence) – is different from the omnipresence of created spiritual beings, including the soul, which can be wholly in more than one place at the same time, but not everywhere. But he can establish with hardly any argument that God alone is eternal, because he alone of all things lacks not only an end to his existence but also a beginning (110:17–18). At this stage, then, Anselm envisages God's eternity as perpetuity of some sort.

Before Anselm takes up the subject of divine eternity again, his course of thinking has taken an important turn. Chapter 14 is an impassioned address to God. "Have I found you, you whom I am seeking?", Anselm asks. He repeats his formula and resumes what he has discovered through it. How then does he not "feel" God, if he has found him? The answer is that he sees God just a little, and not as he is, but when he strains to see God better, he is met by darkness. Chapter 15 uses the formula to explain why this is so. Here Anselm shows – as mentioned already – that that than which nothing greater can be thought is greater than can be thought. The formula itself indicates, then, that it can be filled in only incompletely and sketchily. But Anselm does not abandon the attempt to add some more detail to what he has already established.

Before he returns to the question of divine eternity, Anselm considers whether God is made of parts. Here, what he seems to be doing is to use his formula to probe beyond the limits of what he can fully comprehend. He had previously, as he says, established that God is life, wisdom, truth, goodness, happiness, eternity and every true good. His mind, however, "cannot see so many things in one glance, so as to enjoy them all at once" (Chapter 18, 114:16–17). None the less, he is able to work out that these cannot be considered to be parts of God, but rather, as a whole, they are identical with God. If God were made of parts, then he could be broken up, in thought or in act, and in that case he would not be that than which nothing greater can be thought.

The reconsideration of divine eternity follows on from the recognition that God has no parts. If, Anselm asks, God was and is and will be throughout eternity and "to have been is not to be about to be, and to be is not to have been or to be about to be, how does your whole eternity always exist?" (Chapter 19, 115:7–9). The problem is exactly that he had tackled in the *Monologion*: since God and his eternity are identical, if he exists perpetually he will be broken into temporal parts. There follows the passage quoted above, where Anselm denies that God is in time at all. Does he now, therefore, abandon the view he had put forward a few pages before and in the *Monologion* and opt for a timeless God? The next lines make it clear that he does not. God is not in time (nor in place); rather, they are in him, "For nothing contains you, but you contain all things"

(115:15). If God were timeless, then time would simply have nothing to do with him. But Anselm makes God's eternity closely related to time, although the relationship is the converse of that between a temporal being and time, one of containing rather than being contained. The next chapter shows how much Anselm still thinks of eternity as being like, but far exceeding, the state of something that exists perpetually. There are things other than God that have no end to their existence. How does God differ from them? An advocate of divine timelessness would have a straightforward answer: God would differ from them by existing at no point of time at all. Rather, Anselm notes three types of difference. First, other things that have no end are causally dependent on God. Secondly, they can be *thought* to have an end, whereas God cannot. Thirdly, God's and their eternity is always present as a whole to God, whereas other unending things have neither what is to come nor what has passed. Neither of the first two points at all suggests divine timelessness (indeed, the second makes a close parallel between God and perpetual things), while the third merely repeats Boethius's idea about God's special way of existing, which need not, although it often is, be interpreted in the sense of timelessness. Altogether, Anselm's view of divine eternity in the *Proslogion* seems to be very close to that in the *Monologion*, although the point that God is not *in* time, but contains it, is brought out more explicitly.

If Anselm were to be criticized because he has not made it clear exactly how we are to understand the idea of an eternity that contains all times and in which past, present and future are simultaneous, he could reply that we should expect to be puzzled, because we are trying to grasp aspects not entirely within our comprehension of that which is greater than can be thought. He now (Chapter 22) goes on to look at two further ways – one that Boethius had specially emphasized (*De trinitate* 2) and the other particularly dear to Augustine (e.g. *De trinitate* V, 2) – in which God's way of existing is quite different from that of other things: God is what he is, and he is he who is (exists: *est*). Here he draws on what he has already established by using his formula. Since God is immutable and has no parts, he must be what he is. And God alone, who has no beginning to his existence, cannot be thought not to be, is not dependent on anything else, and is not affected by the flow of time (he "does not have having been or about to be but only being present", 116:22–23), can be said to exist properly speaking and absolutely. There follows a very brief excursion into Trinitarian theology (Chapter 23), a theme that occupies much of the *Monologion*, which does not attempt any rational demonstration that God is triune, but simply introduces the terms that were standardly used to describe the persons of the Trinity (God's "word" for the Son, and his "love" for the Holy Spirit) and proceeds to talk about God using them.

Exemplum meditationis

The chapters that follow do not, at least in a straightforward sense, take the philosophical argument any further. They are dedicated to describing the good that God is from the point of one who enjoys it but looks forward to enjoying it more completely in another life. They are, that is to say, an evocation of heavenly bliss, a piece of metaphysical prose poetry as remarkable in its achievement as anything earlier in the *Proslogion*, even the famous Argument.

A reader might accept the strange beauty of these sections, and of the long prayer-like first chapter of the work, but regard them as belonging to an intellectual enterprise distinct from that which has been the subject of this essay: the *Proslogion* would be seen as a philosophical jewel in a golden setting of religious rhetoric. But such an approach would be misguided. The prayerful prose poetry is not confined to the beginning and end of the piece. Chapter 14 is written in this style, and Chapter 17, dedicated to showing that the perfect objects of the five senses are in God in a way that words cannot describe, is in the same vein. More importantly, the manner of writing in these chapters recurs almost everywhere, although more sporadically, and Anselm's stance with regard to his human audience, on the one hand, and his explicit addressee, God, is the same at the work's moment of most prayerful abandon as in its toughest argument. The readers are bystanders. Their onlooking is tolerated, invited even, but they are there to observe Anselm at thought and at prayer (for him there is no distinction between praying to God and the type of thinking about him exemplified in the *Proslogion*). In the preface to the *Monologion*, Anselm explains that he was asked by his fellow monks to provide an "example of meditation" on God's essence. In the *Monologion*, though, Anselm gave them something much nearer to a treatise, setting out in the third person how someone, without revelation, could establish the various truths of the Christian faith. In the *Proslogion*, Anselm provides what they had asked. We are invited to follow Anselm, the speaker, throughout, as he draws himself closer, through his process of reflection, to God, to whom he is addressing his thoughts.

The recognition that the *Proslogion* is the record of a meditation has a bearing on how the famous argument is read. There was a time when the interpretation of the argument by Karl Barth had many followers. Barth (1960) insisted that Anselm was *not* attempting to propose a rational proof of God's existence, and that that than which nothing greater can be thought is a name of God. Most scholars now agree that Barth's analysis reflects his own theology more than Anselm's. But, like many influential but misleading views, it contains an important element of truth. Anselm is not putting forward a textbook proof of God's existence. He is inviting others to follow his own thought process, in which he engages, not as an atheist or agnostic needing a rational argument to make him believe that God exists, but as a firm believer who regards the discoveries about God he makes through his course of rational reflection as the fruits of divine illumination. The *Proslogion* is a work of practical philosophy, a series of spiritual exercises (like much ancient Greek philosophy; see Hadot (1995)), which lead Anselm himself, and the onlooking reader vicariously, towards God. As such, it needs to be read as a whole, not pulling Chapters 2 and 3 from their context, and not trying to separate the argumentative from the prayerful, meditative sections.

Anselm's second thoughts

Is it not, then, one of the great ironies of the history of philosophy that, except for a few specialists, almost no one is interested in reading the *Proslogion* as a whole? The Ontological Argument, well known but frequently criticized in the Middle Ages, has become an object of fascination since the great early modern philosophers, Descartes, Spinoza and Leibniz, made it their own – in a version distant from Anselm's – and modern thinkers have prided themselves on formulating ever more elaborate versions of the Argument, which is like a trap, captivating the ingenuity of philosophers. Yet there is a deeper irony.

The first person to respond to the *Proslogion* was the otherwise unknown monk, Gaunilo of Marmoutiers, who wrote his *Reply on Behalf of the Fool*, a critique of the argument of Chapter 2, shortly after the work was finished, and was answered by Anselm himself. The exchange has usually disappointed historians of philosophy. Gaunilo is often taxed with not having properly understood Anselm's reasoning, while Anselm, in turn, is certainly guilty of answering Gaunilo's strongest arguments inadequately (cf. Wolterstorff 1993). This objection (*Reply* 6) takes the form of a parody argument: an argument that is intended to have exactly the same structure as Anselm's Chapter 2, but in which instead of the formula "that than which nothing greater can be thought" there is substituted "the island than which none greater can be thought". (Gaunilo's formulation is, in fact, a good deal looser than this, but he clearly intends to parody Anselm's proof.) If Anselm's pattern of argument allows us to prove the existence of an ideal island (an ideal palace, an idea lawnmower – there will be no end to the examples), there must be something wrong with it. The onus, then, is on Anselm to show why the substitute formula changes the argument and makes it unacceptable. But Anselm merely *asserts* (*Reply to Gaunilo 3*, 133:6–9) that there is nothing at all that can be substituted for that than which nothing greater can be thought and preserve the cogency of the argument. Later philosophers have come to his rescue by providing reasons why the notion of an x such that no greater x can be thought does not make sense if the x is spatiotemporal, or if x is any specific sort of a thing (an island, a palace or whatever), because it is impossible to say what characteristics would belong to the greatest conceivable x. It is still a matter of debate whether these answers are satisfactory.

There may well be more philosophical interest than has been suspected in other parts of the exchange between Anselm and Gaunilo. In this essay, which is devoted to the *Proslogion* itself, there is space merely to indicate one way in which Anselm continues here a pattern of development in his thinking already evident in the steps of his initial presentation of his famous Argument. I suggested above that, by Chapter 4, Anselm is already in deep trouble with his idea that that than which nothing greater can be thought is "in the intellect" of the Fool. At the end of that chapter, he seems to be reformulating his argument so as to avoid the whole apparatus of existence in the intellect contrasted with existence in reality:

> For God is that than which nothing greater can be thought. Whoever understands this well, understands indeed that he exists in such a way that he is not able not to exist in thought. Whoever, therefore, understands that God exists in such a way, cannot think that he does not exist. (104:2–4)

One of Anselm's main concerns in his *Reply* seems to be, not to answer Gaunilo directly, but to reformulate the Argument along the lines suggested by this passage from Chapter 4. So, for example, he begins his counter-attack with this entirely new version of his reasoning:

(24) That than which nothing greater can be thought   [Premise]
      cannot be thought except as being without a beginning.
(25) Everything which can be thought to exist and does   [Premise]
      not exist can be thought to have a beginning.
(26) Therefore that than which nothing greater can be   [24, 25]
      thought cannot be thought to be and not be.
(27) Therefore, if that than which nothing greater can be   [26]
      thought can be thought to exist, it exists from necessity.

Given Anselm's Aristotelian view of modality, according to which there are no synchronic alternative possibilities, and what is, is necessarily, when it is (cf. Knuuttila 1993: 1–18 and *passim*), this is an elegant and powerful argument.

Premise (25) can, arguably, be justified, because – on this view of modality – the only way in which something could be thought to exist, when it does not, would be by beginning to exist at some time. Whatever, though, its strengths and weaknesses, this piece of reasoning illustrates very well how, by the time he writes his *Reply*, Anselm has entirely abandoned his attempt to put his Argument using the semantics of existence in the intellect and in reality. And the argument about God as being without a beginning is not the only example. Indeed, the *Reply* is characterized by an almost obsessive wish to reformulate the proof without making the semantic assumptions of Chapter 2. If Gaunilo was the first person to be trapped in the logical web spun by the imaginary encounter between Anselm and the Fool, Anselm himself was the second.

Notes

1. All references to Anselm's works, unless otherwise indicated, are to the pages:lines of Volume I of Schmitt 1938–61.

Bibliography

Adams, M. McCord 2000. "Re-reading *De grammatico* or Anselm's Introduction to Aristotle's *Categories*", *Documenti e studi sulla tradizione filosofica medievale* 11, 83–112.

Adams, R. 1971. "The Logical Structure of Anselm's Argument", *Philosophical Review* 80, 28–54.

Barnes, J. 1972. *The Ontological Argument*. London: Macmillan.

Barth, K. 1960. *"Fides quaerens intellectum": Anselm's Proof of the Existence of God in the Context of his Theological Scheme*, London: SCM.

Charlesworth, M. 1965. *Anselm's Proslogion*. Oxford: Oxford University Press.

Davies, B. & B. Leftow (eds) 2004. *The Cambridge Companion to Anselm*. Cambridge: Cambridge University Press.

Davies, B. & G. R. Evans 1998. *Anselm of Canterbury: The Major Works*. Oxford: Oxford University Press.

Dronke, P. (ed.) 1988. *A History of Twelfth-Century Western Philosophy*. Cambridge: Cambridge University Press.

Foreville, R. (ed.) 1984. *Les mutations socio-culturelles au tournant des XIe-XIIe siècles*, Spicilegium Beccense 2. Paris: Éditions du Centre National de la Recherche Scientifique.

Fredborg, K. M. 1988. "Speculative Grammar", in *A History of Twelfth-Century Western Philosophy*, P. Dronke (ed.), 177–95. Cambridge: Cambridge University Press.

Gersh, S. 1988. "Anselm" , in *A History of Twelfth-Century Western Philosophy*, P. Dronke (ed.), 255–78. Cambridge: Cambridge University Press.

Hartshorne, C. 1965. *Anselm's Discovery: A Re-Examination of the Ontological Proof for God's Existence*. La Salle, IL: Open Court.

Henry, D. 1967. *The Logic of Anselm*. Oxford: Oxford University Press.

Holopainen, T. J. 1996. *Dialectic and Theology in the Eleventh Century*. Leiden: Brill.

Hopkins, J. M. 1972. *A Companion to the Study of St Anselm*. Minneapolis, MN: Minnesota University Press.

Hick, J. & A. C. McGill (eds) 1968. *The Many-Faced Argument: Recent Studies on the Ontological Argument for the Existence of God*. London: Macmillan.

Kapriev, G. 1998. *. . . Ipsa Vita Et Veritas. Der "Ontologische Gottesbeweis" und die Ideenwelt Anselms von Canterbury*. Leiden: Brill.

Klima, G. 2000. "Saint Anselm's Proof: A Problem of Reference, Intentional Identity and Mutual Understanding", in *Medieval Philosophy and Modern Times*, J. Hintikka (ed.), 69–88. Dordrecht: Kluwer. [Preprint available at www.fordham.edu/gsas/phil/klima/anselm.htm (accessed Oct. 2004).]

Knuuttila, S. 1993. *Modalities in Medieval Philosophy*. London: Routledge.

Leftow, B. 1991. *Time and Eternity*. Ithaca, NY: Cornell University Press.

Le Goff, J. 1990. *The Birth of Purgatory*, A. Goldhammer (trans.). London: Scolar Press.

Lewis, D. 1970. "Anselm and Actuality", *Noûs* 4, 175–88. Reprinted with a postscript in Lewis (1983: 21–5).

Lewis, D. 1983. *Philosophical Papers*, vol. 1. Oxford: Oxford University Press.

Luscombe, D. E. & G. Evans 1996. *Anselm: Aosta, Bec and Canterbury*. Sheffield: Sheffield Academic Press.

Malcolm, N. 1960. "Anselm's Ontological Arguments", *Philosophical Review* 69, 41–62.

Marenbon, J. 1988. *Early Medieval Philosophy (480–1150): An Introduction*, 2nd edn. London: Routledge.

Marenbon, J. 2003. *Boethius*. Oxford: Oxford University Press.

Marenbon, J. (forthcoming) "Les Catégories au début du Moyen Âge", Proceedings of 2002 Categories Conference (Geneva), A. De Libera *et al.* (eds).

Millican, P. 2004. "The One Fatal Flaw in Anselm's Argument", *Mind* 113(451), 437–76.

Oppenheimer, P. E. & E. N. Zalta 1991. "On the Logic of the Ontological Argument", in *Philosophical Perspectives 5: The Philosophy of Religion*, J. Tomberlin (ed.), 509–29. Atascadero, CA: Ridgeview. [Preprint available at http://mally.stanford.edu/ontological.pdf (accessed Oct. 2004).]

Oppy, G. 1995. *Ontological Arguments and Belief in God*. Cambridge: Cambridge University Press.

Plantinga, A. (ed.) 1968. *The Ontological Argument: From St. Anselm to Contemporary Philosophers*. London: Macmillan.

Plantinga, A. 1974. *The Nature of Necessity*. Oxford: Oxford University Press.

Schmitt, F. S. (ed.) 1938–61. *S. Anselmi Cantuariensis archiepiscopi opera omnia*. Edinburgh: Thomas Nelson. [Vol. 1: Seckau; Vol. 2: Rome.]

Schufreider, G. 1978. *An Introduction to Anselm's Argument*. Philadelphia, PA: Temple University Press.

Southern, R. 1963. *St Anselm and his Biographer: A Study of Monastic Life and Thought*. Cambridge: Cambridge University Press.

Southern, R. 1990. *Saint Anselm: A Portrait in a Landscape*. Cambridge: Cambridge University Press.

Southern, R. & F. S. Schmitt 1969. *Memorials of St. Anselm*. Oxford: Auctores Britannici medii aevi 1.

Vuillemin, J. 1971. *Le Dieu d'Anselme et les apparences de la raison*. Paris: Aubier Montaigne.

Wolterstorff, N. 1993. "In Defense of Gaunilo's Defense of the Fool", in *Christian Perspectives on Religious Knowledge*, C. S. Evans & M. Westphal (eds). Grand Rapids, MI: Eerdmans.

Further reading

The Latin text of Anselm's works is edited in Schmitt (1938–61); the *Proslogion* and *Monologion* are in Volume 1. Charlesworth (1965) provides Schmitt's text of the *Proslogion*, Gaunilo's critique and Anselm's response, all with a facing English translation, a useful introduction and a quite thorough philosophical commentary. Charlesworth's translation is reproduced along with Anselm's other important works in Davies and Evans (1998). A translation of the *Proslogion*, Gaunilo's critique and Anselm's response is available on-line at http://www.fordham.edu/halsall/basis/anselm-gannilo.html. On Anselm's life, cultural context and role as a churchman, Southern (1963) and Southern (1990) are indispensable. Hopkins (1972) is useful as a general guide to Anselm's writings, and Henry (1967) gives a fascinating although demanding exposition of his logic, especially that of *De grammatico*. For the wider philosophical background, see the important study by Toivo Holopainen (1996); Marenbon (1988) might also be useful. Holopainen (1996) is good, too, on Anselm's methodology, as is Gersh (1988). Papers on many aspects of Anselm, including the *Proslogion*, are found in Foreville (1984), and Luscombe and Evans (1996).

The literature on the ontological argument is vast, although there is very little at all written on the *Proslogion* as a whole. One of the most thorough studies, which keeps close to Anselm's text, is Kapriev (1998). Klima (2000) combines historical accuracy with logical acuity. One of the very few authors to bring out the importance of the meditative element in the *Proslogion* is Schufreider (1978). A close, logical study of Anselm's argument is provided in Barnes (1972), and a fully formal version of the argument in Adams (1971). See also Oppenheimer and Zalta (1991). Two detailed studies of the argument, from very different philosophical perspectives, are those by Hartshorne (1965) and Vuillemin (1971). A very recent contribution to the debate is Millican (2004). There are two useful anthologies: Plantinga (1968) includes translations of the early modern versions and criticisms of the Argument as well as some recent articles; Hick and McGill (1968) concentrate on the (then) modern literature. Recently, philosophers have been especially interested in modal versions of the Argument. Malcolm (1960) (also reprinted in Plantinga (1968: 136–59)) helped to start this trend, and the most important contribution to it is in Plantinga (1974: 196–221). A different, modal tack is found in Lewis (1970, 1983). Oppy (1995) provides an extremely thorough and philosophically acute survey of the many different forms the Ontological Argument has taken, and of the objections to them. Oppy summarizes his views in an article for the on-line *Stanford Encyclopedia of Philosophy* (www.seop.leeds.ac.uk/entries/ontological-arguments (accessed Oct. 2004)). Davies and Leftow (2004) appeared when this chapter was in proof: it contains important essays on the ontological argument, perfect being theology and many other topics.

On the treatment of time and eternity, by the far the best study is in the chapter on Anselm in Leftow (1991).

8

Aquinas
Summa Theologiae

Paul O'Grady

Introduction

The presence of a book whose title translates as "Summary of Theology" might seem odd in a list of great works of philosophy. Yet Aquinas's major work does make a significant contribution to the history of philosophy and has had wide-ranging influence on many philosophers. However, the initial puzzlement one might feel about the title is reflected in the different kinds of scholarly responses to Aquinas's work. Over the centuries, some philosophers have delighted in attacking Aquinas as the philosophical representative of the Catholic Church, and in so doing exposing the perceived errors and perniciousness of that institution. Others have treated Aquinas's writings as almost holy writ and have exhibited excessive reverence and lack of critical distance in their appreciation of his thought. In both approaches there has been a layer of non-philosophical baggage obscuring the philosophical merits or demerits of Aquinas's work.

This issue is ongoing and is reflected in recent scholarship on Aquinas. While there has been some excellent work investigating the philosophical value of Aquinas's thought, much recent work focuses on Aquinas as a theologian and seeks to downplay the independent philosophical value of his writing. Some of this seeks to counterbalance readings of Aquinas that treat him anachronistically and ignore the historical context of the production of his work. However one can be hermeneutically faithful to that context while simultaneously treating his work as a contribution to the history of philosophy.

The division in Aquinas scholarship between those who read him as a philosopher and those who seek to read him as primarily a theologian often reflects substantively different views on the relationship of faith to reason. Many philosophers will cavil at the very idea of faith and reject as incoherent the notion of revealed theology. Others want to argue that faith and reason are, in a certain sense, incommensurable approaches to reality and that therefore those with faith see the world in a way that is different from those who do not and rely solely on reason. Aquinas differs from both these positions. He wants to value *both* faith and reason. He thinks that human reason, as part of nature, is good and is an important aspect of human flourishing. He simultaneously holds that there are some beliefs that cannot derive from reason alone, but that are nevertheless reasonable to hold; that is, those beliefs that are held on faith are compatible with reason. In this respect Aquinas articulates a surprisingly robust account of reason (certainly when contrasted with other religious thinkers such as later Augustine or Kierkegaard) and is a thinker whom non-believers can argue with, rather than wonder about from an incommensurable perspective.

This intellectual robustness is evident in his philosophy of religion (on the existence and nature of God), and also in his accounts of the general nature of reality, human existence, cognition, philosophy of action, freedom, emotion, virtue, natural law theory and aesthetics and in specific points of philosophical theology (the Trinity, the Incarnation). In the following sections of this chapter I wish to examine: the historical context of the *Summa Theologiae*; its general structure; its account of the relationship of faith and reason; the existence of God; the nature of God; human existence; and ethics; and then conclude with some reflections on its place in the history of philosophy.

The historical context

The term "scholasticism" is often used to characterize the philosophy of the mid- and late-medieval period. Etymologically this term derives from the Latin for "school". One main characteristic of scholastic philosophy is its corporate nature; a large number of individuals work together with shared approaches and methods to achieve common goals. Because of this, scholastic philosophy exhibits a high degree of professionalism and technicality and can be quite difficult to read.

After the end of the Hellenistic period, education, including higher education, in western Europe was kept alive chiefly in monastic schools. These were conservative contexts where innovation was discouraged and the main focus was the preservation of ancient learning. Apart from the court of Charlemagne (the so-called Carolingian Renaissance), philosophy in the West began to find a role for itself in the cathedral schools of the late eleventh and early twelfth centuries. After a basic training in the seven liberal arts (grammar, logic, rhetoric, arithmetic, geometry, astronomy and music), scholars in these schools moved on to theological studies. However, philosophers such as Anselm of Canterbury began to deploy certain philosophical arguments in the service of theology, drawing on the Aristotelian tradition in logic. In the early twelfth century, Peter Abelard brought to prominence the discussion of the nature of universals (i.e. what is the reference of general terms such as "truth" or "goodness") and associated epistemological questions about how such things could be known. Abelard applied this kind of reasoning more systematically to theological topics but was opposed in this by conservatives, such as Bernard of Clairvaux. The latter part of the twelfth century saw a resurgence in the study of the works of Aristotle. Aristotle's works had been lost to western Europe (the Athenian schools of philosophy were shut down by the emperor Justinian in 529 CE and the scholars took their texts eastwards) and the dominant style of philosophy up to the mid-twelfth century was a neo-Platonism chiefly mediated by Augustine, Boethius and Pseudo-Dionysius the Areopagite, and adapted to Christianity. Islamic and Jewish scholars in Spain had access to Aristotelian texts, however, and by the late twelfth century these were being translated into Latin, causing a revolution in theological and scientific thought.

By the beginning of the thirteenth century the scholars of Paris banded together into a guild and constituted the first university. The appearance of this new form of educational institution coincided with the Aristotelian influx. The university had a number of faculties, with Arts as the basic one and Theology, Medicine and Law as higher faculties. Initially there was some resistance to the study of Aristotle, since it was regarded as inimical to Christian belief. Aristotle defended the eternity of the world and the lack of personal immortality, and had no role for revealed religion. Yet Aristotelian views in logic, philosophy of language, epistemology, psychology, ethics and metaphysics were fascinating the scholars of early thirteenth-century Paris. Soon the curriculum of the Arts faculty was completely dominated by Aristotelianism. The Theology faculty, largely wedded to an older neo-Platonist heritage, looked on nervously at this development.

The modes of education in the university heavily influenced the genres in which philosophy was written. The basic form of teaching was a reading of a text (*lectio* – lecture) in which the basic meaning of the text was outlined and then further layers of interpretative meaning were found. Hence one genre of philosophical writing was the commentary. Another mode of teaching was the disputation. Postgraduate students debated with one another in a set pattern under the supervision of a master: a thesis was proposed; objections were levelled against it; and the proposer defended his thesis and then answered the objections. The master adjudicated the dispute. The logical validity of the argumentation was paramount, as was the citation of authorities. However, it was clearly accepted that the argument from authority cut little ice in philosophy, while it was more important in theology. Special disputations were held twice yearly at the university, accompanied by festivities, where the masters, or tenured professors, disputed with each other, often on extemporized topics (*disputationes quodlibitales*). A disputed issue was written up as a *quaestio*. *Quaestiones* could have a number of subsidiary issues contained within them and so were subdivided into articles. The article was the basic unit of philosophical pedagogy, often arising as a puzzle from the reading of some text, and seeking an argumentative adjudication of some disputed point. The text of Aquinas's *Summa Theologiae* contains thousands of such articles, each a vignette of dialectical argumentation.

Thomas Aquinas was born in Roccasecca, south of Naples, probably in 1225. Educated at Monte Cassino Abbey in his early years, he studied at the University of Naples from 1239 and there gained an early education in Aristotelian philosophy. In Naples he encountered a new religious movement, the friars of the Dominican Order, who were committed to poverty, study and preaching, and he joined their ranks in 1244. He studied at Paris and also at Cologne with Albert the Great, a scholar committed to the use of Aristotle in the development of Christian theology. Returning to Paris in 1252 he entered the theology faculty and graduated as a Master of Theology, the highest degree in the university. He taught in Paris until 1259, and then moved to Italy, where he remained for the next ten years. During this time he taught within Dominican houses of study, completed the *Summa Contra Gentiles* and started the *Summa Theologiae* (*c.*1265). In 1269 Aquinas returned to Paris to engage in controversy about Aristotle. A movement in the arts faculty argued that key Aristotelian views were incompatible with Christian belief (called variously Radical Aristotelianism or Latin Averroism). Aquinas argued on two fronts: against the conservative theology faculty for the legitimacy of Aristotle and against the Radical Aristotelians on the correct interpretation of Aristotle. Aquinas's usually impassive prose erupted into anger against those "who speak in corners or in the presence of boys who do not know how to judge about such difficult matters, but let him write against this treatise if he dares" (*De Unitate Intellectus Contra Averroistas*, #124). In late 1273 something happened to Aquinas. His biographer recounts that he had a religious experience and ceased writing (or dictating at furious speed to secretaries). Perhaps he had a stroke. Not in good health, he travelled, as ever by foot, to defend the use of Aristotle in theology at a church council in Lyons. His aged teacher, Albert the Great, set out from

Cologne to join in his defence. Aquinas never got there, dying in the Cistercian abbey of Fossanova, not far from his birthplace. The *Summa Theologiae* was left incomplete when he died, aged probably just under 50, but his *oeuvre* amounted to several million words. Despite its lack of completion, the *Summa Theologiae* is regarded as his masterwork, summarizing and developing his earlier work and providing a complete, logically articulated, theistic worldview.

The structure of the *Summa Theologiae*

Because of the *quaestio*-structure of articles in the *Summa*, casual readers are often confused about Aquinas's actual views. Every article begins with objections to the view he wants to defend, followed by the citation of an authority in agreement with his view, a reasoned defence of the position and a reply to the objections. So the first views canvassed in every article are those Aquinas actually opposes.

The *Summa* is divided into three main divisions and written in the rather technical Latin of the medieval university, which avoided rhetorical flourish in order to render clear the structure of argument. The first part (*Prima Pars*) deals with God and Creation. The second part deals with human action and ethics and is itself subdivided into two further sections. The first part of the second part (*Prima Secundae*) looks at general theoretical issues about human action while the second part of the second part (*Secunda Secundae*) examines specific virtues and vices. The third part (*Tertia Pars*) looks at specifically Christian topics, such as the Incarnation and the role of sacraments. There is much material of philosophical interest throughout all these discussions, whether explicitly philosophical treatments of, say human cognition, or the application of philosophical principles in theological discussion, for example about the Incarnation.

There is a standard method of referring to texts in the *Summa Theologiae*, giving the part, the question and the article. For example, Aquinas has a rejection of the Platonic account of knowledge as reminiscence in his discussion of how human beings know physical realities. The discussion is contained in the first part, question 84, article 3. This is usually abbreviated as Ia q.84 a.3. A further specification as to which part of the article (the objections, the body of the article or the replies to objections) may also be given.

Interpreters have noted the neo-Platonic structure inherent in the overall shape of the work. It exhibits an overarching pattern of exit and return (called *exitus–reditus*), initially discussing God as the source of all creation and then examining the response of rational creatures to God. There is disagreement about how exactly the *exitus-reditus* schema fits all parts of the *Summa*. However let's examine the less controversial issue of the general topics discussed in the work.

In the *Prima Pars*, q.1 deals with the nature of *Sacra Doctrina*, a term usually translated as theology, and situates this study in the context of the Aristotelian model of science. Questions 2–26 deal with the existence and nature of God, while qq.27–43 deal with Trinitarian theology (in passing yielding insights to Aquinas's views on mind and aesthetics). Creation in general is discussed in qq.44–6 (where, perhaps surprisingly Aquinas allows for the philosophical possibility of the eternity of the world). Angels provide some interesting speculative problems in qq.50–64. Not being connected to matter and so not having any senses, there are puzzles about how such beings could know physical realities and indeed how they differ from one another. Other aspects of creation are discussed in qq.65–74 and a sustained discussion of humanity fills qq.75–102. The *Prima Pars* ends with providence and the governance of creation in qq.103–19.

The *Prima Secundae* starts with the ultimate goal of human actions, happiness (*beatitudo*) (I-IIae qq.1–5) and then presents an analysis of human action (qq.6–21), followed by a treatment of emotions (qq.22–48). A general discussion of human dispositions, virtues and vices occupies qq.49–89. Law is the topic of qq.90–108, while grace finishes the *Prima Secundae* in qq.109–14.

The *Secunda Secundae* uses the general theoretical framework established above to deal with specific virtues and vices. The theological virtues of faith, hope and charity are found in II-IIae qq.1–46, while the cardinal virtues, prudence, justice, courage and temperance, are dealt with in qq.47–170. This part ends with a discussion of forms of life (qq.171–89) and in so doing returns again to a treatment of *beatitudo*, which had opened the whole second part.

The *Tertia Pars* starts with a discussion of the Incarnation (IIIa qq.1–26) and goes on to treat the life of Christ (qq.27–59). Following this is a discussion of sacraments in general (qq.60–65), with specific sacraments treated in qq.66–90, where the work ceases.

Faith and reason

A reasonably standard way of reading Aquinas on faith and reason has been to hold that he had a two-tier system. On this view, he developed a philosophical system that established the rationality of belief in God, followed by a theological system whose revealed basis was rendered reasonable by the philosophical part. The philosophical system was held to be largely Aristotelian and led seamlessly to the theological conclusions built upon it.

For a number of reasons this view has been discarded by many scholars. The supposed Aristotelianism of Aquinas has been shown to be shot through with a large admixture of neo-Platonism. But more importantly, whatever the philosophical provenance of his system, many scholars now think that Aquinas himself didn't envisage his work as having such a fundamental split between philosophy and theology, faith and reason, or indeed nature and grace. First, there is the fact that the arguments for the existence of God (Ia q.2 a.3) play such a small part in the overall work, a mere single article in the context of the thousands contained in the whole work. The parallel discussions in the *Summa Contra Gentiles* (Part 1, Chs 13–15) offer longer and more developed arguments. If Aquinas is presenting such a two-tier system, the lower part seems very slender. Secondly, Aquinas accepts the psychologically compelling point that most people do not hold religious beliefs on the basis of abstract metaphysical arguments (Ia q.1 a.1). That is, very few people hold the religious beliefs that they do on the basis of reaching the conclusion of a metaphysical argument. Aquinas notes that the reasoning involved is too abstruse for most people, would take too long and is wide open to the possibility of human error. So this idea of first providing a philosophical basis and then developing a theological superstructure is alien to his thought. This then leaves the puzzle: how exactly does he view the relation between philosophy and theology?

A simple initial answer is to say that philosophy belongs to the realm of human reason operating on its own, while theology uses certain resources unavailable to human reason (Ia q.1 a.8). Philosophy uses sense-perception and reasoning, while theology supplements this with revelation. But why accept revelation? What are Aquinas's views on the nature of faith?

Aquinas holds that faith is a virtue (II-IIae q.4 a.5). That is, it is a disposition or stable intellectual habit in individuals. It differs from knowledge in that one is not intellectually compelled to accept the relevant beliefs. In knowing something, the intellect is compelled to hold the specific belief as being true. In holding something on faith, there is not the same kind of intellectual compulsion involved. However, unlike opinion, beliefs held on faith do not waver; there is a stability about them (II-IIae q.1 a.4). Opinions are those beliefs that are not truly known, and about which we change our minds. Why does one hold a belief firmly when there is not intellectual compulsion behind it?

Aquinas distinguishes between two notions of the object of faith: the material and formal (II-IIae q.1 a.1). The material object of a belief is the actual content of the belief. The formal object of a belief is the method or the process by which it is held. So the formal object of a certain kind of mathematical truth may be geometrical reasoning, while the material object is, say, Pythagoras's theorem. The material object of faith, for Aquinas, is the articles of the Christian creed. The formal object of faith is God, understood as the revelation in Christ. Aquinas holds that this revelation is authoritative, it is God's self-revelation.

Yet so far a sceptic might reject all this as question-begging, and point out that unless one initially believes in God, none of this makes sense. Aquinas can agree with this, but nevertheless consistently hold to the position just outlined. The reason for this is that he maintains an exclusivity between faith and reason (II-IIae q.1 a.5). The same content of belief cannot both be an object of faith and an object of knowledge for the same person at the same time. Knowledge and faith, as attitudes to beliefs, exclude each other. Nevertheless, this doesn't stop the same content of belief (e.g. the existence of God) being an object of faith for one person and an object of knowledge for another, or indeed being an object of faith at one time and an object of knowledge at another, for the same person. However, there are also beliefs that are incapable of being objects of knowledge and can only be held on faith by anyone: for example the Trinity and the Incarnation.

Aquinas believes that the existence of God is one of those beliefs capable of being rationally demonstrated using the standards of Aristotelian science (Ia q.2 a.2). However, most people are not capable of the reasoning involved and so hold it as a matter of faith. The philosophical demonstration of the existence of God for Aquinas is rather like what Carnap would later call a "rational reconstruction" (1967: 61–3). It does not cause a belief, but can subsequently show that the held belief is nevertheless a rational belief. And whatever the rational cogency of the arguments for the existence of God, this seems a phenomenologically accurate account of the acquisition of religious belief. So Aquinas's position is that philosophical argument is not usually a cause of religious belief, and will not indeed be a justification of religious belief for the majority of people not versed in philosophical reasoning. Nevertheless he also holds that it is objectively the case that valid arguments can be made for the existence of God. Because the existence of God can be so demonstrated it is not, in an absolute sense, a matter of faith, since it can be known. In this it differs from beliefs about the Trinity or the Incarnation, which cannot in principle be so demonstrated. Therefore Aquinas refers to the existence of God as belonging to the *praeambula fidei* (Ia q.2 a.1 ad1) or presuppositions of faith, meaning not that many people believe in God on grounds of philosophical reasoning, but that it can be abstractly argued (by those who engage in such activity) that God exists. So what are those arguments?

The existence of God

The kind of argument Aquinas produces for the existence of God is what he calls a *"demonstratio"* (Ia q.2 a.2). This notion derives from Aristotle's notion of demonstrative knowledge. Demonstrative knowledge is genuine, scientific knowledge. It is explanatory in that it explains phenomena on the basis of their causes. The expanded Aristotelian sense of cause (matter, form, maker/begetter and purpose) includes all the relevant factors involved in a complete rational explanation of a phenomenon. The premises of a demonstration are prior to the conclusion, in that they are more general than the conclusion, necessary, and presupposed by the conclusion.

There is a crucial sense in which this conception of knowledge differs from modern, post-Cartesian views. Epistemology, on this viewpoint, does not begin with a need to refute scepticism. A distinction is observed between what can be called the order of discovery and the order of knowledge. The former is the psychological account of how in fact knowledge is acquired. The latter is the objective account of the abstract logical relationships of parts of knowledge to each other. Aquinas's view of demonstration is housed within this latter conception, which might be called externalist in the sense that epistemic relations track objectively standing patterns in reality. Aquinas holds that the existence of God is self-evident in an absolute sense: the very idea of existence is analytically contained in the idea of God, were God properly known. However we don't have a proper idea of God, so the existence of God is not self-evident to us (Ia q.2 a.1).

Aquinas thinks of God as the ultimate level of explanation for reality and intelligibility. However he also holds that God is, in certain specific ways, unknowable to us (Ia q.12 a.1). One can make sense of the claim *that* God exists, but make little headway with filling in the details on *what* God is. The reason for this is the excess of intelligibility and perfection in God – a familiar neo-Platonic theme. Because of this, it is clear that discussions about God don't fit into the standard model of demonstration, which runs from premises to conclusion. Apart from begging the question against atheists by putting the existence of God into the premises of the argument, there is also for Aquinas the issue that we don't really know God.

So Aquinas distinguishes between two kinds of demonstration (Ia q.2 a.2). The first kind is the normal one, where the argument moves from premises to conclusion and is called *demonstratio propter quid*. The second kind, however, runs from conclusions back to premises and is called *demonstratio quia*. This kind of argument operates from certain phenomena and argues that these phenomena, when correctly rationally understood, require the existence of some further reality. That is, this kind of argument works from effects to causes (although, importantly, it doesn't just simply assume that the phenomena are effects and hence gets easily to a cause, it argues for this). Thus our knowledge of God is not by direct acquaintance, as it were, but rather by deduction from effect back to cause.

Aquinas holds that there are five such arguments that can be used to get from certain phenomena in the world to the existence of God, famously known as the "*quinque viae*" or the five ways (Ia q.2 a.3). The arguments have some common features. They begin with an uncontroversial observation of some feature of phenomenon in the world: for example, change or causation. From this an argument is made to a singularity, which is required in order for that phenomenon to exist. So there is an argument for a first cause of change, or a first cause *simpliciter*, and Aquinas will often employ a denial of infinite regress in this kind of argument. The first way starts with change (*ex parte motus*); the second causation (*ex ratione causae efficientis*); the third possibility and necessity (*ex possibili et necessario*); the fourth from grades of being (*ex gradibus qui in rebus inveniuntur*); the fifth from order (*ex gubernatione rerum*).

The short text of the five ways is probably the most-discussed part of Aquinas's work in the English-speaking world, having generated a great deal of discussion and numerous objections over the ensuing seven centuries. However some oft-repeated objections are not really germane. Many philosophers object to the conclusion of each way, which goes along the lines of "... and this everyone calls God", pointing out that even if there were a first cause, this is very far from what most people call God. However, this is to pluck the text out of its context. Aquinas devotes the 13 questions that follow to filling out what he means by "God". As one commentator puts it, Aquinas is expressing the grammar of deity in these questions, filling out the meaning of the term "God". The five ways are a starting place, the establishment of something singular and odd, which is further clarified in the subsequent discussion. Hence to cavil at the end of each of the ways without taking account of the following sections is to deal with the text unfairly. Another standard objection is to Aquinas's denial of an infinite regress, holding that he simply begs the question in doing this. Yet most philosophers think that showing that a position leads to an infinite regress is one of the strongest ways of refuting that position; it is the equivalent of a philosophical knock-out. So what most philosophers accept in practice agrees with Aquinas's point here. In general they deny the plausibility of infinite regress, despite their countenancing it in this instance. A further objection is that the arguments rely on outmoded physics. Aquinas accepts Aristotelian physics; many of the arguments he uses first appear in Aristotle's *Physics* and so are superannuated. There is no easy answer to this; a treatment of each argument individually is required, which is beyond the scope of this chapter. However we can look more closely at the first of the arguments (which Aquinas holds is "more obvious" (*manifestior*), than the others) to get a sense of how he argues.

The argument begins with the claim that things move (have *motus*) in the world, as is evident from sensory input. The claim is then made that whatever is moved is moved by something else, other than itself. This is argued for in the following way. Aquinas accepts an analysis of change in terms of potency and actuality. Potency is a capacity to act in a certain way and actuality is the bringing about of a potency. The change from potency to act is brought about by something that is itself actual. Thus the potentially x is made actually x by something that is actual. Now something cannot be both potentially and actually x at the same time in the same respect: these exclude each other. Hence, whatever moves something potentially x to being actually x, cannot be that very thing that is potentially x; it has to be something else. Thus Aquinas argues for the claim that whatever moves is moved by something else. Since an obvious counter-example is found in self-moving animals, it seems clear that Aquinas understands the claim to refer to parts within a whole: that movement in animals is analysed into potency–act interactions at a sub-level and furthermore that the genesis of animals themselves can also be explained in this potency–actuality manner. Each instance of *motus* requires some antecedent operation of something in actuality. With this established, Aquinas claims that this cannot slide into an infinite regress. In a later discussion Aquinas distinguishes two kinds of infinite regress. The first is a sequence in which there is only an accidental relationship between the predecessor and successor in the sequence. In his example, an eternal craftsman may use an infinite sequence of hammers as each one gets worn out. Each hammer follows on the next, but with no real connection between them. This is contrasted with a sequence in which features of the elements in the sequence depend on the preceding ones (Ia q.46 a.2 ad7). Aquinas's claim is that unless there is a first in this sequence, which is not itself dependent, then there will be no subsequent members. Therefore, in the first way Aquinas argues for a first cause of *motus*, which is an unmoved mover. The "God-like" propeties of this metaphysical singularity have to be elaborated in the next sections.

It is not immediately obvious that this argument rests on outdated physics. It is clear that the analysis of motion by potency and actuality is not one that has survived into the modern era in physics, but on its own this doesn't invalidate that distinction as a metaphysical tool. Aquinas defends a philosophical position that is metaphysically realist, essentialist, committed to a correspondence theory of truth, a realist account of causation and an objectivist account of knowledge. In so far as one rejects any of these one will find problems with Aquinas's position. A great deal of twentieth century philosophy has challenged any number of these positions, but more recently a renewed interest in metaphysics has made Aquinas's views less far from mainstream interests and hence less likely to receive undeserved cursory dismissal.

The nature of God

Despite his being correctly understood as a leading theistic philosopher, one of the odd things about Aquinas is his insistence on our relative lack of knowledge about God. He says at the start of the discussion of God's nature "Because we cannot know what God is, but rather what he is not, we have no means for considering how God is, but rather how he is not" (Ia q.3). In one of his favourite images (deriving from Aristotle) he refers to human thought about God as being equivalent to bats blinking in the sunlight, unable to grasp the source of illumination (Ia q.12 a.1). The reason for this is not any defect in God, but the relative poverty of our intellectual capacities. This is not, of course, to say we know nothing about God, but to signal our cognitive limitations in this area.

Having argued for the existence of a metaphysical singularity as the ultimate explanation of phenomena such as change, causation and so on, Aquinas next moves to discuss a very puzzling feature of that singularity; namely, its simplicity (Ia q.3). To modern eyes, simplicity is often considered a defect or a lack: incapacity to achieve complexity or sophistication. So in what sense is God simple? Aquinas argues for God's simplicity by maintaining that there is no composition in God; God has no internal distinctions. This can be understood as involving a number of different claims. There are no spatial parts in God (Ia q.3 a.1). All spatial things admit of composition and can undergo dissolution. God is not the kind of thing that can disintegrate, as there are no physical parts in God. Furthermore there are no temporal parts in God. God exists in eternity, meaning that God exists outside the temporal sequence. God exists in an eternal present that does not admit past or future (Ia q.10 a.2). This lack of temporal composition may provoke puzzlement, but it pales in comparison to some of the other implications of divine simplicity.

There is no distinction between accidental and essential properties in God (Ia q.3 a.3). An accidental property is one that could change while its bearer remains the same (e.g. I get a sun-tan but I still remain myself); essential properties can't change without the nature of the bearer changing (e.g. I lose my brain). God has no accidental properties (at least no intrinsic accidental properties – he has many non-intrinsic ones, such as being discussed in this sentence). So Aquinas holds that all divine properties are essential. However, divine simplicity further holds that there is no genuine distinction between God's essential properties. That is, suppose God is good and God is all-powerful (both standard theistic claims). By the doctrine of simplicity there is no difference between these properties. If God indeed has intellect and will, then they are exactly the same thing. Finally, in the most extreme implication of the claim, there is no distinction in God between essence and existence (Ia q.3 a.4). Aquinas holds that everything else has such a distinction. No thing has an essence that includes its own existence. However in the case of God, his essence and his existence are not distinct. This means that God is not *a* being, not even a very powerful one. Beings are metaphysically constituted by essence and existence. God is in a different league, so to speak, understood as Being-Itself, non-dependent being: "the substance of God is therefore his being" (Ia q.3 a.4). Being-Itself (*ipsum esse subsistens*) is not a being (*ens*).

This cluster of positions, entailed by divine simplicity, seems extremely counter-intuitive even to theists, let alone non-theists. For example, God isn't in time, so apparently there's no difference between his supposed communication with Moses and with the Apostles, several centuries later. Furthermore, by collapsing the essential attributes of God to one – namely, existence – God seems to have become a strange amorphous thing, rather like the cosmic porridge sometimes ascribed to contemporary anti-realist philosophers. And besides, since everyone (supposedly) knows that existence isn't a real property, defending divine simplicity in this way seems to be the height of folly. Nevertheless simplicity is at the heart of Aquinas's metaphysical vision of reality and is used by him to outline a surprisingly coherent and robust position, which can sustain responses to the counter-intuitive implications it apparently entails.

Aquinas thinks of God as being the ultimate metaphysical explanation of the cosmos. So in one sense God is apart from everything else that exists. In another sense God sustains all things in being and so is connected to them as cause of their existence. Aquinas holds that no thing in the world has the explanation of its existence in itself. In that sense everything is contingent: it might not have existed. However in the singularity of God, which is the origin of all intelligibility and order, there is no distinction between essence and existence. God's essence is to exist. This is not graspable in any detail by human intellect; it can just be known *that* it is so. Aquinas does not think that existence is a property of things in the way that colour and weight are. In this he agrees with Frege (1959: §53), holding that existence is, so to speak, a second-order predicate. However unlike deflationists who go on to dismiss the significance of such an understanding of existence, Aquinas thinks that existence is *"inter omnia perfectissimum* [the most pefect of all]" (*De Potentia Dei* q.7. a.2 ad9). This recalls Wittgenstein's remark from the *Tractatus Logico-Philosophicus*: "It is not how things are in the world that is mystical, but that it exists" (1961: 6.44). Aquinas thinks of existence as a metaphysical principle, a fundamental aspect of reality. In all created reality this principle is separate from essence, but in uncreated reality they are identical. God is pure, self-subsistent existence.

From this position Aquinas can begin to answer some of the apparent problems arising from divine simplicity. Human intelligence deals with the primal simplicity of God by thinking about it under different descriptions or different facets. He uses a distinction similar to Frege's later distinction between sense and reference (Frege 1952). We think about the same reference using different senses (like the Morning Star and the Evening Star referring to the same planet, Venus). The difference between the senses has to do with human understanding. So when theists speak of God's knowledge or God's will they are referring to what is ultimately simple and unified, but are picking out different facets of that unity *in relation to them* (Ia q.13 a.4). Any differentiation is a feature of human thought. So speaking of divine attributes makes sense while speaking of human understanding of God, while affirming that God is simple in himself (and hence beyond human understanding). Also by affirming that God exists outside time, in eternity, it is possible to resolve certain puzzles about God's putative communication with human beings (Ia q.10). God exists in a timeless present, but can relate to the temporal sequence from there. God acts in that instant, but the effects of that act can be temporally distinct in time. So God can communicate with people at different times and places without impugning his metaphysical simplicity.

Simplicity can offer a solution to other puzzles about God's nature. One problem is that God's infinite knowledge seems incompatible with human free will. Aquinas affirms that people have free will; otherwise there would be no point to morality (Ia q.83 a.1). However, if God knew in advance that I would write this chapter, then it seems I had no real choice in writing it. This puzzle is resolved by denying that God's infinite knowledge entails *foreknowledge*. God knows from the vantage point of eternity and knows things as they happen, in a single instant on his side. We know in a temporal sequence on ours. With two time frames the challenge to free will doesn't arise; God doesn't *foreknow* anything, since God isn't in the temporal sequence. God knows things as free agents enact them (Ia q.14 a.13).

Another problem is whether God is constrained by a standard of goodness independent of him (Plato's famous *Euthyphro* problem) (Ia q.6). If this is not the case, then it appears that what is good or bad is capriciously determined by God's decision-making. It just happens that God has decided that torturing the innocent for fun is a bad thing; in a different possible universe it could be good, which seems to go against many people's intuitions about goodness. On the other hand, if God is constrained by an objective notion of goodness independent of him, that seems to go against intuitions about deity. God shouldn't be so constrained and any being who is so constrained is not God. However, divine simplicity holds that God's existence and God's goodness are ultimately identical. So there is an objective content to the nature of goodness based in God's nature and Aquinas avoids the twin problems of capriciousness and independence of God.

Aquinas's discussion of God's nature is of interest to religious believers and is controversial among them, as many want to hold that God does exist in time, or exhibits genuinely distinct properties. Philosophers of a more sceptical outlook can find much of interest in the conceptual moves Aquinas makes to render coherent his position, supplying, for example, ammunition for debates between libertarians or compatibilist positions on free will. Whether persuaded by them or not, the first 46 questions of the *Prima Pars* contain a great deal of interest to philosophers.

Human nature

Aquinas discusses humanity in general in Ia qq.75–89 and moves on to his analysis of human actions, emotions and their relation to morality in I-IIae qq.1–54. His general account of the metaphysical constitution of human beings draws heavily on Aristotle, but is not simply a restatement of those views. Aquinas appropriates Islamic neo-Platonist interpretations of Aristotle on mind and uses them to articulate an account of humanity that allows for post-mortem continued existence of individual human beings. What is most interesting about his account is that he explicitly rejects Platonic mind–body dualism and articulates a different view, thereby showing that theists need not necessarily be dualists. Aquinas wrote this account of human nature just before 1268, when he composed his commentary on Aristotle's *De Anima* and a year before he returned to teach at Paris, where controversy about human nature and the exact interpretation of Aristotle led Aquinas to write his polemical work *De Unitate Intellectus Contra Averroistas*.

He takes two key distinctions from Aristotle, which appear as basic structural features of his thought. The first is the analysis of material entities into matter and form. Form is the principle of organization in any being that makes it what it is. Applying this to living things, there is a basic principle that makes them what they are: their form. The form of living things is called soul (*anima*) and distinguishes them from inanimate things (Ia q.75 a.1). Living things exhibit different kinds of capacities, increasing in level of sophistication. Plant souls are the source of nutrition and growth. Animal souls are the source of these in animals, plus movement and sensation. Human souls add the further level of rationality, the capacity for abstract reasoning (Ia q.78 a.1). The second Aristotelian distinction used by Aquinas is that of potency and actuality. Originally a way of analysing change, it can be used in the explanation of mind. The human soul's distinctive feature is its capacity for abstract reasoning, so the notion of soul and mind coincide in humans. The human mind has both a passive or potential and active or agent aspect.

The active operates on things to be known and processes them in a certain way for the potential part to receive (Ia q.79 a.2–3).

Aquinas articulates a close relationship between sense and intellect. The senses receive stimulation from the external world. They are impressed with the forms of extra-mental entities. Sometimes this can be purely physical (as when the skin becomes hot), but sometimes this goes beyond the purely physical, as when the eye takes in a colour. Information passes from the world to the eye, the eye takes in the form of the external object, but not the matter (the eye doesn't actually become the same colour). This is called the reception of the sensible species (Ia q.78 a.4). However, this is still a physical change in a sense-organ, albeit a change of form. A further level of explanation is the formation of a phantasm. The senses produce phantasms ("likenesses of particular things", I q.84 a.7) and this is what is available to conscious experience. (Having a sense informed but without having a phantasm seems to capture the idea of a sense being stimulated but there being no conscious awareness of this, as with an anaesthetic). So sensory cognition involves sensory stimulation, the reception of species by the senses and the formation of sensible phantasms.

Intellectual cognition is a further operation on top of this and presupposes sensory cognition. Phantasms convey information about individuals, whereas genuinely intellectual cognition is of universal aspects of things. Aquinas gives his account of universals in explaining how intellectual cognition occurs. The agent intellect abstracts from the phantasms the universal or general features contained in them. Analogous to what happens with the sense, this is called an intelligible species and such intelligible species are received and understood in the passive intellect (Ia q.85 a.1). Conscious awareness of this intelligible species is brought about by the formation of a mental concept, known as the *verbum*. So, for Aquinas, universals exist in the mind, but nevertheless they pick out genuinely existing features of things in the world. Individual dogs are what exist in extra-mental reality, while the intellect forms the universal "dog" by abstracting the common, general features that individual dogs have in common, which make them dogs. Aquinas criticizes the Platonic account of universals for attributing to extra-mental reality those features that properly belong to the mind (universality, immateriality) (Ia q.85 a.3). A key point that Aquinas emphasizes is that sensible and intellectual species are not *what* the mind knows. Rather the mind knows the extra-mental world *by means of* such species, "sensible species are not what is sensed; rather they are that by which sensation takes place" (Ia q.85 a.2). Hence his account of the mind–world relation, although empiricist, is not representationalist in the manner of the eighteenth-century empiricists. The sceptical problem of bridging the gap from representation to world does not arise.

Islamic discussions of Aristotle's *De Anima* had argued that the agent intellect is one for all humankind (*Avicenna*) and further that the passive intellect is likewise one (*Averroes*). They construed these as abstract realities existing quite independently of human agents. Furthermore they denied any possibility of individual immortality, since all aspects of personal identity ceased on the death of the individual. This position came to be known as monopsychism: there being one mind for all humans. Aquinas argued against monopsychism and for individual immortality.

Using Aristotle's matter–form analysis of physical beings, Aquinas argued that there is just one substantial form per entity, the master-form, which determines what the thing is, and in living things this is the soul (Ia q.76 a.3). As noted earlier, there are levels of complexity in souls, and more sophisticated souls subsume the lower operations within themselves (hence human souls govern nutrition, movement and so on, as well as intellect). There is just one soul per living thing, governing multiple functions. Hence Aquinas argues for the operation of agent and passive intellect as functions of individual souls and rejects as unnecessary any appeal to purported external realities. With an argument for the unity of soul in each individual and an account given of intellectual cognition, Aquinas is in a position to argue for the immortality of individual souls.

Aquinas sets up a position that stands between materialism and dualism. He rejects ancient materialism, holding that these ancient philosophers were limited in the conceptual choices available to them (Ia q.75 a.1). He also rejects Plato's view that the soul is tied to a body in an incidental way (Ia q.89 a.1). Soul and body are related as form and matter. Hence soul is distinct from matter. But in this sense of separation from matter, so are the forms of any material thing and such forms do not persist after the dissolution of the thing (for example, a dog has a substantial form, which is distinct from matter, but this does not persist after the death of the dog). A further argument is required.

Aquinas finds such an argument in the proper function of the human soul: the exercise of rationality. The intellect acquires forms in a way different to the way senses receive forms. It abstracts universal features and creates concepts. Aquinas claims that this requires that the soul has no admixture of matter in it (Ia q.75 a.1). In order to know the nature of all physical bodies, that which knows must not have that nature itself. Aquinas's claim is that if it did, its own physical nature would obstruct it from knowing all other things (using the example that a sick person with an infected tongue can't accurately taste things). As part of this line of reasoning Aquinas also holds that reasoning uses no specific bodily organ (Ia q.75 a.2).

Having established that the rational soul is necessarily non-physical he then argues that it nevertheless is subsistent: that it can exist independently of the body. It has a distinctive activity (reasoning) and only things that actually exist subsistently have such activities. Yet Aquinas holds that the soul is not the person (Ia q.75 a.4). The soul is only part of a person, in the way that a hand or an eye is a part. It is not the entire person. Thus Aquinas's account of postmortem existence holds that while the soul can persist in existence after the body, this is an unnatural state. The soul's natural state is to be united to a body, so Aquinas thinks that ultimately it will be reunited with a resurrected body.

Aquinas's central contention is that human reasoning requires some aspect of us that is non-physical. He presents this in a way that isn't simply substance dualism. However, his lack of knowledge of the role of the brain in cognition seems to cut against his chief argument: that nothing physical can exhibit the conceptual plasticity required for true cognition. Furthermore his notion of a resurrected body, for which no details are given, raises more problems than it solves. Despite these clear problems, Aquinas's account of human nature helps clarify the conceptual geography of the issues, at least in showing that materialism and dualism are not the only possible options available.

Ethics

Aquinas's work is highly systematic in that a number of basic principles, distinctions and philosophical options recur constantly. His basic metaphysical account of reality and the anthropology just outlined directly influence and structure his view of morality. Metaphysics underpins ethics. His view of moral evaluation focuses more on issues of *being* rather than *doing*. That is, his concern is far more with the formation of character and cultivation of good dispositions than with specific isolated acts; a concern with being a good person rather than simply doing good things; with moral well-being rather than obligation or duty. In this he is influenced strongly by Aristotle. As a part of this, it is significant to notice that the emotions play a significant role in moral matters and ought not to be ignored or suppressed.

The way in which his metaphysical views impinge on morality is that Aquinas thinks of morality as being teleological. The universe is an intelligible place and human actions, as part of that universe, are explicable as being directed to some end. His analysis of the end of human action occupies II-IIae qq.1–5. Aquinas distinguishes human actions (those actions exhibiting reason and will) from acts of human beings (random or capricious acts, e.g. scratching one's head). The former comprise the kind that is morally significant. Given that there is a plurality of possible ends for human actions, Aquinas thinks that subsidiary ends can be subsumed under the single ultimate one of happiness (*beatitudo*).

Human actions are directed towards what makes one happy, or, more precisely, towards that which one perceives as likely to produce happiness. Humans act towards an end that is seen under a certain aspect. However, there is room for wide discrepancy between the perceived good and the actual good. An alcoholic perceives the next drink as a good, whereas in fact it is a source of damage to him. Happiness consists in acting to realize what is truly good for us.

Aquinas gives a detailed and subtle account of the mechanics of human action in II-IIae qq.6–21. The main discussion concerns the interaction of intellect and will. He articulates an account that makes elaborate distinctions, but that simultaneously emphasises the close interplay of intellect and appetite in human action. He distinguishes ends and means, and levels within these are outlined. Acts of willing, enjoying and intending are distinguished from each other. Consenting to means and choosing means are distinguished. The relation of complete acts to component elements is discussed. Some critics of Aquinas's account of human action have rejected it for its sheer complexity, maintaining that such intricacy is not available to introspection. However Aquinas's account is not meant to be available to introspection. It is a reconstruction of the elements involved in action, not all of which may be phenomenologically occurrent in the agent's consciousness. This kind of analysis of action is merely another facet of the radically non-Cartesian nature of his philosophy: consciousness is not the distinguishing feature of the soul, epistemology is not the starting place of philosophy, and self-knowledge is not best delivered by introspection. Many twentieth-century philosophers have wrestled with and disentangled themselves from their Cartesian heritage to arrive afresh at such views.

With such an analysis of the elements of human action in place, how does one go about making a moral evaluation of it? Aquinas holds that there are different factors that must be taken into account. There is the intention in the act, which he calls the "object" of the act. This gives the action its distinctive character; it is what makes the act the kind of act it is (he compares the object of an act to the species of a being) (I-II q.18 a.1). However, one must also consider the circumstances in which the act is performed, which may modify the moral worth of the act. For example, studying, which may be considered a good thing, would be viewed differently if one does it while someone nearby is in mortal danger, and one could save the person, but does nothing about it (I-II q.18 a.2). Circumstances are compared to accidents, which help individuate an entity. Finally, there is the end of the act, the goal at which it strives. One might contrast object and end as means and end; so, for example, singing well might be the object of an act and winning a competition might be the end. Each one of these three – intention, circumstances and end – has to be appropriate in order for an act to be judged morally good. However, as mentioned above, Aquinas tends not to focus on specific acts *per se* and indeed affirms elsewhere "The teaching on matters of morals even in their general aspects is uncertain and variable. But still more uncertainty is found when we come down to the solution of particular cases" (*Sententia Libri Ethicorum*, Bk2 Lect 2 #259). Aquinas devotes much analysis to patterns or dispositions to act; namely, virtues and vices. But before that, he discusses human emotions in I-IIae qq.22–48.

Emotion is treated under the label "Passions of the Soul". A passion is something that someone undergoes. Passions involve somatic or bodily features and are a response to some external stimulus. Aquinas thinks of them as being fundamentally a kind of tendency built into human nature, but one that can be modified by acts of will and by the intellect. Aquinas thinks of emotion as primarily pertaining to appetite and will, and so he can be categorized as giving a non-cognitivist account of emotion: he explicitly opts for the view that emotion pertains more to appetite than cognition. That being said, the close interaction of will and intellect for Aquinas, and the ultimate superiority of intellect over will, mitigates the non-cognitivism in his account of emotion. Emotion always operates in a complex where intellect plays some role. The history of the interaction of will, intellect and emotion is the history of one's character formation. Emotions are not to be repressed, on Aquinas's moral theory, but rather have to be properly ordered. This happens through moral education, which is the inculcation of virtues in the moral agent: that is, training one in dispositions to act well. Aquinas's account of virtue takes up the largest number of questions in the entire *Summa*. I-IIae qq.49–89 deals with virtues and vices in general, while II-IIae qq.1–170 deal with specific virtues and vices in exhaustive and indeed exhausting detail.

A virtue is "a good quality of the mind by which we live rightly, of which no one can make bad use" (I-IIae q.55 a.4). A virtue is a disposition (*habitus*) that leads to good; a vice is a disposition leading to evil. They are not simply natural instincts, since the exercise of virtue always involves willing and is always open to the possibility of going in the opposite direction. Hence a constitutional disposition to anger or placidity is not itself virtuous or vicious; rather, the virtue is an acquired disposition that might build on natural dispositions.

Virtues divide into intellectual and moral. Intellectual virtues are those dispositions of mind that lead us to reason well, and they can be speculative or practical. Moral virtues are those related to our appetites and are regarded by Aquinas as more truly virtues than the intellectual ones. That is so because virtues are not merely capacities, but dispositions, ingrained impulses to act. And so the closer connection of moral virtue to the right ordering of appetite makes them virtues absolutely (*simpliciter*), rather than virtues relatively (*secundum quid*). Some intellectual virtues may just remain at the level of a capacity, rather than an impulse to act. The point of this discussion is that for Aquinas a good moral action is one that should come easily to the agent; they have an in-built disposition with appropriate emotional accompaniments to do the good. It is a vision of ethics very far removed from one based on abstract duty or law.

Aquinas does, famously, talk about natural law. However, while happiness, will, emotions and virtues are intrinsic features of human morality, law is something that is extrinsic, that acts on us from without (as is grace – an important theological aspect of his thought discussed just after law at I-IIae qq.109–14). Law is defined by Aquinas as a "rule and measure of acts, by which man is induced to act or is restrained from acting" (I-IIae q.90 a.1). Aquinas believes there is an eternal law, which is divine reason (I-IIae q.91 a.1). Given his meta-physical identification of goodness and being in God, to assert the existence of eternal law is to say that the basic principles of goodness are inscribed into the fabric of being. Rational beings, reflecting on the nature of reality, can partici-pate in that eternal law: "this participation of the eternal law in the rational crea-ture is called the natural law" (I-IIae q.91 a.2). The basic principle of the natural law is known in a way similar to the basic principles of being. It is regarded as a self-evident truth, like the law of non-contradiction (I-IIae q.94 a.2). The prin-ciple is "Good is to be pursued and done, and evil is to be avoided". This works as a fundamental apodictic fulcrum on which all moral reasoning moves. However, Aquinas concedes that as one tries to elaborate the details of this system, there is room for uncertainty. While the speculative intellect deals with necessary features of reality and so can achieve certainty, "the practical reason ... is busied with contingent matters, about which human actions are concerned; and consequently although there is necessity in the general principles, the more we descend to matters of detail the more frequently we encounter defects" (I-IIae q.94 a.4).

The philosophical significance of Aquinas

Aquinas is regarded as the greatest of the medieval philosophers. He did not deal as closely with logical and linguistic issues as Abelard, Duns Scotus or Ockham, but his metaphysics, philosophical psychology, philosophy of action, ethics and political theory provide a powerfully integrated philosophical system. After his death in 1274, his work was attacked by conservative theologians (being con-demned in 1277) and by Scotus and Ockham, among others. He influenced such late-medieval figures as Meister Eckhart (1260–1327) and Dante Alighieri (1265–1321). The Dominican school defended and articulated his thought, with such figures as Capreolus (1380–1444), Cajetan (1469?–1534), De Sylvestris

(1478–1528), Vitoria (1486–1546) and De Soto (1494–1560) writing commentaries on it.

The development of modern science and the turn to subjectivity inaugurated by Descartes led to an eclipse of interest by the general philosophical world in the kind of philosophy presented by Aquinas. However, its influence persisted in unusual ways. Brentano's discussion of intentionality, which exercised such a profound impact on phenomenology, owes much to Aquinas's discussion of cognition. Heidegger was familiar with Aquinas's work and arguably his distinction between Being (*Sein*) and beings (*Seinde*) owes something to Aquinas. Analytical philosophy, influenced by empiricism and scientism and deeply suspicious of metaphysics, regarded Aquinas's work as a quaint relic of medieval culture. However in the later twentieth century, various movements in philosophy, including in analytical philosophy, make Aquinas's work much more congenial to modern readers. First, a general rejection of Cartesianism makes contemporary concerns closer to those of Aquinas. Secondly, a significant number of analytical philosophers now think that metaphysics is once again a respectable enterprise. Thirdly, desires to transcend the interminable Humean–Kantian deadlock in ethics have led to a renewal of interest in virtue ethics and the kind of philosophy of action presented by Aquinas. Finally, the recent renaissance of work in philosophy of religion, and especially in philosophical theology, looks regularly to Aquinas as a source and interlocutor.

There are indeed aspects of Aquinas's work that cannot be salvaged. As a representative of his age he endorsed astrology, slavery and various dubious views about women. Some of these undoubted anachronisms do seem seriously to affect his views; for example, his account of sexual morality is skewed by mistaken biology. However, such is the case with any author from a different age and this should not obscure the greatness of his achievement. The *Summa Theologiae* is an outstanding work of philosophy and theology, and renewed philosophical interest in it is indicated in the number, variety and quality of recent studies of it.

Bibliography

Editions of works by Aquinas

Summa Theologiae, 61 vols, Blackfriars Edition. London: Eyre & Spottiswoode, 1964–80.
Summa Theologiae: A Concise Translation, T. McDermott (ed.). London: Eyre & Spottiswoode, 1989.
Aquinas: Selected Philosophical Writings, T. McDermott (ed.) Oxford: Oxford University Press, 1993.
Aquinas: Selected Writings, R. McInerney (ed.). Harmondsworth: Penguin, 1998.

Other references and further reading

Anscombe G. E. M. & P. Geach 1961. *Three Philosophers*. Oxford: Basil Blackwell.

Burrell, D. 1979. *Aquinas, God and Action*. Notre Dame, IN: University of Notre Dame Press.

Burrell, D. 1986. *Knowing the Unknowable God*. Notre Dame, IN: University of Notre Dame Press.

Carnap, R. 1967. *The Logical Structure of the World*. Berkeley, CA: University of California Press.

Copleston, F. 1991. *Aquinas*. Harmondsworth: Penguin.

Davies, B. 1992. *The Thought of Thomas Aquinas*. Oxford: Oxford University Press.

Davies, B. 2002. *Thomas Aquinas: Contemporary Philosophical Perspectives*. Oxford: Oxford University Press.

Eco, U. 1988. *The Aesthetics of Thomas Aquinas*. London: Radius.

Finnis, J. 1998. *Aquinas*. Oxford: Oxford University Press.

Frege, G. 1959. *The Foundations of Arithmetic*. Oxford: Basil Blackwell.

Frege, G. 1952. "On Sense and Meaning", in *Translations from the Philosophical Writings of Gottlob Frege*. Oxford: Basil Blackwell.

Gilson, E. 1994. *The Christian Philosophy of St. Thomas Aquinas*. Notre Dame, IN: University of Notre Dame Press.

Jenkins, J. 1997. *Knowledge and Faith in Thomas Aquinas*. Cambridge: Cambridge University Press.

Kenny, A. 1980. *Aquinas*. Oxford: Oxford University Press.

Kenny, A. 1993. *Aquinas on Mind*. London: Routledge.

Kenny, A. 2003. *Aquinas on Being*. Oxford: Oxford University Press.

Kretzmann, N. & E. Stump (eds) 1993. *The Cambridge Companion to Aquinas*. Cambridge: Cambridge University Press.

McInerny, R. 1982. *St. Thomas Aquinas*. Notre Dame, IN: University of Notre Dame Press.

Pasnau, R. 2002. *Thomas Aquinas on Human Nature*. Cambridge: Cambridge University Press.

Pope S. (ed.) 2002. *The Ethics of Aquinas*. Washington, DC: Georgetown University Press.

Sigmund, P. 1988. *St. Thomas Aquinas on Politics and Ethics*. New York: Norton.

Stump, E. 2003. *Aquinas*. London: Routledge.

Torell, J-P. 2000. *Saint Thomas Aquinas, Vol.1: The Person and his Work*, R. Royal (trans.). Washington, DC: Catholic University of America Press.

Van Steenberghen, F. 1980. *Le probléme de l'existence de Dieu dans les ecrits de S. Thomas d'Aquin*. Louvain-la-Neuve: Editions de l'Institut Superior de Philosophie.

te Velde, R. 1995. *Participation and Substantiality in Thomas Aquinas*. Leiden: Brill.

Velecky, L. 1994. *Aquinas's Five Arguments in the "Summa Theologiae Ia,2,3"*, Kampen: Kok Pharos.

Weisheipl, J. 1974. *Friar Thomas d'Aquino: His Life, Thought and Work*. Garden City, NY: Doubleday.

Wippel J. 2000. *The Metaphysical Thought of Thomas Aquinas*. Washington, DC: Catholic University of America Press.

Wittgenstein, L. 1961. *Tractatus Logico-Philosophicus*. London: Routledge & Kegan Paul.

9

Duns Scotus
Ordinatio

Richard Cross

Duns Scotus's life and works

Beyond a few details, little is known of the life of John Duns Scotus (*c*.1266–1308). Both the generally accepted date and place of his birth are speculative. According to scholars, 1266 is most likely, given one date that is secure, namely, that of his ordination to the priesthood in Northampton on 17 March 1291. Under canon law, 25 was the earliest age allowable for ordination. The Bishop of Lincoln (in whose huge diocese both Northampton and Oxford were then located) conducted an earlier ordination on 23 December 1290. Thus, assuming that Scotus was ordained at the first opportunity, this makes his birth sometime between late December 1265 and mid-March 1266. Scholars now hold that the "Duns" in his name should be understood to refer to the town of Duns just north of the border between England and Scotland, in Berwickshire, curiously only a few miles away from Hume's birthplace.

His ordination in Northampton implies that Scotus was in Oxford by 1291. Another concrete reference places Scotus in Oxford in 1300. Scotus's name appears in a letter, dated 26 July, as one of 22 friars presented to the bishop of Lincoln for a licence to hear confessions. The list of names includes Philip Bridlington as the incoming Franciscan regent master (i.e. full professor) in theology. Bridlington was regent master for the year 1300–1301. And we know that Scotus took part in a disputation under Bridlington during this year. These facts probably imply that Scotus remained in Oxford until at least June 1301.

As part of their training for the professorship, theology bachelors were required to lecture on the *Sentences* of Peter Lombard (*c*. 1100–60), a kind of theological textbook consisting largely of discussion of conflicting sources from the early Church Fathers – predominantly Augustine – ranged under a series of theological topics. We know that Scotus was busy revising the earliest portion of his lectures in or very shortly after 1300, because of a reference he makes in that year to events that took place in 1299, a reference that entertains a hope for the future that was almost immediately frustrated (namely, that Islam would founder) (*Ord*. prol., pt 2, qu. un., n. 112 (Duns Scotus 1950–: 1:77)). This suggests that he lectured on the *Sentences* during the academic year 1298–99. Two books of this early *Lectura* survive, and the series formed the basis for Scotus's ongoing revision of his lectures for publication: the so-called *Ordinatio*, the subject of this chapter.

We know from an early manuscript now in the library at Worcester Cathedral that Scotus was in Paris in the academic year 1302–3, lecturing for a second time on the *Sentences* in order to qualify for a chair in Paris. These lectures survive in the form of student notes corrected by the lecturer: a *reportatio examinata*. Scotus was forced to leave France, along with some 80 other pro-papal friars, in June 1303. The expelled students were allowed to return to Paris after April 1304. In 1305, Scotus became regent master in theology at Paris. From this period date Scotus's *Quodlibetal questions*: a series of disputed questions, originating in the lecture hall, on issues raised "on anything by anyone [*de quolibet a quolibet*]" – a standard academic exercise held by a regent master during Advent and Lent in the university calendar. Scotus was moved to Cologne in 1307 to teach at the Franciscan house of studies there, where he died the next year, on what is traditionally believed to be 8 November 1308.

Scotus was a member of the Franciscan order. Like the Dominicans, the Franciscans were founded in the early thirteenth century, and these two mendicant orders had a considerable presence in the newly established universities. Scotus was by profession a theologian. But, like many scholastic theologians, he had a substantial purely philosophical output, most notably series of questions on various Aristotelian books: the *Categories*, *On Interpretation*, *Sophistical Refutations*, *On the Soul*, *Metaphysics*, thought (with the exception of the last three books of the *Metaphysics* questions (7–9)) to be early works of Scotus's, dating from the 1290s. These are questions, not commentary, and Scotus uses Aristotle's text as a springboard for a range of questions of philosophical interest to himself. But his most important and famous work is his *Ordinatio*, a heavily revised version of his Oxford lectures on the *Sentences*. The *Ordinatio* covers a vast amount of purely philosophical material, in this context largely, though not exclusively, used to clarify strictly theological questions.

The presence of questions on Aristotle is important, for what most distinguishes theology in the thirteenth and fourteenth centuries from preceding centuries is the massive and pervasive influence of the newly recovered works of Aristotle. It is quite clear that Aristotle's interest in logic and intellectual coherence chimed in with trends already beginning in the twelfth century, most notably exemplified in the work of Peter Abelard (doubtless known to the young Peter Lombard). And Aristotle provided a vision of the universe far less speculative, and far more philosophically sophisticated, than any of the rival theories known at the time (most notably Platonic). The impact on theology was remarkable, and was doubtless responsible for much that was best and most distinctive about medieval theology, most importantly its focus on philosophical and logical cogency.

Duns Scotus's *Ordinatio*

The *Ordinatio*, as we have seen, is primarily a theological work, and its order was dictated by the treatment of various issues in Peter Lombard's *Sentences*. As Peter Lombard left his work, it was divided into four books – roughly on God (largely the Trinity, and then going on to questions about the nature of God), creation (including material about human nature), Christ and salvation (including ethics), and sacraments, respectively – each of which was divided into about 250 chapters. In the early thirteenth century, each book was further divided into "distinctions" – groups of six or so chapters – not disturbing the order of Lombard's chapters. There are thus some 40 or 50 distinctions in each book. As theologians in the later thirteenth and early fourteenth centuries approached their lecturing task, they tended to use the distinctions as springboards for raising their own questions on the relevant topics, not remaining necessarily very close to Lombard's text; indeed, in the later Middle Ages the number of questions raised on each book was considerably reduced and detached from the structure of Lombard's work, and the length of each question made correspondingly longer. The lectures in this case became increasingly specialized, focused merely on certain questions of current theological dispute. But Scotus, while not remaining close to the substance of Lombard's discussions, tends to raise questions related to most of the distinctions. Since the work is fundamentally theological in character, philosophical discussions tend to be dotted around in different and sometimes unexpected places. Most important for the purposes of metaphysics, Scotus's undoubted philosophical *forte*, are distinctions 2 and 3 of Book 1, and distinctions 2 and 3 of Book 2.

After a brief discussion of the nature of theology, and of Augustine's distinction between use and enjoyment (Prologue and Book 1, distinction 1, reflecting the opening discussion of theology by Peter Lombard), Scotus's distinction 2 in Book 1 deals with the existence of God and an attempt to prove the doctrine of the Trinity. Distinction 3 deals with cognition, under the general heading of God's knowability. Distinctions 4–7, 8–16, 18–21, 23–29 and 31–4 deal with more specialized Trinitarian issues, raising complex metaphysical questions on the issues of substance, person, universals, causal powers and human cognition. Distinction 8 discusses divine simplicity, and allows Scotus to develop at length his own theory of properties and of distinctions between properties. Distinction 17 deals with the virtue of charity (love), and questions about the nature of quality in general. Distinction 22 tackles the problem of talking about something that is not fully knowable (i.e. God); and distinctions 30 and 35–44 deal with other divine attributes, including (particularly in distinction 39, left merely in a provisional state by Scotus) complex discussions on future contingents and the relationship between God and modality. Book 2 was left incomplete by Scotus. Distinction 1 contains a discussion of the doctrine of creation. Distinction 2 deals with the temporality, location, motion and possible activity of created immaterial beings such as angels, including a discussion of the problem of self-motion. Distinction 3 provides a systematic account of individuation and the question of universals. Distinctions 4–11 deal with miscellaneous questions on angelic activity, including further material on free will and cognition. Distinction 12 – the key discussion of the reality of matter – is missing, and needs to be read in the earlier *Lectura* version. Distinctions 15–25 likewise were never revised by Scotus, and do not appear in the modern critical edition (earlier editions contain completions made by some of Scotus's early disciples). Distinctions 26–9 deal with grace, and 30–37 with sin and original sin. The remaining distinctions of Book 2 – distinctions 38–44 – discuss various other topics in moral theology, including intention, conscience, goodness, and malice.

Distinctions 1–22 of Book 3 cover questions concerned with the doctrine of the Incarnation – the union of divine and human natures in Christ – and contain, particularly in the opening distinctions, important further clarifications on the notions of substance and essence, discussions of the logic of propositions (to avoid formulations likely to imply heretical positions on the question of the Incarnation) and – surprisingly in the context of the Immaculate Conception of Mary – further discussions on atomism and the limits of spatial and temporal continua. The remaining distinctions (23–40) cover other virtues and, near the end (distinctions 37–40), natural law. Almost all of Book 4 is devoted to the seven sacraments (baptism, Eucharist, confession, confirmation, unction, ordination and marriage). Distinctions 14–42 on the last five of these contain important discussions of various moral and legal issues; the discussions of baptism (distinctions 3–7) and the Eucharist (distinctions 8–13) including treatments of various physical and metaphysical questions, particularly, in the case of the Eucharist, substance and accident, and the nature of place. The opening two distinctions deal with sacraments in general, and focus on questions about causality: what could cause a sacrament, and how could the sacrament cause its effect? The remaining distinctions of Book 4 (distinctions 43–50) cover the question of the resurrection of the dead and last judgement. It is here that Scotus includes his most extended treatment of human beings as composites of body and soul (distinctions 43–4). Questions about the possibility of a disembodied soul knowing something are dealt with in distinction 45, and Scotus spends much of the remaining distinctions discussing questions of justice and mercy.

Scotus devotes anything between one and sixteen questions to each distinction, and each of these questions follows a complex dialectical structure, found in embryonic form in Lombard's text, and echoing the disputation structure of much medieval teaching. A series of arguments against the position to be defended is followed by one or more arguments in favour. Most medieval commentators then quickly turn to their own solution of the question, and then provide replies to the original objections. In Scotus, this argumentative structure is taken to considerable extremes. The main discussion of the topic is usually used by Scotus to raise further series of objections and the extensive discussion of opposing views, often followed by replies judged by Scotus to be unsound, replies to these replies, and so on, before finally getting to Scotus's own view. And, in good philosophical fashion, he often likes to consider specious arguments in favour of his own view too, and reply to these. Following a discussion in Scotus is not always a straightforward matter, and certainly not in those portions of his work that still lack a critical edition.

The end result is vast: at a rough calculation, somewhere in excess of one and half million words, 15 thick folio volumes projected in the new and still incomplete critical edition of Scotus's theological works (Scotus 1950–). This is a remarkable achievement given the number of other small- and large-scale works produced by Scotus in the course of a writing career of no more than 15 years, although not atypical of the extraordinary achievements of the greatest scholastic writers. The text itself presents unique editorial difficulties. Scotus did not finish his revisions by the time he died, and his many students attempted to produce a clean, finished text by interpolating and deleting material available to them. The modern editors of the critical edition of Scotus's theological works believe that they have identified a manuscript (Assisi, Bibliotheca Communale, MS 137) that contains a copy of Scotus's own working text, complete with accurate copies of Scotus's own additions, marginal notes and deletions. They are basing their edition of the text on this manuscript. In what follows, I supplement the discussion with material from the earlier *Lectura* in those cases in which Scotus did not even begin his editorial work on this earlier text.

The existence of God (*Ordinatio* Book 1, distinction 2)

The chapters of distinction 2 of Book 1 of Lombard's work are general ones about God's Trinitarian nature, and thirteenth-century theologians tend to use their questions on the opening distinctions to raise not only preliminary questions about the Trinity but also questions about the possibility of proving God's existence. Scotus follows this practice, proposing not only that it is possible to prove God's existence but also that "persuasive" arguments can be found in favour of the view that God is a Trinity (on these, see Cross 2005). The proof for God's existence is – as with many topics in Scotus – of considerable complexity and subtlety. Scotus is very concerned that as many of Aristotle's criteria for a scientific proof, laid out in the *Posterior Analytics*, be satisfied: for Scotus these are self-evidence, certainty, necessity and explanatoriness (*Ord*. prologue, pt 4, qu. 1–2, n. 208 (Duns Scotus 1950–: 1:141; see Aristotle, *Posterior Analytics* 1.2 (71b9–12)). If something is self-evident, then either it is *a priori* or it is immediately empirically obvious (*Ord*. bk 1, dist. 2, pt 1, qu. 1–2, n. 15 (Duns Scotus 1950–: 2:131)); something is certain if and only if it is not open to doubt; and explanatory if and only if it gives some sort of *causal* explanation (construing "causal" here very broadly, to cover all of Aristotle's four causes: efficient, final, material and formal). Necessity is more complex; something is necessary in this context if and only if it is such that it is required by the causal constitution of the actual world.

Clearly, no cosmological argument can be explanatory, since a cosmological argument is by definition an argument from effect to cause; the premises do not give a *causal* explanation of their conclusion. But Scotus believes that he can find an argument whose premises satisfy the remaining three requirements (namely, self-evidence, certainty and necessity). The relevant premise is, "Some producible nature exists". What Scotus means is not that there exists an individual producible thing. He is talking about a nature (or property, as we would say), and the claim is that this nature (*being producible*) is, given the causal constitution of the actual world, instantiable. This premise is thought of by Scotus to be both self-evident and certain. It is necessary, too, in the sense that, given the causal constitution of the actual world, it cannot fail to be true. And for Scotus, the premise immediately implies "Some nature able to produce exists": again, not a genuinely existential claim about individuals, but merely the claim that this nature (*being able to produce*) is instantiable (*Ord*. bk 1, dist. 2, pt 1, qu. 1–2, n. 56 (Duns Scotus 1950–: 2:161–2; ed. and trans. in Duns Scotus 1987: 44)). This in turn implies "Some first nature, able to produce, exists", by which Scotus means that the nature *being a first thing able to produce* is instantiable (*Ord*. bk 1, dist. 2, pt 1, qu. 1–2, n. 43 (Duns Scotus 1950–: 2:151–2; ed. and trans. in Duns Scotus 1987: 39)). According to Scotus, this conclusion is entailed by the second on the grounds that an infinite regress of causes is impossible (*Ord*. bk 1, dist. 2, pt 1, qu. 1–2, n. 53 (Duns Scotus 1950–: 157–9; ed. and trans. in Duns Scotus 1987: 41)). Hence if, given the causal constitution of the actual world, *being able to produce* is instantiable, then so too (as a matter of necessity) is *being a first thing able to produce*.

The next step in the argument aims to show that this nature is in fact instantiated: thus, "Something simply first, able to produce, exists" (*Ord*. bk 1, dist. 2, pt 1, qu. 1–2, n. 58 (Duns Scotus 1950–: 164–5; ed. and trans. in Duns Scotus 1987: 46)). Scotus does this by drawing on his assumption that something is possible if and only if all the causal conditions in the real world for its existence are satisfied. Possibility is thus tied to causal powers, and if something is possible, then whatever the relevant causal explanation, that explanation must be *real* (if it were not real, the *explanandum* would not be possible: its very possibility is tied to the existence of a real explanation). Any first efficient cause is really possible, and its explanation is intrinsic to itself. Some such efficient cause must, then, be real, otherwise there would be no explanation for any causal relations lower down the causal chain. Thus Scotus devotes most of his time at this stage in the argument to showing that there is no feature of the real world incompatible with the existence of a first efficient cause. The very odd assumption here, spelt out clearly enough elsewhere by Scotus, although never defended, is that it is non-existence, rather than existence, that somehow needs explaining: "Nothing can not-be, unless something positively or privatively incompossible with it can be" (*Ord*. bk 1, dist. 2, pt 1, qu. 1–2, n. 70 (Duns Scotus 1950–: 2:170; ed. and trans. in Duns Scotus 1987: 49)). Since nothing is incompatible with the existence of a first cause, and since the explanation of a first cause is somehow intrinsic to it, a first cause exists. Scotus then argues similarly for the existence of a final goal of activity (*Ord*. bk 1, dist. 2, pt 1, qu. 1–2, nn. 60–2 (Duns Scotus 1950–: 2:165–7; ed. and trans. in Duns Scotus 1987: 47–8)), and a maximally excellent being (*Ord*. bk 1, dist. 2, pt 1, qu. 1–2, nn. 64–6 (Duns Scotus 1950–: 2:167–8; ed. and trans. in Duns Scotus 1987: 48–9)).

The argument – not, it seems to me, one of Scotus's happier contributions to philosophy – is located at something of a distance from Aristotelian arguments for an unmoved mover: the argument that, since there is motion, and since both self-motion and an infinite regress of movers is possible, there must be an unmoved first mover. Scotus, on the contrary, believes there is nothing contradictory about the notion of self-motion: something can certainly have the power to move itself, or to change itself in various ways. All it needs is the possession both of the relevant active power, and of the relevant passive capacity (Scotus, *Ord.* bk 2, dist. 2, pt 2, qu. 6, nn. 444, 453–63 (Duns Scotus 1950–: 7:351–2, 358–62); for the definitive modern discussion, see King (1994)).

Modality and the freedom of the will
(*Ordinatio* Book 1, distinction 2; Book 1, distinction 39)

Throughout Book 1, various issues about modality arise in passing, and Scotus shows himself to be, as one modern commentator has put it, something of a Janus figure (Calvin Normore in Williams 2003: 156). On the one hand, Scotus works out a clear account of the logically possible that relies on no more than the notion of formal compatibility (thus giving something like the notion of a possible world, doubtless occurring in Leibniz as the result of his reading of later Scotist writers); on the other, Scotus very often makes modalities dependent on states of the actual world, thus looking back to the old Aristotelian account of modality that tends to reduce modal operators to temporal ones (the necessary is the everlasting; the possible is what is at some time actual). The understanding of the modalities in the proof for God's existence shares something of both views.

One of the places where Scotus makes use of his new "logical" account of modalities is in his attempt to prove that the first cause must have both intellect and will. As he sees it, the existence of contingency in the world requires that the first cause be able to cause contingently, in a non-deterministic way. The reason is that God is the primary cause of every creaturely action; thus if God caused deterministically, no creaturely activity would be contingent (*Ord.* bk 1, dist. 2, pt 1 qu. 1–2, n. 80 (Duns Scotus 1950–: 2:176–7; ed. and trans. in Duns Scotus 1987: 54)). Scotus offers an introspective proof of creaturely freedom, claiming that we know by experience that we could, in precisely the same circumstances as those in which we did *a*, have done not-*a* (*Ord.* bk 1, dist. 39, qu. 1–5, n. 16 (Duns Scotus 1950–: 6:417–19)).

As Scotus sees it, sustaining this "contra-causal" account of freedom requires the notion of logical possibility, and he introduces such a notion precisely as part of the defence of the first cause's possession of will:

> I do not here call contingent everything that is neither necessary nor everlasting, but that whose opposite could have happened when this did. For this reason I did not say "something is contingent", but "something is caused contingently".
>
> (*Ord.* bk 1, dist. 2, pt 1, qu. 1–2, n. 86
> (Duns Scotus 1950–: 178; ed. and trans. in Duns Scotus 1987: 55))

"Contingent" is to be understood as that whose non-existence does not entail a contradiction; that is to say, the relevant sense of the modality is (roughly speaking) logical, or broadly logical. The significance of the simultaneity claim is that contingency – and modality in general – is "understood to involve a consideration of several alternative states of affairs with respect to the same time" (Knuuttila 1982: 353). Such alternative states of affairs are in some sense possible, and, consistently with this, Scotus elsewhere makes it clear that the relevant sense of "possible" also approximates to what we would think of as logical, or broadly logical, possibility: "the possible is that which does not include a contradiction" (*Ord*. bk 1, dist. 2, pt 2, qu.1–4, n. 196 (Duns Scotus 1950–: 249)). This approach contrasts with older, Aristotelian accounts of modality, according to which modalities are understood fundamentally as expressing temporal facts about the real world. Commentators sometimes call this account of modality "diachronic", and contrast it with Scotus's new "synchronic" modalities.

Scotus uses this synchronic account of modality in his development of a notion of contra-causal freedom, most clearly found in the (late) final book of the *Metaphysics* questions. According to this account, a free power is "not determined of itself, but can cause this act or the opposite act, and act or not act" in the selfsame circumstances (*In Metaph*. bk 9, qu.15, n. 22 (Duns Scotus 1997–: 4:680–1)). These features entail, for Scotus, that a free power can "determine itself" in both ways (that is, both to act rather than not act, and to act in one way rather than another: *In Metaph*. bk 9, qu. 15, n. 32 (Duns Scotus 1997–: 4:683)), and that it does this on the basis of its "unlimited actuality" (such that it is not, or need not be, in passive potency to any causal activity external to it: *In Metaph*. bk 9, qu. 15, n. 31 (Duns Scotus 1997–: 4:683)). As far as I can see, this account of freedom requires the notion of synchronic contingency (considering alternative states of affairs with respect to the same time), since it requires the notion of real alternatives at one and the same time. Furthermore, this understanding of alternative possibilities, according to Scotus, entails the notion of contra-causal freedom. The reason is tied in with Scotus's residual Aristotelianism on the question of modalities. As we saw above, Scotus believes that positing the existence of something both contingent and uncaused would generate a formal contradiction. So *real* contingency – contingency in the real world, as Scotus believes to be observable – requires a real free power. This does not mean, of course, that every logical possibility has to correspond to some real power in the world; "not all logical possibilities are real alternatives in the actual world", and thus realization "in the actual world is no longer the criterion of real possibility" (Knuuttila 1982: 354). The importance of these groundbreaking innovations, both in modal logic and in the theory of freedom, can hardly be overestimated, passing from Scotus to the later scholastics, and thence into modern philosophy through Leibniz and Kant.

Cognitive empiricism and transcendental concepts
(*Ordinatio* Book 1, distinction 3)

Scotus's influence on Leibniz and thence on the rationalist tradition in philosophy is evident in another area of his thought that crops up in distinction 3 of Book 1 of the *Ordinatio*. In this distinction, Scotus lays out his theory of how we know God, and indeed of knowledge more generally, as the presupposition for the more specialized theological theory. Basically, Scotus proposes a system of transcendental concepts under whose extension all real and possible things fall. Concepts are meanings of words, and the network of concepts is reducible to some basic, non-overlapping concepts irreducible to any others, and thus not interdefinable. But Scotus's account of the acquisition of such concepts is robustly empiricist, holding that all of our concepts are derived more or less directly from our sense experience. He is thus quite unlike some of his early modern successors on this question. So before I talk about the transcendental concepts, I shall talk about the general empiricist theory of concept-acquisition defended in distinction 3.

Strictly epistemological questions were not much to the fore in the Middle Ages. In line with most of his contemporaries, Scotus is more concerned with the mechanism by which concepts are acquired than with the distinction between knowledge and mere true belief (a point made nicely by Robert Pasnau in Williams (2003: 285)). The assumption underlying this attitude is Aristotelian: that in some way reality is intrinsically intelligible, and that the human mind is capable of understanding it. Basically, Scotus holds that we form general concepts by abstraction from sense-data. This process is a cognitive *activity*: part of the mind is such that it is able to operate in this way, and part of the mind is the passive recipient of the abstracted concept or "intelligible species" (*Ord.* bk 1, dist. 3 pt 3, qu. 1, nn. 359–60 (Duns Scotus 1950–: 3:216–18)). This is not a "magical" or "mystical" process; unlike some of his contemporaries, Scotus does not hold that the forms of extramental objects somehow come to exist in the mind. Aquinas, for example, is usually understood to maintain that having such a form actually in the mind is to have knowledge of the extramental object. For Scotus, what is made to exist in the mind is a representation of the extramental object; the extramental object is known by means of this mental object (*Ord.* 1.3.3.1, nn. 382, 386 (Duns Scotus 1950–: 3:232–3, 235)). The causality here is *efficient*, not *formal* (as in the Thomist account); it involves the notion that the extramental object is causally connected to the internal representation, rather than the bare notion of Aquinas's that the form of the external object somehow comes to exist in the mind. And an (efficiently) causal account is just what most modern realist theories rightly think is required here. This marks an important move in the direction of a representationalist theory of knowledge, one that Scotus feels bound to make because of the mysteriousness of the non-representational theories known to him. Scotus does not of course think that the representation need be an *image* of the thing known, or indeed "physically" like it in any way at all. Quite the contrary: the real property in which the object is represented is something quite unlike the object itself.

Scotus's theory of cognition is the first to exclude any appeal to divine influence (contrast *inter alia* Socrates' "divine sign", Plato's recollection, and Aristotle's external agent intellect). As Pasnau notes, "This marks a turning point in the history of philosophy, the first great victory for naturalism as a research strategy in the philosophy of mind" (Williams 2003: 303). Scotus holds that divine illumination – or some analogous supernatural process – would not be a sufficient guarantee of knowledge. Pasnau summarizes: "Scotus's bold – but reasonable – claim is that if the human mind were intrinsically incapable of achieving certain knowledge, then not even divine illumination could save it" (Williams 2003: 301: see especially *Ord.* bk 1, dist. 3, pt 1, qu. 4, nn. 219–45 (Duns Scotus 1950–: 3:133–48)).

In addition to concepts of various natural kinds, Scotus holds that we have by abstraction more general concepts too: transcendental concepts, transcending Aristotle's categorical scheme and thus natural kinds too. That there are such transcendentals – particularly being, goodness, truth, and beauty, supposedly attributes of everything that there is – is something of a medieval commonplace. But Scotus develops the theory in a radically new direction, and makes the development of the theory central to his theory of how it is possible to have knowledge of reality, and particularly of God. Basically, Scotus proposes that there is a complex network of concepts arranged hierarchically as genus and species, ultimately traceable to certain irreducibly simple, non-overlapping "genera", and irreducible, non-overlapping "specific differences" (*Ord.* bk 1, dist. 3, pt 1, qu. 3, nn.131–7 (Duns Scotus 1950–: 3:81–5; ed. and trans. (n. 137 only) in Duns Scotus 1987: 4)). The origins of this theory lie in Porphyry's famous "tree": his attempt to analyse each one of Aristotle's categories as a descending series of ever more specific genera, with (taking the category of substance as an example) *substance* at top, and the most specific species of substances at the bottom (*man, cat, dog, tree* and so on (Porphyry 1887: 4–5; ed. and trans. in Spade 1994: 4)). The medieval theory of the transcendentals modifies this scheme, continuing the hierarchy above the categories, such that (for example) *being* is the supreme "genus" of all the categories. Being in turn entails, and is coextensive with, unity, as it also is with truth and goodness (i.e. desirability). Scotus proposes a series of disjunctive transcendentals, each pair coextensive with *being*: necessary-or-contingent, actual-or-potential, infinite-or- finite, cause-or-caused, prior-or-posterior, independent-or-dependent, absolute-or-relative, goal-or-goal-directed, simple-or-composite, one-or-many, exceeding-or-exceeded, substance-or-accident, same-or-diverse, equal-or-unequal (for this list and a discussion of the disjunctive transcendentals, see Wolter (1946: 138–61)). On Scotus's understanding, the disjunctive transcendentals are the relevant "differences" of the "genus" of being. Each of these transcendentals will be wholly simple, not interdefinable. The same follows of the various "specific differences" that appear all the way down the modified scheme (classically, "rational" as the specific difference of "man").

As Scotus sees it, some such scheme is necessary for our knowledge of God, among other things. We gain concepts by abstraction from the creatures that we encounter. So unless there were concepts under whose extension both God and creatures fell, then it would not be possible for us to know anything about God at all. For example, Scotus argues that, if we are to consider whether or not God is a finite or infinite being, our concept of being must be the same in the two cases, and thus be a concept under the extension of which both finite and infinite beings fall (*Ord.* bk 1, dist. 3, pt 1, qu. 1–2, n. 27 (Duns Scotus 1950–: 3:18; ed. and trans. in Duns Scotus 1987: 20)). In fact, of course, it is, according to Scotus, proper to God to be an infinite being (*Ord.* bk 1, dist. 3, pt 1, qu.1–2, n. 51 (Duns Scotus 1950–: 3:34; ed. and trans. in Duns Scotus 1987: 41)). So this position entails that both God and creatures fall under the extension of the same concept. Basically, this amounts to saying that the concept's contents are the same in the cases under consideration: namely, God and his creatures. This theory is sometimes known as the univocity theory: rather than hold that the only relation between concepts under whose extension God falls and concepts under whose extension creatures fall is *analogy*, Scotus holds that God and creatures fall under the extension of some concepts that are identically the same in both contexts.

By claiming that being, the most general of all concepts, is univocal, Scotus is able to solve a long-standing problem at the heart of Aristotelian metaphysics: how it can be that, as Aristotle claimed, being-as-being is the subject of metaphysics, given that metaphysics includes the study of both material and immaterial substances. Being-as-being is common to all substances (and accidents too, for that matter); both material and immaterial substances thus fall under the scope of human cognition, admittedly in rather different ways.

In recent years this theological and philosophical teaching has been the subject of some controversy among theologians and others who have been motivated by worries about what is sometimes called (following Heidegger) "ontotheology". As usually understood (although not necessarily so by Heidegger), this is the view that there is something more ultimate than God: in this case, being. And this seems absurd. (For a fuller account of the criticism, see Cross (2001).) Of course, the criticism involves mistaking a cognitive theory for a metaphysical one. Scotus's point is that, if creatures are to know God at all, it needs to be the case that God falls under the extension of certain concepts. The theory certainly should not be understood to imply that there is some real thing – Being – more ultimate than God. Indeed, for Scotus the non-disjunctive transcendentals are really no more than *concepts*: they do not pick out real, extramental, properties of things; they are simply ways in which we can successfully think about the substances presented to us. What Scotus has in mind is that there is a real prop-erty – *infinite wisdom*, for example – that is proper to God, and another, different real property – *finite wisdom*, for example – proper to creatures. But these two real properties have nothing real in common; (unqualified) *wisdom* is just a vicious abstraction.

As noted above, Scotus holds that concepts are the meanings of words. Indeed, his univocity theory entails as much. This theory is not currently in vogue, partly because it seems to make it difficult to use words unless their meanings are fully understood. But Scotus would not accept this objection to the traditional theory. He holds that it is perfectly possible to use words successfully and accurately even in cases where the concepts meant by the words are not properly understood at all (*Ord.* bk 1, dist. 22, qu. un., nn. 4–11 (Duns Scotus 1950–: 343–7)). This is obviously true. We can talk successfully about water without knowing that it is H_2O; I take it that Scotus, among many others, did this himself. Being a success-ful language-user does not require being a perfect language-user; it does not require a full understanding of the meanings of the words used. As Scotus realized, this does not in itself undermine the view that concepts are the meanings of words. And Scotus thinks that there is good reason for accepting that concepts are indeed the meanings of words. One of Scotus's most compelling reasons for his theologi-cal position is simply that deductive arguments require unambiguous middle terms; the only way to exclude ambiguity is to accept the univocity theory, and thus that concepts are, at root, the meanings of words, identically the same in different statements (*Ord.* bk 1, dist. 3, pt 1, qu. 1–2, n. 36 (Duns Scotus 1950–: 3:24; ed. and trans. in Duns Scotus 1987: 23); the point is made more clearly at *Lect.* bk 1, dist. 3, pt 1, qu. 1–2, n. 113 (Duns Scotus 1950–: 16:226–7)).

Varieties of distinction and identity (Book 1, distinctions 2 and 8)

When outlining some of Scotus's claims about divine properties, I claimed that whereas *wisdom*, for example, is a vicious abstraction, nothing other than a concept, *divine wisdom* is a "real property". By a "real property", I mean a property that is in some sense or another a real *constituent* or *component* of the thing that possesses it, as opposed to an account of properties that would reduce all properties to mere linguistic or conceptual items: predicates, or whatever. Let me label this reductive strategy "nominalism" (by which I mean, here, nominalism about (particular) *properties*, not about universals). Scholastic philosophers, following Aristotle, distinguish two radically different kinds of property: essential properties and accidental ones. Essential properties are those that define a thing as the sort or kind that it is; accidental properties are all other properties of a thing. Setting aside complexities about necessary but non-defining properties, the so-called "*propria*" of a substance (of which different philosophers had different things to say), it was certainly not controversial in the Middle Ages to treat accidental properties of a thing as in some sense themselves real entities, albeit ones fully dependent for their reality on the substances on which they depend and in which they inhere. Thinkers towards the end of the thirteenth century were beginning to adopt the view that the essential properties of a thing should be thought of in something like this way as well: not as *inherent* particulars, because they are permanent features of the substances that they intrinsically compose, as it were, but at least as *dependent* particulars, together inseparably composing a complete substance. Setting aside the problem of universals – to which I shall return below, because Scotus has many very important things to say on the subject – such properties, both accidental and essential, were generally thought of as particulars (for accidents, see below; for essential properties, see Cross (2005: 103–11)). As Scotus sees the issue, substances are collections of such essential properties. Bearing in mind the standard definition of "man" as "rational animal", we might think of Socrates, for example, as the collection of his animality and his rationality. Scotus, again taking up some suggestions in late-thirteenth-century theologians such as Henry of Ghent, holds that such properties – Socrates's animality and his rationality – are *formally distinct* from each other. Scotus deals with the formal distinction in Book 1, distinction 2, and with its application to the divine attributes in distinction 8.

Roughly speaking, Scotus believes that a formal distinction is the kind of distinction that obtains between the necessary properties of a thing on the assumption that nominalism about properties is false. It is easiest to understand in contrast to the notion of a real distinction. Scotus basically believes that really distinct things are separable (see *Quod*. 3, n. 15 (Duns Scotus 1639: 12:81), for the necessity of separability for real distinction; *Ord*. bk 2, dist. 1, qu. 4–5, n. 200 (Duns Scotus 1950–: 7:101), for the sufficiency of separability for real distinction). More precisely, he thinks at least that really distinct things are the kinds of thing that either are capable of being independent *supposita* (absolutely non-instantiable or non-exemplifiable non-relational subjects of properties – Socrates and Plato, for example), or are uniquely properties of such things (Socrates's humanity and Plato's humanity). Formal distinctions obtain between the necessary properties of any one such *suppositum* (Socrates's rationality and Socrates's animality). Scotus here presents the distinction as one that obtains between not things but *formalities* – little or diminished things – and the sort of distinction is not real but somehow diminished too (*Ord*. bk 1, dist. 2, pt 2, qu. 1–4, nn. 400–4 (Duns Scotus 1950–: 2:355–7)). These formalities are inseparable, and thus really identical with each other. Their formal distinction results from the fact that they are different properties: not sharing the same definition, even if in some cases interdefinable:

> "To include formally" is to include something in its essential notion, such that if there were a definition of the including thing, then the thing included would be the definition or a part of the definition. Just as, however, the definition of goodness in general does not include wisdom, neither does infinite [goodness include] infinite [wisdom]. There is therefore some formal non-identity between wisdom and goodness, inasmuch as there would be distinct definitions of them if they were definable. But a definition does not only indicate a concept caused by the intellect, but the quiddity of a thing: there is therefore formal non-identity from the side of the thing, which I understand thus: the intellect forming this [sentence] "wisdom is not formally goodness" does not cause, by its act of combining, the truth of this combination, but it finds the terms in the object, and a true act is made by their combination.
>
> (*Ord*. bk 1, dist. 8, pt 1, qu. 4, nn. 192–3
> (Duns Scotus 1950–: 4:261–2))

Formal distinction, according to Scotus, is compatible with real identity, because the necessary properties of a thing are not themselves things, or separable from their subject. (Indeed, the domain of formally distinct items is limited to that of really identical items in the required sense.) The relation of real identity is what explains the unity of these properties with each other, and the real identity itself is (in normal cases) explained by the identity of the *suppositum* whose properties they are. Thus, what explains the real identity of my necessary properties with each other – the real identity of my rationality and my animality, for example – is just that they are properties of me. Considered in abstraction from their unity in me, they would not be unified with each other (*Ord*. bk 1, dist. 8, pt 1, qu. 4, nn. 219–20 (Duns Scotus 1950–: 274–5)). As I have argued elsewhere, the relation of real identity between different properties is in all formal respects the same as the relation of compresence in modern metaphysics; indeed, among many of those metaphysicians who believe in what are now labelled "tropes" – that is to say, particular properties – the relation of compresence does exact duty for Scotus's relation of real identity between formally distinct properties (see Cross 2005: part 2, §5.1). Just as in the modern relation of compresence, Leibnizian requirements for identity are not satisfied; Scotus would hold that the indiscernibility of identicals obtains only if the domain is restricted to substances as such, and does not obtain if the domain includes the *properties* of substances (my rationality and my animality, for example, are really identical but, because of the formal distinction between them, certainly not indiscernible; indeed, their very discernibility is what grounds the distinction between them).

The passage just cited makes it clear why Scotus might want to posit a formal distinction between wisdom and goodness as necessary properties of a thing. But why would he want to extend this to God too? The basic reason is connected with the theory of univocity outlined above. If it is the case that God's wisdom and wisdom in a creature fall under the extension of the same concept – and likewise for other such pairs of properties too – then it must be the case that a distinction between wisdom and any other relevant attribute obtains *globally*, and thus obtains in the case of God as well as the case of creatures.

Universals and individuation (*Ordinatio* Book 2, distinction 3)

Scotus puts his formal distinction to a great deal of use. One of the most important contexts is that of his theories of universals and individuation, found in distinction 3 of Book 2. It is often felt that Scotus's most important contribution to philosophy lies in this area. Scotus's account of individuation is justly famous: his belief, unprecedented in any previous philosopher, is that in order to explain individuation it is necessary to posit completely non-qualitative "haecceities": "thisnesses". Understanding this position requires that we first of all understand Scotus's theory about universals. Basically, Scotus accepts two different theories about universals, one applicable uniquely in the case of the Trinity (one divine essence shared by three persons), and one applicable in the case of creatures. What distinguishes the two theories is that the universal divine essence is indivisible – *numerically* singular, and thus numerically identical in each of its exemplifications – whereas all other common essences are divisible, and thus identical in each instantiation in some *non-numerical* way (*Ord.* bk 2, dist. 3, pt 1, qu. 1, nn. 37–9 (Duns Scotus 1950–: 7:406–8; ed. and trans. in Spade 1994: 65–6)). The origins of the teaching are found in Avicenna's *De Prima*

Philosophia (bk 5, ch. 1; Avicenna 1977–83: 2:228–34). This latter sense of identity – Scotus calls it the "less-than-numerical identity" of a common essence or nature (*Ord.* bk 2, dist. 3, pt 1, qu. 1, n. 8 (Duns Scotus 1950–: 7:395; ed. and trans. in Spade 1994: 59)) – is rather mysterious; modern theories of universals tend to hold that universals are numerically identical in their exemplifications (for a brief but explicit statement of the contrast between medieval and modern views, see Armstrong (1978: 112)). But this view was almost unknown in the ancient and medieval worlds (other than in the mysterious context of the Trinity; Plato's Forms are, after all, *extrinsic* to their exemplifications in a way that most theories of universals deny of universals). For from the time of Aristotle onwards, indivisibility was (for perhaps obvious reasons) held to be the mark of particularity, and divisibility the mark of universality. And the notion of less-than-numerical identity, first formulated by Scotus, is simply an attempt to give some account of the unity relevant to such a divisible entity.

Why accept that such common natures are real: humanity as such, for example, distinct from humanity in this or that instantiation of it? Scotus offers a variety of arguments, all of which presuppose that there are in some sense real (i.e. non-conventional) kinds: the world is really known by us, and really carved up into kinds more or less in the way that we suppose. The following is typical:

> According to the Philosopher, *Metaphysics* V, the chapter on relation [c. 15, 1021a9–12], the same, the similar and the equal are all based on the notion of one, so that even though a similarity has for its foundation a thing in the genus of quality, nevertheless such a relation is not real unless it has a real foundation and a real proximate basis for the founding. Therefore, the unity required in the foundation of the relation of similarity is a real one. But it is not numerical unity, since nothing one and the same is similar or equal to itself.
>
> (*Ord.* bk 2, dist. 3, pt 1, qu. 1, n. 18
> (Duns Scotus 1950–: 398); ed. and trans. in Spade 1994: 61))

The point here is that relations of similarity between two particulars cannot be self-explanatory; they must have some explanation (some "real foundation") in the things that are similar. This, I take it, is among other things an argument against resemblance nominalism. But it is also supposed to be an argument against the view that a universal could be numerically identical in each instantiation. Since it is the universal that is supposed to explain the relation of similarity, positing that the universal is numerically identical in each instantiation might lead to the conclusion that the universal in each instantiation is similar *to itself*. But, Scotus notes, similarity is not a reflexive relation.

And this gives us some sort of answer to the position that common natures are indivisible. Elsewhere, Scotus argues that if created natures were not divisible on instantiation, then these instantiations would themselves be, in effect, numerically identical:

> This opinion posits that that one substance [namely, the universal], under many accidents, will be the whole substance of all individuals, and then it will be both singular and this substance of this thing [x], and in another thing [y] than this thing [x]. It will also follow that the same thing will simultaneously possess many quantitative dimensions of the same kind; and it will do this naturally, since numerically one and the same substance is under these [x's] dimensions and other [y's] dimensions.   (*Reportatio Parisiensis* bk 2, dist. 12, qu. 5, n. 3 (Scotus 1639: 11:326)[1]

I have tried elsewhere to make this argument more plausible (see Cross 2003). For now, what is worth noting is that Scotus is clearly supposing that numerically singular things are paradigmatic candidates for being subjects of properties, in line with the basic Aristotelian association of indivisibility with particularity.

Scotus believes, then, that common natures – humanity as such, for example – must be divisible. Clearly, particular substances are not divisible. This indivisibility, according to Scotus, requires explanation (*Ord.* bk 2, dist. 3, pt 1, qu. 4, n. 76 (Duns Scotus 1950–: 426–7; ed. and trans. in Spade 1994: 76); see Park 1988). The reason is that the divisible entity whose division into the relevant kinds of (indivisible) parts is being explained is itself real. Humanity as such, for example, is (as we have just seen) real. So the explanation for indivisibility must therefore reside in something that is real too. And since indivisibility is being explained, the explanation must be something in itself irreducibly indivisible. But anything qualitative (quidditative, in the technical medieval vocabulary) is shareable and thus divisible in the required sense. So the explanation must lie in something non-quidditative: and the only candidate, according to Scotus, is a "thisness" or haecceity (*Ord.* bk 2, dist. 3, pt 1, qu. 5–6, n. 169 (Duns Scotus 1950–: 474–5; ed. and trans. in Spade 1994: 101)).[2] A haecceity is a non-quidditative property or feature of an individual, explaining its indivisibility. As a consequence of explaining indivisibility, Scotus believes, the haecceity can also explain a substance's numerical distinction from all other things. Indeed, although he believes that what fundamentally needs explaining is indivisibility, he believes too that the capacity of a haecceity to explain indivisibility is itself explained by a haecceity's capacity to distinguish one thing from another. According to Scotus, numerical distinction – as opposed to (say) specific distinction – entails that each of the things distinguished has numerical singularity. And numerical singularity entails indivis-ibility (into subjective parts). For what allows a common nature to be divided is its possession of less-than-numerical unity. Numerical unity entails indivisibility (see *Ord.* bk 2, dist. 3, pt 1, qu. 5–6, n. 186 (Duns Scotus 1950–: 483; ed. and trans. in Spade 1994: 106)).

Scotus uses his formal distinction to give an account of the metaphysical constitution of a substance that includes both nature and haecceity. After all, both nature and haecceity are real. But they are – in any given substance – inseparable, and neither is in itself anything like a *suppositum*: indeed, each is more like a property of a thing than a thing (each is, we might say, a "formal-ity"). Among the formally distinct constituents of an individual substance are both nature and haecceity:

> [The haecceity] is the ultimate reality of a being ... Thus whatever is common and yet determinable can still be distinguished (no matter how much it is one thing) into several formally distinct realities of which this one is not formally that one. This one is formally the entity of singularity and that one is formally the entity of the nature. These two realities cannot be distinguished as "thing" and "thing" ... Rather when in the same thing, whether in a part or in the whole, they are always formally distinct realities of the same thing.
>
> (*Ord.* bk 2, dist. 3, pt 1, qu. 5–6, n. 188
> (Duns Scotus 1950–: 483–4; ed. and trans. in Spade 1994: 107))

And in line with this, Scotus holds that a thing's nature (the common nature in the particular thing) and its haecceity are really identical, and that this relation of real identity is what ties nature and haecceity together.

Material substance (*Ordinatio* Book 2, distinction 2; Book 3, distinction 2; Book 4, distinction 11)

In Book 2, distinction 2, Scotus deals with a range of problems about angels. It might look odd to look here for information about material substance. But Scotus uses the questions about angels to deal with a variety of issues connected with atomism. For angels are (according to the medievals) spiritual substances, and a feature of such substances is the lack of any sort of spatial extension. This raises interesting questions about their motion (people who believe in angels tend also to believe that such beings can "move" around the universe, causing effects at different places). For Aristotle held that spatial extension was a necessary condition for motion, since motion requires traversing a distance less than the extension of the moving substance before traversing a distance equal to the extension of the moving substance, a condition that cannot be satisfied by something spatially indivisible. Scotus uses the whole issue as an arena to reject atomism. The conclusion is standardly Aristotelian, although Scotus's reasons add something to the tradition. Against the notion that a continuum is divisible *everywhere*, he reasons that the evident fact that a continuum is divisible anywhere certainly does not entail that it is divisible everywhere; indeed, the very notion of a division requires something "left over", as it were (*Ord.* bk 2, dist. 2, pt 2, qu. 5, n. 288 (Duns Scotus 1950–: 279–80)). And Scotus maintains that the incommensurability of the diagonal with the side of a rectangle is sufficient to disprove atomism, as long as the atoms are thought of as existing side by side (*Ord.* bk 2, dist. 2, pt 2, qu. 5, nn. 327–30 (Duns Scotus 1950–: 296–8): on this, see Cross (1998: 116–38)). It was not until the middle of the fourteenth century that anyone (at least in the West) thought that atoms could be (as we would say) "densely ordered", such that between *any* two there is always a third.

These arguments have antecedents in the Islamic theological tradition. More distinctive are Scotus's arguments in favour of the reality of matter. Hard-line Aristotelians on this question maintain that matter is "pure potency": the bare capacity to exist under any set of essential properties or (in the technical language) substantial *form*. Scotus argues that this is contradictory; if matter is supposed to persist from its being under one form to its being under another, then it must have some constant actuality that is proper to it and entirely its own. After all, in the Aristotelian position, the identity of matter appears to be entirely fixed by the identity of form, and on this view, it makes no sense to speak of the *same* matter under successive forms (*Lect.* bk 2, dist. 12, qu. un., n. 11 (Duns Scotus 1950–: 19:72–3): for a discussion, see Cross (1998: 13–33)). Equally, Scotus supposes that substantial form – that set of properties that, in addition to matter, constitutes a material substance – must have some kind of reality too. For along with matter it is a constituent of a real substance; and as such it must be as real as the other constituent. And the two are separable, at least in the sense that the matter can exist without the form (*Lect.* bk 2, dist. 12, qu. un., nn. 54–6 (Duns Scotus 1950–: 19:90); for a discussion see Cross (1998: 34–46)). They are thus really distinct things, constituting one substance (*Ord.* bk 3, dist. 2, qu. 2, n. 9 (Duns Scotus 1639: 7:80)). In line with the conscious reifying strategy, Scotus has no problem affirming a plurality of substantial forms in one substance, responsible for explaining distinct and separable features of that substance (for example, the persistence of a body, although not an animal, over death) (*Ord.* bk 4, dist. 11, qu. 3, nn. 25–56 (Duns Scotus 1639: 8:629–54); see Cross 1998: 55–71).

In effect Scotus posits two overlapping accounts of the constitution of material substance: in more or less traditional Aristotelian terms of matter and form (though allowing the possibility of a plurality of substantial forms), and in terms of his own view of substances as collections of properties. As he would see it, these would correspond to different levels of analysis – physical and metaphysical, respectively – and are used to explain different features of the substance: its capacity for change and destruction, and its kind-membership, respectively. This duality of explanation might look problematic, but in fact Scotus's accounts of the reality of matter and form, and of the formal distinction, allow the potential messiness to be tidied up. For we might most helpfully think of the relation between these two different accounts in terms of relations between two different (really distinct) sets of necessary properties within one and the same substance: those constituting its matter, and those constituting its form. Scotus holds that the whole substance somehow "emerges from" or "supervenes on" (as we would say) these lower-order components (matter and form, respectively). Indeed, he spends some time wondering what it is that distinguishes a substance from the mere aggregate of its matter and form. And his answer is that a substance has properties different in kind from any mere aggregate of its parts. An aggregate, Scotus believes, cannot have any properties that are not also properties of one or (the mere sum of) more of its constituents; a substance, contrariwise, has properties that are distinct from the properties of one or more of its constituents (*Ord.* bk 3, dist. 2, qu. 2, n. 8 (Duns Scotus 1639: 7:79); for a discussion see Cross (1998: 77–93)).

Substance and accident (*Ordinatio* Book 4, distinction 12)

Scotus, then, is not unhappy about reifying some of the constituents of a substance, namely, its matter and form. He believes too that the non-essential properties of a substance need to count as things as well. One reason is that they are separable, in the sense that the substance can survive without any given accident (although perhaps not without every one of them). Indeed, Scotus believes that the doctrine of transubstantiation entails that – at least by divine power – accidents can exist without substances too (*Ord.* bk 4, dist. 12, qu. 1, n. 9 (Duns Scotus 1639: 8:717)).[3] A further, more compelling reason for the reification of accidental properties has to do with Scotus's account of the conditions necessary for causation. Something that causes an effect must be real: indeed, it must be more than just a formality, for formalities are no more than the minimal constituents of a fully fledged thing, and do not seem to be the sorts of entity with the robust existence required of causes. They are, perhaps, more like powers than the things that exercise those powers. Now, a substance is composed of such formalities, and as such can explain certain of its effects. But in itself the substance cannot explain those effects that are the result of contingent or accidental features of it, for in itself it does not include such features. But there clearly are effects of substances that are the result of some of their accidental features. To explain this, Scotus reasons, accidents must be real, in the sense of having causal effects of their own (*Ord*. bk 4, dist. 12, qu. 1, n. 16 (Duns Scotus 1639: 8:720); for a discussion of the whole issue, see Cross (1998: 94–115)).

Natural law (*Ordinatio* Book 3, distinction 37)

The precise nature of Scotus's ethical theory has been the subject of considerable and sometimes heated debate. At best, there is an agreement that Scotus's account of the radical freedom of the will in ethical contexts means that virtues do not play the strongly explanatory role in ethics that they do in Aristotle, not because virtues are not character forming, but because they cannot sufficiently explain actions. Even the virtuous can act badly, and one virtue can be possessed wholly in the absence of another (for discussion, see Bonnie Kent's essay in Williams (2003: 352–76)). This emphasis, then, leads to a more rule-based ethical system than is found in Aristotle. But these rules are, with some exceptions, the result of positive, not natural, law. Basically, Scotus accepts a classic move in natural law theory – namely, that something's *nature* might be such as to generate obligations towards itself – but restricts this to the case of God and his nature. Thus, he holds that obligations to love and obey God belong "properly" to natural law (*Ord*. bk 3, dist. 37, qu. un., n. 6 (Duns Scotus 1639: 7:898; ed. and trans. in Wolter 1986: 277)). But no obligations respecting creatures are like this. If they were, then either God would be bound to will them, or he would not be so bound. In the first case God would fail to be free with regard to his creature-directed actions. And this would make his actions dependent on the natures of creatures; which in turn would mean that God failed to be wholly unconditioned, such that he could not be affected by anything external to him. But this contradicts Scotus's view that every divine creature-directed action is contingent. In the second case, God could will against some of his obligations, and this really would make him bad. But it is impossible for him to act badly. So there cannot be any obligations placed on God – with regard to the actions he directs towards creatures – prior to any act of his will. I take it that the way Scotus sets up the disjunction – lack of freedom versus (moral) badness – entails that there really are no restrictions on how God can behave to his creatures in relation to these creature-directed actions, and thus that he can command creatures as he will, at least with regard to their behaviour towards each other. (Scotus makes these points most clearly at *Lect*. bk 1, dist. 39, qu. 1–5, n. 43 (Duns Scotus 1950–: 17:492–3).)

This position has the theological advantages of a divine command theory (there is no danger that goods relative to creatures could be a source of obligation that somehow binds God), while avoiding the incoherence of most such theories (namely, the impossibility of generating an obligation to obey God without either a vicious regress or vicious circularity). But of course it suffers from the other major disadvantage of divine command theories: the worry that God's commands are (or could be) completely arbitrary. This worry is intensified if we recall that Scotus sometimes talks as though the natures of creatures are such that, without divine command, they would generate certain obligations (see e.g. *Ord*. bk 1, dist. 17, qu. 1–2, n. 63 (Duns Scotus 1950–: 5:164; ed. and trans. in Wolter 1986: 207)), obligations that God is not bound to respect, and that he could presumably command against.

Conclusion

Scotus has had his fair share of admirers and detractors over the years. The poet Gerard Manley Hopkins, for example, thought of him as

> Of realty the rarest-veinèd unraveller; a not
> Rivalled insight, be rival Italy or Greece.

("Duns Scotus's Oxford")

The American pragmatist C. S. Pierce thought him one of the "profoundest metaphysicians that ever lived" (Wolter 1990: 23). At the Reformation, Scotus came to represent in the minds of some of the Church Reformers the very worst of scholastic pedantry and logic-chopping. In his native Scotland, a prey to extreme Presbyterianism in the sixteenth century, it was a criminal offence to call a lawyer a "Dunce": an explicit reference to Duns Scotus. His writings were considered even by his contemporaries to be dense and difficult to understand, earning him almost immediately the soubriquet "subtle doctor" (*doctor subtilis*). In less partisan times, we can see that Scotus was undeniably a philosophical thinker of rigour and originality. He was one of the most innovative of all medieval philosophers, and arguably one of the most creative speculative metaphysicians ever seen. It is not an exaggeration to suggest that philosophical ideas discovered or developed by Scotus set a good part of the agenda for both rationalist and empiricist philosophies in later centuries.

Notes

1. See also *Ord*. bk 2, dist. 3, pt 1, qu. 1, nn. 37, 41 (Duns Scotus 1950–: 7:406–7, 409–10; ed. and trans. in Spade 1994: 65–7).
2. Scotus does not use the term "haecceity" in the *Ordinatio*. He talks rather about the individual difference, or individual entity. But he does elsewhere talk about this entity as a haecceity (a term of Scotus's own invention). For the change in terminology, see Stephen Dumont's essay in Sileo (1995).
3. In the light of his reifying strategy, this is not quite as bizarre as it might seem on a more normal account of accidental properties.

Bibliography

Primary sources

Avicenna. 1977–83. *Liber de philosophia prima sive scientia divina* [*Metaphysics*], S. van Riet (ed.). Louvain, Peeters; Leiden: Brill.

Duns Scotus. 1639. *Opera Omnia*, Luke Wadding (ed.). Lyon.

Duns Scotus. 1950– . *Opera Omnia*, C. Balić *et al.* (eds). Rome: Typis Polyglottis Vaticanis.

Duns Scotus. 1987. *Philosophical Writings: A Selection*, A. B. Wolter (ed. and trans.). Indianapolis, IN: Hackett.

Duns Scotus. 1997– . *Opera Philosophica*, G. J. Etzkorn *et al.* (eds). St Bonaventure, NY: The Franciscan Institute.

Frank, W. A. & A. B. Wolter 1995. *Duns Scotus: Metaphysician*. West Lafayette, IN: Purdue University Press.

Porphyry. 1887. *Isagoge et in Aristotelis Categorias commentaria*, A. Busse (ed.). Berlin: Reimer.

Spade, P. V. 1994. *Five Texts on the Mediaeval Problem of Universals: Porphyry, Boethius, Abelard, Duns Scotus, Ockham*. Indianapolis, IN: Hackett.

Wolter, A. B. 1986. *Duns Scotus on the Will and Morality*. Washington, DC: Catholic University of America Press.

Secondary sources

Armstrong, D. M. 1978. *Nominalism and Realism*. Cambridge: Cambridge University Press.

Bos, E. P. (ed.) 1998. *John Duns Scotus (1265/6–1308): Renewal of Philosophy*. Amsterdam: Rodopi.

Cross, R. 1998. *The Physics of Duns Scotus: The Scientific Context of a Theological Vision*. Oxford: Clarendon Press.

Cross, R. 1999. *Duns Scotus*. Oxford: Oxford University Press.

Cross, R. 2001. "'Where Angels Fear to Tread': Duns Scotus and Radical Orthodoxy" *Antonianum* **76**, 7–41.

Cross, R. 2003. "Divisibility, Communicability, and Predicability in Duns Scotus's Theories of the Common Nature" *Medieval Philosophy and Theology* **11**, 43–63.

Cross, R. 2005. *Duns Scotus on God*. Aldershot: Ashgate.

Honnefelder, L., R. Wood & M. Dreyer (eds) 1996. *Duns Scotus: Metaphysics and Ethics*. Leiden: Brill.

King, P. 1992. "Duns Scotus on the Common Nature and the Individual Differentia", *Philosophical Topics* **20**, 50–76.

King, P. 1994. "Duns Scotus on the Reality of Self-Change", in *Self-Motion from Aristotle to Newton*, Mary Louise Gill & James G. Lennox (eds), 229–90. Princeton, NJ: Princeton University Press.

Knuuttila, S. 1982. "Modal Logic", in *The Cambridge History of Later Medieval Philosophy*, N. Kretzmann, A. Kenny & J. Pinborg (eds), 342–57. Cambridge: Cambridge University Press.

Knuuttila, S. 1993. *Modalities in Medieval Philosophy*. London: Routledge.

Park, W. 1988. "The Problem of Individuation for Scotus: A Principle of Indivisibility or a Principle of Distinction?" *Franciscan Studies* **48**, 105–23.

Ryan, J. K. & B. Bonansea (eds) 1965. *John Duns Scotus 1265–1965*. Washington, DC: Catholic University of America Press.

Sileo, L. (ed.) 1995. *Via Scoti: Methodologica ad mentem Ioannis Duns Scoti. Atti del Congresso Scotistico Internazionale, Roma 9–11 Marzo 1993*, [Proceedings of the International Scotistic Conference, Rome, 9–11 March 1993]. Rome: Antonianum.

Tweedale, M. M. 1999. *Scotus vs. Ockham: A Medieval Dispute over Universals*, 2 vols. Lampeter: Edwin Mellen.

Williams, T. (ed.). 2003. *The Cambridge Companion to Duns Scotus*. Cambridge: Cambridge University Press.

Wolter, A. 1946. *The Transcendentals and Their Function in the Metaphysics of Duns Scotus*. St Bonaventure, NY: Franciscan Institute.

Wolter, A. 1990 *The Philosophical Theology of John Duns Scotus*. Ithaca, NY: Cornell University Press.

Further reading

The critical edition of Scotus's *Ordinatio* (Duns Scotus 1950–: vols 1–16) has now (in 2005) reached the end of Book 2. The editors have published alongside it the earlier *Lectura*, Scotus's first draft of the work (Duns Scotus 1950: vols 17–20). Books 3 and 4 of the *Ordinatio* are found in Duns Scotus (1639: vols 7–10). Scotus's philosophical works are projected in the five volumes of Duns Scotus (1997–), of which three have thus far been published. Important English translations of material in the *Ordinatio* include Duns Scotus (1987), Frank and Wolter (1995) (largely duplicating Duns Scotus (1987), although with helpful commentaries on the texts chosen), Spade (1994) and Wolter (1986). The best place to start reading the secondary literature on Scotus is Williams (2003), and Bos (1998), Honnenfelder *et al.* (1996) and Sileo (1995) provide essential and up-to-date collections of essays. For Scotus on universals and individuation, Tweedale (1999), a translation of all the relevant texts, with detailed paragraph by paragraph commentary, is essential (although difficult and complex) reading.

10

William of Ockham

Summa Logicae

Peter King

Introduction

Ockham's *Summa logicae* (*The Logic Handbook*), written *c.* 1323, is a manifesto masquerading as a textbook.[1] Its aim, Ockham disingenuously declares in his Preface, is merely to help beginning students in theology avoid elementary difficulties in logic. His undeclared aim is far more ambitious. In the *Summa logicae* Ockham puts forward a new philosophical programme designed to supersede the views of his contemporaries and predecessors, views that come in for extensive and trenchant criticism in the course of its many pages. We call that programme and the movement it engendered "nominalism". Its guiding principle is the conviction that only concrete individuals exist, and hence that any other purported entities are no more than names (*nomina*), traditionally expressed as the maxim not to multiply entities beyond necessity, a formulation known as "Ockham's razor". This principle has a wide range of application, and it has deep theological as well as philosophical consequences. The *Summa logicae* lays out in systematic detail Ockham's account of logic and language, providing him with the necessary groundwork for applying his razor.[2]

Ockham's goal in the *Summa logicae*, then, is to expound and promote his nominalist programme in the context of developing a rigorous account of logic and language. The *Summa logicae* follows the traditional division of logic: Part I is devoted to terms and is concerned with semantics; Part II is devoted to sentences, which are made up out of terms, and is concerned with truth; Part III is

242

devoted to arguments, which are made up out of sentences, and is concerned with inference—a subject so extensive that Ockham divides it into four sections, dealing respectively with the syllogism, demonstrative proof, 'topical' reasoning (broadly speaking) and fallacies. Most famous is Part I, in which Ockham wields his semantic theory as a razor against other philosophical views; Part II and Part III build on it and for the most part are directed at narrower logical aims. Accordingly, after giving some background against which to measure Ockham's achievements, I shall concentrate on matters treated in Part I: the machinery of semantic theory, including terms and their reference, and its deployment against universals and most of the Aristotelian categories. A brief look at Ockham's account of sentences and argumentation will round out the picture.

Background

The history of logic in the Middle Ages begins with its inheritance from antiquity, and is largely due to the work of a single man, Boethius (480–524/5), who translated Porphyry's *Isagoge* into Latin along with Aristotle's *Categories* and *Peri hermeneias*, and wrote commentaries on them. He wrote summary treatments of the categorical syllogism, the hypothetical syllogism, topics and topical inference, and logical division; and he wrote a commentary on Cicero's work on topics. Thus from the beginning of the Middle Ages philosophers had a working knowledge of logical rules and practices. But the virtues of Boethius's work, attempting to encapsulate the whole of logic in a form readily assimilated without prior training, were also its defects: there was little explanation of why the rules and practices were what they were; no account of logical metatheory worth mentioning; an almost complete neglect of some areas of logic, such as modal and tense logic, proof theory and fallacies. Succeeding generations therefore inherited a systematic discipline without an account of its foundations.

This they set about to provide, once the dust had settled on the collapse of the western Roman Empire and civilization re-established itself in western Europe. Progress was slow until early in the twelfth century, when the first great logician since antiquity, Peter Abelard (1079–1142), turned his attention to the project. In the course of his controversial life Abelard tried to create a new semantic foundation for logic, and wrote with a logician's insight on matters such as the nature of conditional inference, how the theory of topics is connected to the theory of valid argument, and much else. Above all, Abelard seems to have started an original tradition in logic; its achievements were represented in the systematic manuals of logic of the mid-thirteenth century written by

Peter of Spain, William of Sherwood and Lambert of Auxerre. These authors expounded an account of logic based on *supposition theory*, in which logical rules were shown to be derived from deeper principles in the philosophy of language (or sometimes the philosophy of logic itself).

This was the first phase of supposition theory. A complete account of logic that was neither derived from nor even, strictly speaking, inspired by antiquity, it was an original achievement hammered out over the course of centuries. However, for reasons we do not know, this native development of logic went into eclipse after the middle of the thirteenth century. There is little trace of it at the inception of high scholasticism; it is not found in Aquinas, Bonaventure, Albert the Great, Duns Scotus or others. They had shifted their attention to the effort to create a workable Christian Aristotelianism, and the main issues they confronted were theological rather than logical. So matters stood for several decades. Then came Ockham.

Ockham was born in the late 1280s, in the village of Ockham, so called from Oak Hamlet, in Surrey, perhaps Woking today. His early years are lost to history. It is likely he was given to the Franciscan Order at a young age and taken to its London house, known as Greyfriars, for his education. (We first glimpse Ockham in 1306 when he was ordained a subdeacon.) If he was on the regular schedule, Ockham would have begun studying theology around 1310. We do not know where he began his studies, but at the end of the decade, probably by 1317, he was a student at the University of Oxford, lecturing on Peter Lombard's theology textbook and writing his own commentary on it. Ockham did not complete his studies at Oxford. Instead, he returned to Greyfriars around 1321, where in the course of the next three years he wrote commentaries on Porphyry's *Isagoge* as well as on Aristotle's *Categories*, *Peri hermeneias*, *Sophistical Refutations* and *Physics*. He also wrote a short treatise on predestination and foreknowledge, and conducted a series of 'quodlibetal' debates (open-question sessions). At the end of this period Ockham wrote the *Summa logicae*, presumably as a summary of how he thought logic, and by extension philosophy as a whole, ought to be done.

Mental language and signification

Ockham regards logic as a *scientia sermocinalis*, that is, as an organized body of knowledge concerned with meaningful language (I.2). But it is not empirical linguistics. Its proper subject, according to Ockham, is not conventional "natural" languages such as English or French but rather what makes them possible in the first place: mental language. Ockham holds that thought is literally a language: a familiar thesis in contemporary philosophy. While there were authoritative precedents in the writings of Aristotle, Boethius and Augustine, Ockham seems to have been the first to work out the details of the proposal.

Following Aristotle's lead, Ockham holds that there are three distinct levels of language: *written*, *spoken*, and *mental*, associated respectively with the activities of writing, speaking and thinking. Each is a fully developed language in its own right, with vocabulary, syntax and formation-rules. The three levels are hierarchically ordered, and the ordering is piecemeal rather than holistic; particular inscriptions are conventionally correlated with particular utterances (since the phonetic representation is up to us), which in turn are conventionally correlated with particular concepts (since we may say *red* or *rouge* to express a given concept). Ockham calls both instances of conventional correlation "subordination". Unlike the inscriptions and utterances that make up spoken and written languages, however, the concepts that are the basic vocabulary of mental language are non-conventionally correlated with things in the world. A concept, Ockham holds, is naturally linked to that of which it is the concept. This is a point about the nature of concepts: what it is to be the concept-of-ϕ is bound up with being ϕ, and not, for instance, ψ. Hence concepts are by definition related to the things of which they are the concepts.[3] Ockham explains this relation as a matter of similarity or likeness, maintaining that the concept of a rabbit (say) is naturally similar to rabbits, or at least more naturally similar overall to rabbits than to anything else.[4] The natural relation between concepts and their objects is the foundation of Ockham's semantics. He identifies it with the semantic property of (natural) "signification": roughly, meaning. Concepts naturally resemble their objects, and thereby signify those objects. The utterances subordinated to a given concept signify what the concept naturally signifies, and so too in turn the inscriptions subordinated to them. Hence a spoken word does not signify the concept to which it is subordinated; instead, it signifies what the concept signifies, although conventionally and derivatively rather than naturally.

Ockham's account of signification is a technical version of a common intuition about language: roughly, that words get their meanings from the ideas they are associated with, with the additional proviso that ideas are more fundamental. Hence in speaking we encode our thoughts in spoken or written form to communicate them externally, and the meaning of a word is what it brings to mind when it is heard.

Mental language therefore functions as the semantics for conventional spoken and written languages. It explains what it is for a written or spoken term to have a meaning, namely, to be subordinated to a concept. Furthermore, it explains both sameness in meaning (synonymy) and difference in meaning (equivocation): terms of spoken or written languages are synonymous when subordinated to the same concept(s) in mental language;[5] again, a term in spoken or written language is equivocal if it is subordinated to distinct concepts at one and the same time.[6]

The vocabulary of mental language is made up of concepts, which play a dual role for Ockham. On the one hand, they have a psychological dimension. They are literally the elements of thought: *thinking of* φ just is *having a concept-of-*φ. As such, concepts are the primary building-blocks of thought itself. We acquire them from our interaction with the world, according to Ockham, and an adequate psychological theory should detail the process of concept-acquisition in light of the operation of other mental faculties, such as sense-perception. Thus mental language is at least a partial description of the way human minds actually function. Since the structure of conceptual thought was held to be the same for all thinking beings (God excepted as always), cognitive psychology can be a universal natural science; Ockham understands it to be the foundation for logic.

On the other hand, concepts have a semantic as well as a psychological dimension. As part of a language, concepts are normatively governed and have semantic features that can be considered independently of their psychological properties, and indeed so does mental language *qua* language. For instance, mental language will be universal to all thinking beings, in virtue of the universality of the structure of cognitive thought. Of course, it is universal only with respect to its structure, not its content, since two thinkers may have different (if not disjoint) stocks of concepts, depending on their past causal interaction with the world. To claim universality for the structure of mental language, then, is roughly to say that there is a set of conceptual abilities common to all thinkers, in virtue of which each is a thinker. (Any thinker can combine simple concepts into complex concepts, for example.) Furthermore, the universal language of thought will be "expressively complete": since thinking of φ just is to have a concept-of-φ, anything that can be thought is expressible, and in fact thereby expressed, in mental language; hence anything expressible at all must be expressible in mental language. By the same token, mental language cannot contain any ambiguity, since to do so would require that a concept-of-φ be naturally related to φ and also to some unrelated ψ, which is impossible, since the one does not involve the other. Ockham's psychological realism reinforces this conclusion. Since we think in mental language, an ambiguous term (concept) would mean that we could think something without determinately thinking it rather than thinking something else, which cannot happen. Hence mental language is universal, expressively adequate and free of ambiguity.

Although mental language is a language, it does not have all the features conventional languages such as English or French have. In particular, Ockham holds that mental language includes only those syntactical (grammatical) features that are needed to make a semantic difference to an expression (I.3).[7] For example, pronouns are not required, since at least in principle they could be replaced by the nouns for which they stand (also disambiguating mental sentences). Nor need there be distinct conjugations for verbs, declensions for nouns or gender for nouns. However, nouns must have number and case; verbs must have number, mood, person, voice and tense. These features make a difference to what is said: "Socrates will run" differs from "Socrates has run", for instance. Ockham leaves it open whether we should think of mental language as containing (a) verbs but not their participles, since "Socrates runs" can replace "Socrates is running" everywhere, or (b) one single verb, namely the copula, which can be combined with the participles of all other verbs for the converse reduction, putting "Socrates is running" in place of "Socrates runs" everywhere. Since (a) and (b) are semantically equivalent, we should think of mental language as having a deep structure that could be represented by either; the choice of one rather than the other is a matter of our (spoken or written) representation of mental language, not a fact about mental language itself.[8] In addition to nouns and verbs/participles, Ockham argues that conjunctions, prepositions and adverbs are also included in mental language: "The cat is on the mat" differs from "The cat is under the mat", for instance.[9]

The grammar, and hence the formation-rules, of mental language is therefore very like that of ordinary spoken and written languages, with this difference: the syntax of mental language is entirely driven by its semantics, and it contains all and only those features that could make a semantic difference.

Terms

Ockham distinguishes "categorematic" from "syncategorematic" terms, a distinction roughly parallel to the modern distinction between logical and non-logical particles. Unlike modern logicians, who take the difference to be primitive and explicated by syntactic rules, Ockham distinguishes them semantically: a categorematic term has a "definite and determinate signification" as described in "Mental Language and signification" (above), whereas a syncategorematic term has no proper signification of its own but affects the semantic behaviour of any categorematic term with which it is combined (I.4). The categorematic term 'rabbit' signifies rabbits, and provides an unambiguous rule to determine whether some item is signified by 'rabbit' (namely whether it is a rabbit); its signification is therefore definite. Syncategorematic terms, in contrast, do not signify things but instead affect the semantic behaviour of terms that do. 'Every' does not signify anything, unlike 'rabbit' (what item in the world is an 'every'?), but it can be combined with 'rabbit'; 'every rabbit' distributively signifies all the rabbits there are. Since no item in the world, even a rabbit, is an 'every rabbit' (whatever that might be), 'every' clearly makes a semantic difference when combined with 'rabbit'. Hence 'every' is not a categorematic but a syncategorematic term.[10] So too for 'all', 'some', 'not', 'if', 'and', 'or', 'except' and the like, identified nowadays as logical constants.

Syncategorematic terms are present in mental language since they make a semantic difference to the expressions in which they occur.[11] Unlike ordinary concepts, they are not *of* something, for they have no significate; instead, they *do* something when combined with ordinary concepts. In the case of conjunction, for example, the syncategorematic term 'and' forms a new expression out of two categorematic terms, so from 'Jerry' and 'Phil' we get the well-formed expression 'Jerry and Phil'; the psychological correlate is the combination of the concept-of-Jerry with the concept-of-Phil.[12] This expression is itself a term, since it can occur as the subject or predicate of a sentence (the root meaning of 'term' from *terminus*); as we would put it, Ockham takes conjunction to be a term-forming functor operating on (pairs of) simple terms.[13] Because all the parts of the new complex term already exist in mental language, the complex term is not something over and above these parts; nothing needs to be added to mental language to accommodate the new complex term; it can be produced from elements already present prior to their combination. Hence mental language will "contain" the new term in the sense that it will have its constituent parts conjunctively combined.

As with conjunction, so too with other syncategorematic terms. Mental language thus contains primitive ("atomic") elements and complex expressions formed out of them by logical operations. Ockham holds further that this is *all* mental language contains, and hence that every expression in mental language is either primitive or a logical construction out of primitive expressions. Since mental life begins with the acquisition of concepts that are then combined, if mental language were to contain any complex expression not logically constructed from primitives it would have to involve a non-logical mental operator that compounds primitive expressions, but this operator would by definition be a syncategorematic term, since it affects the semantic properties of its constituents taken in combination, and hence it must belong to mental language.[14] Expressions in mental language are therefore completely articulated with respect to their logical structure. The sequence of syncategorematic terms in an expression – the "frame" left behind after deleting the categorematic terms – is its logical form, which can be directly read off any expression. Accordingly, mental language is logically perspicuous, which makes it ideal as the foundation for logic.

However, mental language is not quite a "logically ideal" language of the sort in vogue at the beginning of the twentieth century.[15] Its semantics does not perfectly dovetail with the logical analysis of expressions. To see why not, we need to take a closer look at the signification of primitive and complex expressions.

Consider a complex expression, say 'white rabbit'. Ockham adopts a principle of semantic compositionality: the signification of an expression is a function of the signification of its parts. If 'rabbit' signifies rabbits and 'white' white things, then there seem to be only two plausible candidates for the signification of 'white rabbit', namely the intersection of their significations (so that 'white rabbit' signifies white rabbits) or the union of them (so that it signifies rabbits and white things). The first candidate seems to match our practice. We use 'white rabbit' to talk about white rabbits, after all, and the juxtaposition of the terms might be thought to limit the signification of each to what it has in common with the other. Yet Ockham rejects the first candidate in favour of the second. On the one hand, while we do use 'white rabbit' to talk about white rabbits, that is a matter of how we use the (complex) expression to refer to things, not a matter of its significa-tion; in short, this line of reasoning confuses meaning and reference.[16] On the other hand, the second candidate matches our intuitive understanding of signifi-cation. Hearing 'white rabbit' brings to mind (first) white things and (next) rabbits; hence it signifies white things and rabbits, the union of the signification of its component parts. So, too, in general: Ockham holds that the signification of a complex expression is the sum of the significations of its categorematic parts, the so-called "Additive Principle" (of semantic compositionality).[17]

According to the Additive Principle, the signification of a complex expres-sion is itself complex; the semantics follows the syntax well enough here. The difficulty lies instead in logically primitive expressions. For an ideal language all logically primitive expressions would also be semantically simple. This is not the case for Ockham. In addition to semantically simple primitive terms, Ockham also admits semantically complex primitive terms. He does so because he thinks there is another important distinction to draw among terms.

Signification as described above fits well the meaning of terms where there is some readily identifiable significate to which the term applies. Clear examples are proper names ('Socrates') and common names that are natural-kind terms ('weasel' or 'flower'). Such "absolute" terms, Ockham tells us, have no nominal definition (I.10), which is to say that there is no adequate way to describe what they signify; direct experience of their significates, or at least paradigmatic instances, is necessary to know what the term stands for. Hence some form of knowledge by acquaintance is called for in the case of absolute terms.[18]

There are other terms whose signification is more complex. A term like 'parent', for example, primarily signifies men and women: not all men and women, certainly; only those men and women who have children. It is not possible to characterize what 'parent' signifies without mentioning children. Nevertheless, 'parent' does not signify children the way 'weasel' signifies weasels; 'parent' signifies men and women in virtue of their having children. Although it does call children to mind they are not what it primarily signifies; contrast 'parent' with 'family', which does signify children along with their parents. Ockham says that 'parent' primarily signifies men and women (those who have children) and secondarily signifies their children. In other words, 'parent' signifies men and women, and also connotes their children. Ockham calls such terms "connotative", as opposed to absolute terms like 'rabbit'. Unlike absolute terms, connotative terms do have nominal definitions. The nominal definition of 'parent' is 'man or woman who has at least one child'. This definition, although nominal, provides adequate "knowledge by description" of what a parent is (whether one has ever encountered a parent or not), in contrast to absolute terms, which lack such nominal definitions; no amount of description quite gets at what 'giraffe' signifies, although some descriptions prepare us better for our first encounter than others.

Connotative terms greatly outnumber absolute terms. They include overtly relational terms, such as 'guitarist', 'double', 'wealthy' and 'similar'; all geometrical terms, such as 'figure', 'circle' and 'solid'; psychological terms, such as 'intellect' and 'will'; all terms in categories[19] other than substance and quality, and, especially worth noting, concrete terms in the category of quality: 'white', for example, signifies (white) things and connotes whiteness, being nominally definable as 'thing having whiteness'.[20]

If all logically primitive expressions in mental language were absolute terms, connotative terms could be completely replaced by equivalent nominal definitions involving only absolute terms (in the end), and the semantics of mental language would match its logical structure. However, Ockham explicitly allows some connotative terms to be logically primitive in mental language.[21] Hence logical simplicity does not entirely match semantic simplicity. While logically perspicuous, mental language does not necessarily articulate the complex signification connotative terms may have, or, to the extent that it does, a simple connotative term can be present in mental language along with its complex nominal definition. Thus mental language may contain some redundancy, in the form of synonymous expressions, and so may not be semantically perspicuous.

Connotative terms are one of the weapons in Ockham's arsenal against what he regards as the bloated ontologies of his predecessors and contemporaries. Whereas absolute terms seem to require the existence of their significates, diagnosing a term as connotative rather than absolute gives Ockham a way to avoid the ontological commitments that it would carry if it were absolute. This is particularly important when it comes to the concrete and abstract forms of nouns, which, Ockham holds, have often misled philosophers, for example, in mistakenly taking 'whiteness' to pick out an independent shareable entity, present simultaneously in many white things. But before we can turn to Ockham's programme of ontological reduction (see "Ontological reduction", below), we first need to look at the other semantic notion fundamental to the *Summa logicae*.

Supposition

Signification is a property that terms and, by the Additive Principle, complexes of terms have in their own right; regardless of context they call their significates to mind whenever they occur. But we use terms for more than simply calling things to mind; we use them to talk about things, and indeed usually to talk about the things they signify. (Another way to put the point is to say that terms occur as subjects and predicates in sentences.) This is accomplished by a distinct semantic relation, called "supposition",[22] which accounts for the referential use of categorematic terms.[23]

Supposition and signification thus differ in two ways for Ockham. First, terms retain their signification at all times, whereas they are only used referentially in sentences. Hence a term has supposition only in a sentential context. Secondly, terms can be used referentially in many ways; unlike signification, supposition takes a variety of forms, and it is the business of a theory of supposition to spell out what these varieties are. In practice that amounts to giving a taxonomy of kinds of supposition: a medieval version of "the varieties of reference".

Ockham distinguishes three primary kinds of supposition (I.64): *material*, *simple* and *personal*.[24] Consider the absolute term 'frog', which signifies frogs. We use it to refer to frogs when we say such things as "Waiter, there is a frog in my soup" or "Every frog is green". In these cases 'frog' has personal supposition, since it refers to what it signifies, namely frogs. Clearly there is much to say about whether in a given occurrence 'frog' refers to all frogs, or merely to some frogs, or perhaps to a certain frog; Ockham calls these "modes" of personal supposition, to be investigated shortly.

We can also use 'frog' to refer to things other than frogs. I could use it to refer to pigs, or to the first person I see in the morning, or to red sails in the sunset. These idiosyncratic uses have no particular connection with 'frog' or with frogs, and are plausibly understood as changes in the signification of the term: in the first case it is a new word for pigs, no more sharing a meaning than 'bank' does as the side of a river and as a financial institution; in the second case it acts as a definite description; in the third it picks out a class of things for which there was no single word before. In none of these cases is there anything special about the choice of the term.

Ockham holds that two uses of 'frog' are interestingly related to what it ordinarily signifies, despite not referring to frogs. On the one hand, we say things like "Frog has four letters" and "Frog is a monosyllable". In these cases 'frog' has material supposition, since it refers to the particular inscription (element of written language) or the particular utterance (element of spoken language) *qua* subordinated to the concept-of-frog in mental language (I.67).[25] On the other hand, we say things like "Frog is a genus". According to Ockham, as we shall see in "Ontological reduction" (below), genera are not real items in the world but only concepts; hence 'frog' here has simple supposition, since it refers to the concept-of-frog, not *qua* signifying frogs but *qua* intrinsically general in its signification. More exactly, 'frog' here refers to the particular concept (element of mental language) involved in its ordinary significative use, rather than to what it signifies (I.68).

Since there are only three elements involved in language – the embodied token subordinated to a concept, the concept itself, and what is conceived through the concept – Ockham's division of supposition into material, simple and personal respectively is complete. Yet Ockham does *not* hold that when a term refers to embodied tokens it must have material supposition, or that when it refers to a concept it must have simple supposition, or that it must refer to things in the world if it has personal supposition. The term 'concept' personally supposits for concepts, for example; it does so by means of the concept-of-concept (just as 'pig' personally supposits for pigs via the concept-of-pig), which it picks out in particular, though not *qua* concept-of-concept, when it is in simple supposition, for example, in "Concept is a universal". Likewise 'inscription' personally supposits for inscriptions, including the inscription 'inscription', whereas in material supposition it refers only to the inscription 'inscription' *qua* inscription (namely as ink on paper) rather than *qua* exemplifying the concept to which it is subordinated (the concept-of-inscription). Terms always have personal supposition when they stand for what they signify, taken significatively, and not otherwise (I.64).

Note that 'pig' is one and the same term no matter where it occurs, whether it has personal supposition ("Every pig is pink"), simple supposition ("Pig is a universal"), or material supposition ("Pig has three letters"). Ockham is therefore at odds with contemporary philosophy, which takes quotation to do much of the work of material supposition – to the point where the sentence would have to be written as "'Pig' has three letters". Modern quotation is a term-forming functor that produces a name of that to which it is applied: 'pig' refers to (the term) *pig*.[26] The former refers to a word (or perhaps a tokening of a word), the latter refers to pigs in the world. On the contemporary view, however, the new name produced by quotation is indivisible and has no special relation to the word of which it is a name; much the same effect could be obtained by letting 'A' stand for (the term) *pig*.[27] Ockham's account of material supposition has the virtue of explaining why the cases are not similar.

Material and simple supposition are cases in which the selfsame term is used referentially, although in non-standard ways. Ockham recognizes their importance but devotes most of his energy to working through the modes of personal supposition (I.69–74), which catalogue the ways in which a term can be used to refer to what it signifies.

First, Ockham divides terms with personal supposition into "discrete" and "common" (I.70). Terms with discrete supposition are proper names, demonstrative phrases and definite descriptions, each of which is semantically singular by its nature, signifying exactly one thing, at least on an occasion of its use: for example, 'Orson Welles', 'this fish', 'the present Queen of England'.[28] Hence each can be used to refer only to the very thing it signifies, and if used referentially at all must pick out that very thing. That is, the kind of reference in question for such cases is naming or denoting. Conversely, a term not semantically singular by nature will have common personal supposition. Ockham's distinction more or less matches the distinction between proper and common nouns (or noun-phrases); hereinafter he will be concerned with the referential uses of common nouns or noun-phrases.

Secondly, Ockham divides terms with common personal supposition into "determinate" and "confused" (I.71). He characterizes determinate supposition, and the remaining modes as well, in two ways: by the logical properties an expression has, and by the inferential relations of ascent and descent. Intuitively, a term has determinate supposition when it is used to refer to at least one of the things it signifies. (It may of course refer to more than one.) When Smith says "Some man has been on top of Mount Everest", for example, 'man' has determinate supposition.[29] With regard to an expression's properties, Ockham holds that a term has determinate supposition in subject-position if it is indefinite or in the scope of a particular quantifier not itself in the scope of another logical particle, as 'man' is in the scope of 'some' (but 'some man' is not in the scope of any other syncategorematic term). Furthermore, when a term has determinate supposition, two inferences are licensed: a 'descent' from the general term in the original sentence to individuals by a disjunction of sentences, and an 'ascent' from any individual to the original sentence. Thus "Some man has been on top of Mount Everest" licenses the inference "Hence Socrates has been on top of

Mount Everest, or Plato has been on top of Mount Everest, or ..." descending to singulars; equally, from any one of these disjuncts, such as "Arnold has been on top of Mount Everest", we may legitimately infer "Hence some man has been on top of Mount Everest", ascending to the general claim.[30] A common term that does not have determinate supposition has confused supposition.

Thirdly, Ockham divides terms with confused supposition into "merely confused" and "confused and distributive" (I.73). Again intuitively, a term has merely confused supposition when it is used to talk indifferently about several of the things it signifies, namely when it is used attributively: 'marsupial' in "Every kangaroo is a marsupial" refers to marsupials, in this sentence to whatever marsupials there are that are kangaroos, whichever they may be, indifferently, since none is singled out.[31] Ockham summarizes the situation by saying that sentences containing terms having merely confused supposition do not license inferences descending to singulars under the term via a disjunction of sentences, but they do license descent to a disjunctive predicate, and, like determinate supposition, permit inferences to the original sentence from a given singular. Hence from "Every kangaroo is a marsupial" we cannot legitimately infer "Every kangaroo is this marsupial, or every kangaroo is that marsupial, or ..." but we can infer "Every kangaroo is this marsupial or that marsupial or ...": there is no given marsupial that every kangaroo is,[32] although any given kangaroo is some marsupial or other. The rules Ockham provides to describe the logical properties of expressions containing terms with merely confused supposition are a motley assortment. A term outside the scope of a universal sign has merely confused supposition if it is construed with a term falling within the scope of that sign (as 'marsupial' is construed with 'every kangaroo' above); a term outside the scope of a quantifier but in subject-position has merely confused supposition, *e.g.* 'food' in "Every lawyer gives some food to this cat". (Note that this allows Ockham to handle multiple quantification with relative ease.)

A term having confused supposition but not merely confused supposition must have confused and distributive supposition (I.74).[33] Intuitively, a term has confused and distributive supposition when it is used to refer to every or all of the things it signifies. Hence 'pig' in "Every pig is pink" has confused and distributive supposition, since it is used to refer to every pig (whereas 'pink' has merely confused supposition). The semantic relations involved in distributive confused supposition are clear: reference is made to everything (presently existing) that the term signifies; it is "distributed" over each individual. Ockham's rules for confused and distributive supposition amount to this: a term in subject-position in the scope of a universal quantifier not itself in the scope of another logical particle has confused and distributive supposition, and likewise the predicate in universal negative sentences, as 'piano' in "No wind instrument is a piano". From a sentence with a term having confused and distributive supposition it is legitimate to descend to singulars via a conjunctive sentence, or to ascend from all the singulars. From "Every pig is pink" we can infer (descending under 'pig') "Porky is pink, and Petunia is pink, and Wilbur is pink, and …".

The theory of supposition bridges the gap between signification and truth, providing Ockham with a sophisticated and subtle account of the legitimate referential uses of terms when they are used, in sentences, to talk about things. In addition, it links logic to metaphysics, words to the world; truth depends on successful reference, and supposition theory catalogues the varieties of reference. In contemporary jargon, it is the vehicle of ontological commitment: the measure of what a thinker takes to exist, spelled out in the ineliminable references present in his or her account of the world. This cuts both ways, of course; Ockham can use his semantic theory to show that putative ontological commitments are in fact merely apparent, not genuine. Time for a razor.

Ontological reduction

Ockham's charge is that his predecessors and contemporaries have been misled by grammar into thinking there must be certain sorts of entities: universals (common natures) and items in most of the traditional Aristotelian categories. In the case of the former they misunderstand philosophical terminology and the semantics of abstract names; in the case of the latter they mistake connotative for absolute terms.

The world contains distinct individuals. Trigger, Ed and Silver are horses, each different from the others. They nevertheless belong to the same kind, since each is a horse; traditionally put, they share a common nature, one not shared with goats or geese, although all alike are animals and hence share a common animal nature distinct from the nature common to horses alone. The world is thus divided into genera and species reflecting these shared natures. Hence statements of the form "Horse is a species" will be as true as "Trigger is a horse" and, as we saw in "Supposition" (above), 'horse' is the selfsame term in each sentence. This gives rise to two questions: (i) What do 'horse' and 'species' refer to in "Horse is a species"; and (ii) What does 'horse' refer to in "Trigger is a horse" and "Ed is a horse"? Many philosophers – too many for Ockham's taste – reasoned that in order to make a real difference in the world, 'horse' had to at least connote (if not refer to) some real shared feature that Trigger and Ed and Dobbin each have simultaneously, namely the common nature *horseness*. Thus metaphysically real differences are explained by metaphysically real constituents in things, constituents that can be named by abstract names. In addition to concrete singulars, then, the world also contains real abstract entities.

Ockham will have none of this line of reasoning, finding only bad semantics in it. He divides his response into two parts, the first offering his positive account of genera and species (I.14–17), the second his attack on abstract entities (I.5–9).

According to Ockham, "Horse is a species" is true but has no untoward ontological consequences. 'Horse' in this sentence does not have personal supposition, since it is not used to refer to horses the way it is in "Trigger is a horse"; instead, it has simple supposition. Recall from "Supposition" (above) that a term with simple supposition is used to refer to the concept involved in the term's ordinary significative use, rather than referring to what that concept signifies. Thus 'horse' in "Horse is a species" refers to the concept-of-horse, the very mental particular by which we think of horses; it picks out a word in the language of thought. The term 'species' must therefore personally supposit for the concept-of-horse, among other things, if "Horse is a species" is to be true. On this score it is like the term 'concept', which also personally supposits for concepts rather than non-mental objects. Now, just as "Horse is a species" is true, so too is "Rabbit is a species", "Kangaroo is a species" and so on, but "Trigger is a species" is not. Hence 'species' must refer to items that are somehow general in their nature. Put another way, 'species' signifies general concepts, or technically the lowest-level general concepts characterizing what a thing is: the concept-of-horse, the concept-of-rabbit, the concept-of-kangaroo and so on, but neither the concept-of-Trigger nor the concept-of-animal (a generic rather than specific concept). And just as 'horse' signifies various horses through the concept-of-horse, so too 'species' signifies various species through the concept-of-species, that is, through the concept-of-<lowest-level general concept>.

To the question "What is a species?" Ockham therefore replies: a concept of concepts, what we technically call a "second-order concept" and Ockham technically called "a concept of second intention"; terminology aside, 'species', and likewise 'genus' and 'differentia', classify kinds of concepts, not non-mental things or their real ingredients.[34] Each is itself ontologically singular, although semantically general. No non-individual entities need to be postulated to explain the truth of sentences such as "Horse is a species". His strategy, broadly speaking, is to resolve metaphysical questions by techniques of semantic ascent, so that claims about genera and species are reinterpreted as metalinguistic statements. "Horse is a species", stripped of Ockham's apparatus of mental language, is roughly equivalent to "The term 'horse' is a common noun". To ask what 'horse' picks out in the world beyond individual horses is to mistake this point: to confuse simple with personal supposition.

The objection might be raised to Ockham that even if he is correct about genera and species, there nevertheless must be some real feature in the world underlying the generality of the concepts we legitimately apply. Horses are not merely grouped together arbitrarily, after all; they constitute a natural kind no matter how our conceptual apparatus happens to work. What is more, we need to explain how general terms like 'horse' work, that is, how they signify all and only horses. We can satisfy both by postulating some real metaphysically common entity named by the abstract term 'horseness': each horse is a horse by horseness, which is possessed by horses and nothing else, and likewise the term 'horse' picks out horses because each has or exemplifies horseness.

Ockham's reply to this objection has three parts. First, Ockham offers a detailed psychological account of how concepts are acquired, and what it is for them to signify what they do. The bulk of his account, though, is not given in the *Summa logicae* but in his other writings.[35] Secondly, Ockham argues that there are strong reasons not to postulate any such abstract entities, since theories involving them are inconsistent or at least highly implausible. This is the burden of *Summa logicae* I.15–17. The arguments he gives there are metaphysical, not particularly indebted to his semantics, and are found in much greater detail elsewhere.[36] Thirdly, Ockham thinks this objection is confused about the semantics of abstract terms (I.5–9), mistakenly thinking that an abstract name must name an abstract object. He develops his reply by considering the general case of concrete names, such as 'horse', 'white' and 'parent', as compared to their abstract counterparts 'horseness', 'whiteness' and 'parenthood', in spoken or written languages.[37] Ockham argues that concrete and abstract names might be related in different ways.

On the one hand, a concrete name and its abstract counterpart might be completely synonymous (I.6), that is, subordinated to the same concept or expression in mental language. In this case they each signify exactly the same thing in exactly the same way; the difference between them is wholly an artefact of written or spoken language. So it is for 'horse' and 'horseness', Ockham holds, and in general for absolute terms in the category of substance.[38] 'Horseness' signifies exactly what 'horse' signifies, namely horses. It does not pick out some ingredient or feature in the horse, in virtue of which the horse is a horse, if for no other reason than that horseness is not some feature that a horse has, the way it has colour, but rather a description of what a horse is (I.7). After all, to think that 'horse' signifies a horse in virtue of its possession of some metaphysical property *horseness* is to treat it as a connotative rather than an abstract term, on a par with 'rich' (which signifies human beings in virtue of their possession of wealth). Ockham's view has the surprising result that we can use the abstract term interchangeably with the concrete term, so we can talk about the horsenesses in the stable, or riding a horseness, and so on; we can even say "Horseness is a horse", of course (of course!). As long as we keep in mind that 'horse' and 'horseness' are synonymous, no difficulties, other than some deviant usage, should trouble us. And as in the category of substance, so too in many other categories, although the concrete and abstract names in those categories are connotative rather than absolute. For instance, 'parent' and 'parenthood' in the category of relation are synonymous connotative terms: they each signify human beings who have children, that is, they primarily signify human beings and connote their children. In these cases it is ontologically innocuous to allow the abstract name, since it is an exact synonym of the concrete name; 'horseness' no more fattens the ontology than 'horse' did in the first place.

On the other hand, a concrete name may fail to be synonymous with its abstract counterpart (I.5). This happens in the category of quality, for instance; 'white' and 'whiteness' are not synonyms. The concrete name 'white' is connotative, signifying primarily something white and secondarily the whiteness through which it is white, whereas the abstract name 'whiteness' is absolute, signifying a real individual quality (the possession of which makes its possessor white). Yet even here there is no metaphysically common element. Each whiteness is an individual quality, one in itself and possessed by one substance at most. Two white things are each white, but each is made white by its individual whiteness, not shared with anything else. Hence even when the concrete and abstract names are not synonymous, just as when they are, the abstract name is not the name of an abstract entity but rather the name of an individual, albeit an individual from a category other than substance. Abstract names, therefore, are no support for defenders of metaphysically common entities, for they only ever signify individuals. Realists about universals or common natures are simply misled by the shadow of grammar into thinking that there are such abstract entities.

Ockham's account of concrete and abstract names prompts the question: when are concrete names synonymous with their abstract counterparts, and when are they not? There seems to be no principled difference between the case of 'parent' and 'parenthood', which Ockham declares synonymous, and the case of 'white' and 'whiteness', which he declares non-synonymous. The answer won't affect Ockham's reply to the realist objection, since whether we treat the cases alike or differently we still are not countenancing any abstract entities. So why the difference? In particular, why not treat all the accidental categories uniformly, no matter which way that should be?

The answer is a blend of metaphysics and semantics: Ockham wants to reduce ontological commitments by countenancing as few basic *kinds* of things as possible, which meant paring down the number of the traditional nine 'accidental' Aristotelian categories; he does so by giving paraphrases for sentences involving them. This project is the heart of Part I of the *Summa logicae*, occupying 23 chapters (I.40–62) and a staggering amount of detailed argumentation. In brief, Ockham's conclusions are these: (i) the only categories we need to countenance are substance, quality, and relation; (ii) in each we recognize only individuals; (iii) the sole reason to countenance the category of relation is for the sake of a few entities required for theological reasons having to do with the Trinity, the Incarnation and the Eucharist, although natural reason would not recognize any need for these entities; (iv) only some, not all, entities in the category of quality exist.

Ockham's strategy for categorical reduction is to show that purported absolute terms in a given category are really connotative terms not requiring any ontological commitments. Consider "Socrates is similar to Plato" in some qualitative respect or other. Ockham argues that we do not need to countenance the existence of an entity *similarity* in the category of relation in order for this sentence to be true. Instead, all that is required is for Socrates and Plato each to have a quality of the same sort; the truth of the sentence follows immediately. The only entities that need to exist are Socrates, Plato and their respective individual qualities. Hence 'similar' is a connotative term, primarily signifying substances and secondarily signifying their qualities; the sentence will be true if the qualities are of the same sort and false otherwise. Likewise, Ockham proposes that terms in the category of quantity, such as 'body', are connotative rather than absolute; the nominal definition of 'body', for instance, is "something having parts distant from one another in three dimensions", which signifies substances and connotes their parts, or at least connotes those parts spatially separated from one another.

There is no royal road to reductive ontology. Ockham argues in the *Summa logicae* for the elimination of each category (or sub-category) on a case-by-case basis, appealing to a wide range of considerations and styles of argumentation.[39] For instance, in attempting to determine which qualities are eliminable, Ockham proposes the following technique: if some qualities can be predicated of something "successively but not simultaneously due only to local movement", they need not signify distinct things (I.55), presumably because local movement can itself be explained away in terms of the relative positions of parts of bodies, as described in the preceding paragraph. Yet just as often his arguments are independent of one another. Thus Ockham could be wrong that some qualities exist (he might just not have found the clever paraphrase) or that some entities are eliminable (perhaps relations cannot be paraphrased away as he suggests). Each case is its own battlefield, where most of the blood was spilt upon the publication of the *Summa logicae*.[40]

Sentences and argumentation

Part II of the *Summa logicae* is devoted to sentences and their truth-conditions. Sentences are divided into simple and compound (*hypothetica*) sentences. Simple sentences are paradigmatically illustrated by the assertoric categorical sentence, consisting in a subject-term, a copula and a predicate-term: "Every bat is blood-thirsty".[41] Compound sentences are either conjunctions or disjunctions of sentences. Ockham also allows "consequence" as a type of compound sentence, which combines sentences by means of 'if' and 'then'/'therefore', but he defers treatment of them as being equivalent to inferences among sentences (II.31). That done, the truth-conditions for compound conjunctive or disjunctive sentences are straightforward, the former true if all the conjoined sentences are true (II.32), the latter if at least one is true (II.33). Most of Ockham's efforts are directed to understanding the categorical sentence in all its varieties.

Ockham holds that categorical sentences can be distinguished in four ways: by their quantity, quality, mode and tense. (Contemporary logicians usually recognize only quantity and mode.) With respect to quantity, sentences are universal, particular, singular or indefinite, depending on syncategoremata such as 'every', 'some' and 'none'. With respect to quality, sentences are either affirmative or negative; Ockham recognizes two primitive and independent forms of the copula, one affirmative ('is') and the other negative ('is-not').[42] With respect to mode, sentences may be either assertoric or modal, that is, they may explicitly involve possibility or necessity. Finally, with respect to tense, Ockham recognizes past, present and future tenses as irreducibly different, although a sentence can be about times other than the present due to temporal words that are not part of the copula. Both modal and tensed sentences may involve "ampliation", that is, widening of the domain of discourse to include things that are possible, or future or past, and the like.

Truth-conditions for assertoric present-tense categorical sentences are straightforward. For instance, the particular negative sentence "Some vampires are-not friendly" is true just in case what 'friendly' personally supposits for, namely people who are friendly, does not include anything – note the negative copula – for which 'vampire' personally supposits. Universal affirmatives ("Every S is P") are true when everything their subjects supposit for their predicates also supposit for; particular affirmatives ("Some S is P") when their predicates supposit for at least one thing their subjects supposit for; universal negatives ("No S is P") when the predicate does not supposit for anything the subject supposits for.[43]

Ockham works through several cases in which this basic picture is complicated in some respect. For instance, adding the syncategorematic term 'only' to the singular affirmative sentence "Socrates is running", producing "Only Socrates is running", fundamentally alters its truth-conditions (II.17). Other complicating factors are reduplicative terms, such as 'in so far as' or '*qua*', or terms like 'except'. But he directs most of his efforts to exploring tensed and modal sentences.[44]

Consider the sentence "Something black will be blue". Ockham holds that it may be understood in two distinct ways. On each reading the predicate-term 'blue' personally supposits not for present blue things but, due to the tense of the copula, for future blue things; the subject-term 'something black', however, personally supposits for either (a) present black things, as it would ordinarily, or (b) future black things, which may include some present black things if they are also black in the future (but not otherwise), so that the supposition of the subject follows the temporal shift of the predicate. A similar distinction can be drawn for past-tense sentences. Likewise, modal sentences that have a modal copula such as 'can be' are also susceptible to this dual reading: the subject of "Someone ugly can-be a shoe salesman" may be taken as someone who is actually ugly, or as some non-actual ugly possible man; truth-conditions here, as with the tensed case, will systematically differ.[45]

Modal sentences, unlike tensed sentences, can also be formulated impersonally: "Socrates can run" is the same as "It is possible that Socrates runs". Yet the former sentence looks as though it ascribes a power to Socrates, whereas the latter, when not read as a mere variant of the former, seems to characterize a state of affairs. Ockham calls modal sentences taken in this way "composite", and he takes them to be about what sentences say: "It is possible that Socrates runs" attributes a property to what the sentence "Socrates runs" says (namely *that Socrates runs*), and is true or false depending on whether what it says has the modal quality attributed to it: here, whether "Socrates runs" is possible, that is, describes a possible situation. Thus the truth-conditions of composite modal sentences will track the modal qualities of other, simpler sentences; and there Ockham lets the matter rest, turning to the theory of argumentation.

Part III of the *Summa logicae* is devoted to inference in general, and is longer than Parts I and II combined. To some extent this is a reflection of the exponential complexity of Ockham's subject matter. Since inferences are sequences of sentences that have or lack certain properties, Ockham has to take into account his analysis of the several kinds of sentences and how they can be legitimately combined to produce acceptable conclusions. Of the many topics Ockham addresses I shall mention only two that can give the flavour of his achievements as a logician: syllogistics and the theory of consequences.

By Ockham's day, the logic of the assertoric syllogism had been well worked out, and he accordingly presents it clearly and concisely. It is the springboard for

Ockham's investigation of the modal syllogism. Unlike the assertoric syllogistics, modal syllogistics was neither well understood nor systematic; Ockham helped make it both. He allows composite modal sentences as well as ordinary modal sentences to enter into syllogisms, and he further analyses which syllogisms hold depending on whether a modal sentence is read as affecting the supposition of the subject-term or not. While this might seem to make the resulting theory unmanageable, Ockham offers an elegant reduction of modal syllogistics. For ordinary modal sentences, Ockham proposes modalizing the terms involved and then applying the ordinary assertoric syllogism. Thus Ockham transforms "Socrates can run" into "Socrates is a possible-runner", and the other premises likewise, until we are left with an assertoric syllogism (perhaps with some peculiar subjects and/or predicates). For syllogisms consisting in composite modal sentences, Ockham offers a series of reduction rules that enable assertoric syllogistics to generate valid moods of composite modal syllogistics. All that remains is the admittedly messy job of considering the mixed cases, which do not lend themselves to systematic treatment. But that should not blind us to Ockham's accomplishment in systematizing much of the rest of modal inference.

Modal inference is only one kind of inference. To the extent that Ockham has a general theory of inference, it is found in his treatment of consequences. The rules he offers spell out what is known as a "natural deduction system". The elements of this system are inferences – that is, consequences – which can be used to license arguments.[46] Hence the rules for consequences state legitimate inference schemata. Consider, for example, the first rule Ockham gives for consequences (III.3.2): "There is a legitimate consequence from the superior distributed term to the inferior distributed term; for example, 'Every animal is running; hence every man is running.'" Ockham usually gives his rules in metalogical or schematic terms (often in both ways), referring to inferences that hold in virtue of the logical form of their constituent sentences. Consider the three proposals that an inference or inferential scheme $A \vdash B$ is legitimate when:

(1) The truth of A guarantees the truth of B in virtue of the meanings of the terms in each.
(2) The truth of A guarantees the truth of B in virtue of the forms of A and B.
(3) There is no uniform substitution of non-logical terminology that renders A true and B false.

To the extent that the meanings of the terms in A and B determine the situations – the range of possibilities or models – against which we evaluate our sentences, (1) may provide a semantic dimension to the modal account. Yet (1) will fail to capture formal validity to the extent that meaning is not a formal feature. If it is not, then inferences such as "Every animal is running; hence every man is running" are legitimate by (1) but are not formally valid: they do not hold in virtue of their form but only in virtue of some extrinsic feature, such as the meanings of their terms or the way the world is. (Thus even metaphysical necessity does not entail formal validity.) Logicians today usually adopt (2) or (3). Ockham, however, seems to endorse (1), thereby countenancing a wider scope for logic than formal inference; modern logicians take formal inference to be the whole of logic, whereas for Ockham it is only a part, although an important part. This may explain the wide variety of topics dealt with in Part III, which includes consequences, topics, sophisms, demonstrations, proof theory, paradoxes, obligations and fallacies. Take the last case. Ockham's treatment of fallacies tries to give a systematic theory about the kinds of inferential failure. Such a project makes little sense in the modern understanding of logic as the study of formally valid inference, but it fits well Ockham's more generous notion about what may count as logic.

Conclusion

The *Summa logicae* was Ockham's last look at the issues covered here. In May 1324, shortly after its completion (perhaps even spurring him to complete it), Ockham left England for the Papal residence at Avignon to be examined on charges of "false and heretical teaching".[47] Apart from editing his London quodlibetal debates, and perhaps polishing parts of the *Summa logicae*, Ockham had little to occupy himself with in Avignon. Then in 1327 the Minister-General of the Franciscan Order, Michele di Cesena, arrived in response to his own papal summons, and Ockham's life was irrevocably changed. The Franciscans had been in a long and increasingly bitter dispute with Pope John XXII over the Franciscan renunciation of property and the ideal of voluntary poverty. While conferring with the Pope, Michele di Cesena asked Ockham to look into the poverty question with an eye to recent papal pronouncements on the subject. Ockham dutifully did so, and came to the conclusion that Pope John XXII had exceeded and contravened his own authority, becoming heretical in the process.

Matters deteriorated for the Franciscan delegation at Avignon, and, fearing for their safety, a small group of Franciscans, including Michele di Cesena and William of Ockham, fled Avignon during the night of 26 May 1328, travelling to join the Holy Roman Emperor, Louis of Bavaria, for political asylum. They were excommunicated for leaving Avignon without permission, but were welcomed by Louis, who was in the middle of his own difficulties with Pope John XXII. Ockham spent the rest of his life under German protection, much of it in Munich, writing on political matters, mostly on voluntary poverty, papal authority and the relation of church and state. He died in Munich in 1347, perhaps of the Black Death.

Ockham is not known to have written anything else on logic, or generally on philosophy or theology apart from political matters, after his departure from England. Yet the movement begun by the publication of the *Summa logicae* carried on even in his absence. His work found its own defenders and enthusiasts, and it remained a much-studied work for centuries; between 60 and 70 manuscripts of it survive, remarkable for such a long, often extremely dry, work. We are still tracing its repercussions in the history of logic and philosophy today.

Notes

1. The *Summa logicae* is not completely available in English yet: Part I is translated in Loux (1974) and Part II in Freddoso (1980), with excerpts from each in Spade (1995); Part III has not yet been translated.
2. Ockham's *Summa logicae* was recognized as a work of genius, and provoked immediate responses. Walter Burleigh, Ockham's older contemporary, replied with his *De puritate artis logicae*, and the pseudo-Campsall's *Logica valde utilis et realis contra Ockham* is a line-by-line critique of the *Summa logicae*.
3. More exactly, the concept-of-φ is related to what it is to be φ, which is in turn intimately linked to something's being φ: in order for anything to be φ (whether there are any such things or not) there must be something that is what it is to be φ, which also accounts for how a concept is the concept it is rather than a concept of something else. Strictly speaking signification is not a relation at all.
4. Ockham holds this account in the *Summa logicae* but there are reasons to think he abandons it in the end: see King (2005).
5. This point also explains how translation from one conventional language to another is possible, which is a matter of identifying the relevant utterances or inscriptions subordinated to the same expression of mental language.
6. In contemporary terms, a semantics is a function from well-formed formulae to meanings, sufficiently well-behaved to individuate meanings. It may have further properties as well, such as compositionality, so that the meaning of an expression is a function of the meanings of the constituent parts of the expression. We shall see how Ockham handles such cases in "Terms".
7. Ockham offers as a test for inclusion in mental language whether the truth-value of a sentence can be altered by varying the syntactical feature in question (I.3).
8. Ockham is particularly tempted to use (b) since it makes the statement of logical laws, such as equipollence and conversion, much easier. That is, again, not a deep fact about mental language but about our representation of it.
9. If mental language includes prepositions, then it arguably need not include noun-cases; since there must be scope-markers, the function of grammatical noun-cases could be replaced by explicit prepositions, for example, "The book is Socrates's" (where 'Socrates's' is the possessive genitive) could be eliminated in favour of "The book belongs to Socrates" (where 'belongs to' makes the possession relation explicit).

10. Technically 'every' affects the reference of the term 'rabbit' rather than its signification (we are still thinking only of rabbits in 'every rabbit'); hence the semantic property it affects is not its signification but its supposition (I.4): see "Supposition". A term such as 'fake' alters the signification as well as the supposition of the term with which it is combined: 'fake rabbit' does not signify rabbits at all (and is not used to refer to them). It isn't clear, however, that 'fake' is purely syncategorematic, rather than being at least in part what Ockham calls a connotative term (like 'dead' in 'dead man'): see the discussion later in "Terms".

11. Hence not every element of mental language has signification, strictly speaking.

12. This brief sketch skates over several difficulties. Are syncategorematic terms in mental language concepts at all, or ways of thinking ordinary concepts? How do they have relevant logical properties, such as scope, ordering and the like? Is the conjunction of the concept-of-φ with the concept-of-ψ the concept-of-$<\varphi + \psi>$? Ockham leaves these questions unresolved.

13. Conjunction can also form (compound) sentences out of sentences. Ockham, like other medieval logicians, regards sentential connectives and operators as having a rather different logical character: see the further discussion in "Sentences and argumentation".

14. So described, Ockham's project looks very much like modern logic: a set of atomic expressions and a recursive definition of well-formed formulae by logical construction from atomic expressions. Ockham's treatment of the syntax is driven by his semantics, though, which is the opposite of our modern approach.

15. Trentman (1970) argues that mental language is a logically ideal language for Ockham.

16. For Ockham's theory of reference, see the discussion of supposition in "Supposition". According to the first candidate, the complex expression 'John and Paul' would signify John and Paul, since the syncategorematic term 'and' has the effect of combining the signification of 'John' with that of 'Paul'. But syncategoremata were defined in terms of affecting the semantic properties of the terms with which they are combined, and so we cannot appeal to their effects in determining the signification on pain of circular reasoning.

17. See Spade (1975, 1980).

18. Absolute terms are thus similar to Kripke's rigid designators, involving necessary *a posteriori* criteria.

19. Aristotle held that there are ten categories of things: substance, quantity, quality, relation, action, passion, time, place, position and state. Substances are primary self-subsisting beings; the other nine "accidental" categories classify features that substances may have. Thus Socrates (a substance) has a certain height and weight (quantities); he is the son of Sophroniscus (relation); and so on. Language reflects the world, so Ockham classifies terms by the category they fall under: "son" is a term in the category of relation, "Socrates" a term in the category of substance, "whiteness" in the category of quality. Ockham argues that, contrary to appearances, there really are things in the world in only two of the traditional categories, namely particular substances and particular qualities.

20. 'Whiteness', unlike 'white', is an absolute term naming a singular quality: see "Ontological reduction".

21. See Panaccio (1990, 1991), Tweedale (1992), and Spade (2002).

22. The word 'supposition' is cognate to the Latin *supponere*, literally 'to put underneath' (*sub* + *ponere*), a matter of identifying the referent of a word: a usage apparently indebted to earlier grammarians' describing what a pronoun stands for. It has nothing to do with making an assumption or accepting a hypothesis. A better rendering would be 'reference' itself, but 'supposition' is now the entrenched translation.

23. Ockham's account of supposition applies to terms in all three levels of language – spoken, written and mental – although sometimes obvious qualifications are glossed over; for instance, terms in mental language do not "call things to mind" but simply are the having of those things in mind. I shall ignore such details and talk indifferently about language.

24. Ockham's trichotomy is based on the observation that while we normally use a term to refer to what it signifies (personal supposition), in one way or another, we do not always do so (material and simple supposition), although in the latter cases we do refer to something interestingly related to what the term signifies.

25. Ockham is unnecessarily restrictive here, since he recognizes only two subordinate levels of language. We could just as easily talk about the gestures that are the "material" of sign language, or the raised patterns that make up Braille. The point is that a term has material supposition if it is used to refer not to what it signifies but to whatever encodes its signification in a given medium.

26. Strictly speaking this should be: ''Pig'' refers to 'pig'. Unlike material supposition, quotation can be indefinitely iterated. Contemporary philosophers of language take quotation to be a way of enshrining the distinction between *using* a word and merely *mentioning* it. For Ockham there is no distinction: each is a way of using the selfsame word referentially, although the ways of course differ.

27. Whether a quoted name is indivisible is a matter of debate. The issue is surprisingly subtle, involving deep questions about quantifying into quotation-contexts, *oratio obliqua* and substitutivity, questions that go to the heart of contemporary semantic theory. No consensus has been reached. See Normore (1997) for more discussion of Ockham's account of material supposition.

28. Ockham does not try to spell out what semantic singularity consists in, offering instead grammatical criteria: proper names; demonstrative pronouns, perhaps in combination with common nouns; and the like. Only the last case properly fits Ockham's approach, where 'fish' in "This fish took twenty minutes to catch" has discrete supposition (taking 'this' as purely syncategorematic). Nothing of the sort is possible for proper names, which are necessarily singular; 'Socrates', for example, has no common referential use. Ockham and Burleigh disagreed about discrete supposition, Burleigh distinguishing proper names from demonstrative phrases as simple and complex forms of discrete supposition.

29. This formulation conceals an ambiguity. If we ask Smith "Which man?" we may mean "Which man has been on top of Mount Everest?" or "Which man were you, Smith, referring to?" The former takes 'some man' in Smith's original statement attributively, accepting its truth and wondering which man or men make it so; the latter takes 'some men' referentially, so that Smith is talking about some man or men, and wonders whether they have indeed been on Everest. Each interpretation is possible; modern logicians prefer the attributive reading for the existential quantifier, and medieval logicians, including Ockham, prefer the referential reading for the syncategorematic term 'some'.

30. The inferential conditions for determinate supposition, then, roughly correspond to existential generalization and instantiation. Unfortunately, Ockham's account of ascent and descent does not work as a theory of truth-conditions for quantified sentences.

31. Since merely confused supposition is attributive, working from the truth of the sentence to determine the extension of the predicate, it is in some ways closest to the modern use of existential quantification.

32. In a world with only one kangaroo there is a single marsupial that every kangaroo is, namely the marsupial that is the lone kangaroo. This is true enough, but true due to the facts of the case rather than to its logic, which is all Ockham is concerned with here.

33. Ockham further divided confused and distributive supposition into "mobile" and "immobile", but this refinement is not necessary for our purposes here.

34. The term 'universal' is more general still, since "Genus is a universal" is true (and so for each of the five traditional universals); hence 'universal' must refer to concepts of concepts, and itself be a third-level concept, the concept-of-<concepts-of-concepts>. Ockham fumbles this point in *Summa logicae* I.14.

35. See especially Ockham's Prologue to his *Ordinatio*.

36. Ockham, *Ordinatio* 1 d.2 qq.4–8.

37. In Latin, as in English, abstract nouns are typically formed by taking the concrete noun as the stem and then adding a special suffix: in Latin *-itas* and in English -ity or -ness or -hood, so *equus* (horse) becomes *equinitas* (horseness), for example. But this is merely a grammatical feature that need not reflect any semantic difference in mental language, as Ockham notes (I.5).

38. Ockham thinks that there are theological exceptions to this principle based on the possibility of hypostatically assuming a nature (I.7). We can ignore this complication in what follows.

39. One of his favoured styles of argumentation is by appeal to his razor: if there is no reason to postulate entities of a given sort (since the work can be done by eliminative paraphrase), then such entities should not be postulated. Whether in the end Ockham genuinely eliminates entities or merely remains agnostic about them is a difficult question: see Spade (1998, 1999b).

40. For contemporary discussions of Ockham's reductive programme, see Adams (1987), Freddoso (1991), Tweedale (1992) and Klima (1999), in addition to Spade (1998, 1999b).

41. Ockham also recognizes sentences that have a verb in place of the copula and predicate-term.

42. Is Ockham's view defensible? The answer turns on the significance attached to the distinction between predicate-negation and sentence-negation, which cannot be clearly drawn in modern logic: there is no difference between belonging to the extension of the complement of a predicate and not belonging to the extension of the predicate. Ockham, however, insists on the difference.

43. Ockham adopts the general medieval view that affirmative sentences are false if their subjects are empty, whereas negative sentences are true if their subjects are empty. The former rule guarantees "existential import": a universal affirmative sentence entails a particular affirmative sentence, so that from "Every S is P" it is legitimate to infer "Some S is P". Logicians today, however, represent the logical form of universal affirmatives conditionally, $(\forall x)(Sx \rightarrow Px)$, from which it is not possible to infer $(\exists x)(Sx \ \& \ Px)$.

44. See Normore (1975) for an account of Ockham's modal and tense logic, and Karger (1976) for an account of Ockham's modal logic.

45. Singular modal/tensed sentences do not have the dual reading, since their subject-terms must personally supposit for the unique thing to which they apply.

46. See King (2001) for an extended defence of these claims.

47. The *Summa logicae* was not one of the works considered questionable by the investigating committee; only his theological work was taken under examination. We do not know who brought the charges against Ockham.

Bibliography

Adams, M. 1987. *William Ockham*, 2 vols. Notre Dame, IN: University of Notre Dame Press.

Biard, J. 1989 *Logique et théorie du signe au XIVème siècle*. Études de philosophie médiévale 4. Paris: J. Vrin.

Biard, J. 1997. *Guillaume d'Ockham: Logique et philosophie*. Paris: Éditions du Cerf.

Bottin, F. 2000. "Linguaggio mentale e atti di pensiero in Guglielmo di Ockham", *Veritas* **45**, 349–59.

Brown, S. F. 1972. "Walter Burleigh's Treatise *De suppostitionibus* and its Influence on William of Ockham", *Franciscan Studies* **32**, 15–64.

Chalmers, D. 1999. "Is There Synonymy in Ockham's Mental Language?" See Spade (1999a), 76–99.

Freddoso, A. J. 1991. "Ontological Reductionism and Faith versus Reason", *Faith and Philosophy* **8**, 317–39.

Freddoso, A. J. & H. Schuurman 1980. *Ockham's Theory of Propositions*. Notre Dame, IN: University of Notre Dame Press.

Karger, E. 1976, *A Study of William of Ockham's Modal Logic*, PhD dissertation, University of California at Berkeley.

Karger, E. 1984. "Modes of Personal Supposition: The Purpose and Usefulness of the Doctrine Within Ockham's Logic", *Franciscan Studies* **44**, 87–106.

Karger, E. 1994. "Sémantique et nominalisme", *Philosophiques* **21**, 563–76.

Karger, E. 1996. "Mental Sentences According to Burley and the Early Ockham", *Vivarium* **34**, 192–230.

King, P. 2001. "Consequence as Inference: Mediaeval Proof Theory 1300–1350". In *Medieval Formal Logic: Obligations, Insolubles, and Consequences*, The New Synthese Historical Library 49, M. Yrjönsuuri (ed.), 117–45. Dordrecht: Kluwer.

King, P. 2005. "Rethinking Representation in the Middle Ages". In *Representation and Objects of Thought in Medieval Philosophy*, H. Lagerlund (ed.). Aldershot: Ashgate Press.

Klima, G. 1999. "Ockham's Semantics and the Ontology of the Categories". See Spade (1999a), 118–42.

Loux, M. 1974. *Ockham's Theory of Terms*. Notre Dame, IN: University of Notre Dame Press.

Maurer, A. A. 1999. *The Philosophy of William of Ockham in Light of its Principles*. Toronto: The Pontifical Institute of Mediaeval Studies Press.

Michon, C. 1994. *Nominalisme: La théorie de la signification d'Occam*. Paris: J. Vrin.

Normore, C. 1975. *The Logic of Time and Modality in the Later Middle Ages: The Contribution of William of Ockham*. PhD dissertation, University of Toronto.

Normore, C. 1990. "Ockham on Mental Language". In *Historical Foundations of Cognitive Science*, J. C. Smith (ed.), 53–70. Dordrecht: Kluwer.

Normore, C. 1997. "Material Supposition and the Mental Language of Ockham's *Summa logicae*", *Topoi* **16**, 27–33.

Normore, C. 1999. "Some Aspects of Ockham's Logic". See Spade (1999a), 31–52.

Ockham 1967–1985. *Guillelmi de Ockham opera philosophica et theological*. Edited by Stephen Brown with the assistance of Gedeon Gál. Quaracchi (Ad Claras Aquas), Italy.

Panaccio, C. 1990. "Connotative Terms in Ockham's Mental Language". In Cahiers d'épistémologie 9016: Publications du groupe de recherche en épistémologie comparée, Université du Quebec à Montréal.

Panaccio, C. 1991. *Les mots, les concepts, et les choses. Le sémantique de Guillame d'Occam et le nominalisme aujourd'hui*. Montréal: Bellarmin and Paris: J. Vrin.

Panaccio, C. 1995. "La philosophie du langage de Guillaume d'Occam". In *Sprachtheorien in Spätantike und Mittelalter*, Geschichte der Sprachtheorie, S. Ebessen (ed.), 184–206. Tübingen: Gunter Narr Verlag.

Panaccio, C. 1999. "Semantics and Mental Language". See Spade (1999a), 53–75.

Spade, P. V. 1974. "Ockham's Rule of Supposition: Two Conflicts in his Theory", *Vivarium* **12**, 63–73.

Spade, P. V. 1975. "Ockham's Distinctions Between Absolute and Connotative Terms", *Vivarium* **13**, 55–76.

Spade, P. V. 1980. "Synonymy and Equivocation in Ockham's Mental Language". *Journal of the History of Philosophy* **18**, 9–22.

Spade, P. V. 1990. "Ockham, Adams, and Connotation: A Critical Notice of Marilyn Adams, *William Ockham*", *The Philosophical Review* **99**, 593–612.

Spade, P. V. (trans.). 1995. Selections from Ockham's *Summa logicae*, www.pvspade.com/Logic/docs/ockham.pdf (accessed Oct. 2004).

Spade, P. V. 1998. "Three Versions of Ockham's Reductionist Program", *Franciscan Studies* **56**, 335–46.

Spade, P. V. (ed.) 1999a. *The Cambridge Companion to William of Ockham*. Cambridge: Cambridge University Press.

Spade, P. V. 1999b. "Ockham's Nominalist Metaphysics: Some Main Themes". See Spade (1999a), 100–117.

Spade, P. V. 2002. "William of Ockham". In *The Stanford Encyclopaedia of Philosophy* (Fall 2002), E. N. Zalta (ed.), http://plato.stanford.edu/archives/fall2002/entries/ockham (accessed Oct. 2004).

Trentman, J. 1970. "Ockham on Mental", *Mind* **79**, 596–90.

Tweedale, M. 1992. "Ockham's Supposed Elimination of Connotative Terms and his Ontological Parsimony", *Dialogue* **31**, 431–44.

Further reading

Part I of Ockham's *Summa logicae* is translated in Loux (1974), and Part II in Freddoso and Schuurman (1980); excerpts from both are found in Spade (1995). Part III has not yet been translated. The original Latin text is available as Volume 1 of Ockham's *Opera philosophica* in Ockham (1967–1985). Overviews of Ockham's philosophy are given in Adams (1987), Panaccio (1991), Michon (1994), Biard (1997), Maurer (1999) and Spade (2002). In addition, Spade (1999a) is an anthology containing specialized studies of various aspects of Ockham's philosophy, including chapters on his logic and metaphysics. Readers interested in pursuing particular details about Ockham's logic or his nominalism should also consult works listed in the Bibliography.

Index